COINS
OF THE
INDO-SCYTHIANS, SAKAS &
KUSHANS

COINS
OF THE
INDO-SCYTHIANS, SAKAS & KUSHANS

PART I – INTRODUCTION
PART II – SAKAS
PART III – KUSHANS OR TOCHARI

BY

SIR A. CUNNINGHAM, K.C.I.E.

GYAN

Published by

Gyan Publishing House
5, Ansari Road
Daryaganj, New Delhi-110002
Phone: 011-47034999, 9811692060
E-mail: books@gyanbooks.com

Distribution Network
gyanbooks.com
India, USA, Canada, UK, Australia, France

ISBN : 978-81-212-2219-8 (PB)
First Published, 1888

2nd Impression 2021

Printed at: Gyan Press, Delhi.

Coins
of the
Indo-Scythians, Sakas & Kushans
Author: A. Cunningham

COINS
OF THE
INDO-SCYTHIANS, SAKAS & KUSHANS

PART I – INTRODUCTION

PART II – SAKAS

PART III – KUSHANS or TOCHARI

BY

Sir A. CUNNINGHAM, *K.C.I.E.,*

PART I.

INTRODUCTION.

PART II.

SAKAS OR SACÆ.

PART III.

KUSHANS OR TOCHARI.

COINS OF THE INDO-SCYTHIANS.

PART I.

BY

MAJOR-GENERAL SIR A. CUNNINGHAM,

R.E., K.C.I.E., C.S.I.

REPRINTED FROM THE NUMISMATIC CHRONICLE,

VOL. VIII., THIRD SERIES, PAGES 199—248.

LONDON:

1888.

COINS OF THE INDO-SCYTHIANS.

PREFACE.

On three sides India is protected from invasion; by the Himâla Mountains on the north, and on the east and west by the sea. But on the north-west side, along the line of the Indus, she is open to attack. On this side she was successfully invaded in ancient times by the Persians, the Greeks, and the Indo-Scythians. On this side also, in modern times, she was successfully assailed by the Turks under Mahmud Ghaznavi and Muhammad Ghori, and by the Mongols under Baber.

The Persian rule in N. W. India lasted for about two centuries, from B.C. 500 to 330, from the time of Darius to the invasion of Alexander the Great. The Greek dominion lasted for about three centuries, from B.C. 330 to 26, when the Kabul valley and the Panjâb were conquered by Kujula, king of the Kushân Scythians. The flourishing period of Indo-Scythian rule also lasted for about three centuries, or from B.C. 26 down to the end of the third century A.D.,[1] when it came into contact with the rapidly growing power of the Gupta dynasty of N. India.

---

[1] Pauthier, *Le Thian-tchu, ou l'Inde*, p. 9 note, quoting Ma-twan-lin.

The rise of this great dynasty deprived the Indo-Scythians of N. W. India; but they still retained possession of the Kabul valley and the Panjâb in the north and of Sindh in the south. In the latter country they remained until the seventh century, when they were dispossessed by the Brahman Chach. In the former they remained until the end of the ninth century, when they were displaced by the Brahman Kalar.

The three centuries of Indo-Scythian rule in N. India form a very striking period, as it separates Sanskrit literature into two broadly marked divisions, named by Dr. Max Müller the *ancient* and the *modern*, the former comprising the Brahmanical Veda and the Buddhist Tripitaka, and the latter all other works,[2] including even the Râmâyana and Mahâbhârata, which in their present form are probably not older than the period of Gupta rule.

In the present account I propose to treat at some length of the three centuries of the more flourishing period of Indo-Scythian rule previous to the rise of the Gupta empire. For this period we possess not only a profusion of coins but also a considerable number of inscriptions. For the later period of almost four centuries, from about A.D. 300 down to the advent of the Muhammadans, the materials are comparatively scanty. The coins indeed are numerous, but they are unfortunately of uncertain dates, and their inscriptions, even when expressed in Indian characters, are either limited to single letters or to general titles which give but little useful information. The long legends on most of the silver coins of this period are at present quite useless, as they are expressed in an

---

[2] *India—What can it teach us?* p. 88.

unknown Scythian character, and no doubt also in some Scythian language. According to the Chinese pilgrim, Hwen Thsang, the characters in use to the north of the Indian Caucasus in A.D. 630 were 25 in number, and were written from left to right. Not a single name is known, and as all the characters on the coins are joined together, it is difficult to find out where any particular letter begins or ends. I think that I have discovered the combination that corresponds with the title of *Shâhi*, and as this was the native title the characters should correspond.

In the following account I have aimed at giving a description of all the known coins of the Indo-Scythians, together with such historical notices as I have been able to gather from various sources. I have divided the work into three parts, as follows:—

Part I.—Historical notices of the Indo-Scythians.
Part II.—Notes on the coins of the Indo-Scythians.
Part III.—Descriptive lists of the coins.

There are three minor subjects, which, as they are brief, may be conveniently discussed at once. These are—

1.—The Arian legends on the coins.
2.—The monograms on the coins of the Saka kings.
3.—The monetary systems.

1.—The Arian Alphabet.

When Wilson published his Ariana Antiqua in 1840, no progress whatever had been made in reading the native legends beyond the point where James Prinsep had left it. The native forms of several important names still remained unread, such as Gondophares and Abdagases, and the legend on the reverse of Queen Agathokleia's coin. I was the first to discover the true form of the letter G on the coins of Gondophares and Abdagases in 1841, which I followed up by applying it to the word *Strategasa*, *Στρατηγός*, on the coins of *Aspa Varma*, the son of Indra Varma. The discovery of GH followed immediately afterwards, as this letter is formed by the simple addition of H to G. At the same time I discovered the form of BH in *bhráta-putrasa*, or "brother's son," as the translation of **ΑΔΕΛΦΙΔΕΩΣ** on the coin of Abdagases, and in *bhrátasa*, or "brother," as the translation of **ΑΔΕΛΦΟΥ** on the coins of Vonones and Spalahores. This was followed up by reading the name of *Amogha-bhuti* on the coins of the King of the Kunindas.

The compound character answering to STR I found on the coins of *Hippostratus*, which led to the discovery that the native legend of the coins of Agathokleia gave the name of King *Straton*.

In the proceedings of the Bengal Asiatic Society for April (just received) I find that Dr. Hoernle objects to the readings of *Stratasa* and *Hipastratasa*, on the ground that the *st* of Sanskrit becomes *th* in Pali. This is true for *Eastern* India, but not for Western India and the Panjâb and Kabul, where we know that the people preserved the pronunciation of *st* in the names of the Princes Haustanes and Astes. But the most direct and satisfactory proof is afforded by the different versions of Asoka's inscription. On comparing the *Girnar* version, which is recorded in Indian Pali characters, I find *násti* in Edicts II. and VI. as in the Shâhbâzgarhi text, while the Kâlsi, Dhauli, and Jaugada versions have *náthi*. I find also *asti* and *vista* in Edict XIV. of Girnar and Shâhbâzgarhi where Kâlsi and Dhauli have *athi* and *vitha*.

For Western India I may refer to the inscription of

Chashtan, the *Tiastanes* of Ptolemy, as the most convincing proof that the compound *st* was not pronounced as *th* in Ujain and Surâshtra.

In India also we know that *aswa*, a horse, was shortened to *assa* and *asa* in Pali. But in the west we find *Tushaspa*, the Yavana satrap of Surâshtra under Asoka; and to the west of the Indus we have *Khoaspes*. It will be sufficient, however, to note that the Arian compound letter read as *sp*, is the equivalent of the Greek ΣΠ in the names of *Spalahora* and *Spalgadama*.

I was the first to read the name of *Kushân* on the coin of *Kozoulo Kadphises*, and that of *Khushân* on the coins of *Kozola Kadaphes*, and to identify both with the Greek KOPANO and XOPAN. After this followed the name of *Kanishka* in Court's Manikyala inscription as king of the *Gushâns*.

Two forms of PH were obtained from the coins of Telephus and Gondophares.

CH and CHH I discovered about the same time, by identifying *Chhatrapa* as the true reading of *Kshatrapa*, or Satrap.

SW I found in Mahiswara and Sarva-lokeswara on the coins of Hima Kadphises.

The prefixed R was another valuable discovery, as it led to the correct reading of RM in *dharma*, as well as in Aspa Varma and Indra Varma. Then followed *Sarva* and *acharya*, to which I can now add Gondopharna.

But my chief discovery in the reading of names in the native characters was the decipherment of the names of the Macedonian months Arthamisiyasa, Panemasa, and Apilaesa in three different inscriptions.

In the Indian Pali alphabet I claim the discovery of the title of *Râjine* on the coins of Pantaleon and Agathokles, which had baffled every previous writer. *Râjine* is the Pali form of the Sanskrit genitive *Râjnya*, "of the king." The middle letter *j* had been read by Lassen; but the undulating form of the initial *r* had puzzled him.

I also discovered the true reading of the title of **ZAOOY**, or *zaou*, which had always been read previously as **ZAΘOY**, or *zathou*. It is the Greek rendering of the native title which the Chinese have preserved as *Sha-wu* (*Cha-wou*).

I may add also that the true reading of the name of **BAZO-ΔHO** or Vasu Deva, was due to me. On the small copper coins the name is shortened to **BAZ-ΔHO**, which is the true spoken form of *Bâs-deo*.

It is perhaps curious to note, that though all these readings have now been generally adopted, scarcely one of them has been acknowledged as mine.

The accompanying Plate VII. gives the native names and titles of all the Indo-Scythian kings in the Arian Pali characters, as found upon their coins. The transliterations of all the legends are given in Plate VIII.

2.—Monograms.[3]

The Greek monograms on the coins of the Indo-Scythians are comparatively few, there being only about fifty on the coins of the Saka kings, but not even one on those of the Kushân kings. I am fully aware of the difficulty of any attempt to explain these monograms; but as they occupy a very prominent place on the faces of the coins, I do not think it right to leave them unnoticed. My previous attempt to explain the monograms on the coins of the Greek princes of Bactria and India was con-

[3] For illustrations of monograms see Plate IX.

fessedly tentative. But I still feel that I was right in my original opinion, that *the occurrence of the same monograms on the coins of many consecutive princes of different dates is sufficient evidence to show that they cannot be the names either of magistrates or of mintmasters, and must therefore almost certainly be the names of cities where the coins were struck.*

It has been objected by M. Chabouillet that my early attempt to explain these monograms does not give the name of any one of the seventeen towns of Bactria recorded by Ptolemy. To this I can reply that only six of the thirty known Greek princes of the East were kings of Bactria, and that the number of monograms on their coins can be counted on the fingers. As all the other monograms are found upon coins bearing native legends, they must certainly be referred to the south of the Caucasus. I may note, however, that the letter N, which is found singly on the coins of Antiochus I., Antiochus II., Diodotus, and Antimachus I., perhaps denotes *Nautaka,* where Alexander wintered, as I find a monogram forming NA on the tetradrachm of Antimachus with the head of Diodotus on the obverse.

Mr. Percy Gardner accepts M. Chabouillet's opinion, and adds that I *profess* to have found in the monograms "the names of *most* of the cities of Bactria and the Panjâb." Mr. Gardner has evidently overlooked my actual profession on this point, in which I distinctly state that "I do not suppose that all, or even one half, of the names that occur on the coins of the Bactrian and Arian Greek, are the names of mint cities."

Mr. Gardner then proceeds to state his "entire agreement with M. Chabouillet," that there are but few cities, such as "Odessus, Patræ, and Panormus, which are known to have placed on their coins a monogram to represent their names."

To this argument I reply that as the coins of cities usually give their names at full length, their repetition in the form of monograms was quite unnecessary. There are, however, *many* examples of the names of cities expressed by monograms, but only on those coins where the name itself is not given. I may quote the following:—

1. Monogram forming ΑΚ on coins of Akarnania. (Head, *Hist. Num.*, p. 283.)
2. Monogram forming ΑΝΑ on coins of Anaktorium. (Head, *Hist. Num.*, p. 279.)
3. Monogram forming ΑΡΚΑΔ on coins of Arkadia. (Head, *B. M. Guide*, pl. 23, 37.)
4. Monogram forming ΛΕΟΝΤΙΝ on coins of Leontini. (*B. M. Cat. Sicily*, p. 94.)
5. Monogram forming ΚΡΑ on coins of Kranii. (*B. M. Cat. Pelop.*, p. 80.)
6. Monogram forming ΚΟΡ on coins of Korkyra. (*B. M. Cat. Corcyra*, p. 128.)
7. Monogram forming ΕΡ on coins of Hermione. (*B. M. Cat. Pelop.*, p. 160.)
8. Monogram forming ΣΑ on coins of Samé. (*B. M. Cat. Pelop.*, p. 91.)
9. Monogram forming ΓΑ on coins of Gaza. (Head, *Hist. Num.*, p. 680.)
10. Monogram forming ΠΤΟ on coins of Ptolemaïs. (*B. M. Cat. Ptolemies*, p. lxxxvi.)
11. Monogram forming ΑΧΑΙ on coins of Achaia. (*B. M. Cat. Pelop.*, p. 1.)
12. Monogram forming ΚΛΗ on coins of Kleitor. (*B. M. Cat. Pelop.*, p. 180.)
13. Monogram forming ΜΑΤ on coins of Mateolum. (*B. M. Cat. Italy*, p. 141.)

Monograms for the names of kings are not unknown, as—

ΔΗΜΗΤΡ for Demetrius of Macedon. (Head, *Hist. Num.*, p. 204.)

ΝΙΚ for Nikokreon of Cyprus. (Head, *Hist. Num.*, p. 626.)

ΠΥΡ for Pyrrhus. (Head, *Hist. Num.*, p. 203.)

ΑΝΤΙ for Antigonus of Macedon. (Head, *Hist. Num.*, p. 204.)

ΜΟΑΓ for Moagetes of Kibyra. (*Zeit. f. Num.*, I. p. 330.)

Again Mr. Gardner states his opinion that M. Chabouillet is clearly right in saying that these monograms are usually merely "the private mark of a magistrate or a contractor." That this may have been the case with many of the *cities* of the *West* I freely admit, but we are now dealing with the *kings* of the East, and not with the *cities* of the East. In the East, the right of coinage has always been a royal prerogative, which from the time of Darius Hystaspes has been jealously guarded, and its infringement severely punished. The story of Aryandes as told by Herodotus is familiar to every one.

But both M. Chabouillet and Mr. Gardner have evidently overlooked the case of the well-known coins, called Cistophori, on several of which the names of the cities where the coins were minted are certainly given in monogram, while the names of the magistrates are usually confined to the two initial letters.

1. On cistophori of Adramyteum, monogram forming ΑΔΡΑ. (Head, *Hist. Num.*, p. 446.)
2. On cistophori of Parium or Apameia, monogram forming ΠΑ. (Head, *Hist. Num.*, p. 459.)
3. On cistophori of Pergamus, monogram forming ΠΕΡ. (Head, *Hist. Num.*, p. 462.)

Might not the same system have prevailed in other

countries besides Asia Minor? For instance, on a large copper coin of Alexander, I find the monogram which I have read as *Demetrias* coupled with another forming ΤΗ, and on another copper coin the same *Demetrias* monogram with the letter Δ. If one of these must be the mintmaster's name it certainly cannot be the first, as that monogram is found on the coins of no less than twelve different princes from the time of Demetrius down to Hermæus, or for upwards of a century and a half. Similarly I find a common monogram of the coins of Hippostratus repeated on the coins of Azas. It forms the syllable ΑΡΤ, which I take to be the name of the mint city. On the coins of Hippostratus it stands alone, but on those of Azas it is variously accompanied, sometimes by ΔΙ in monogram, sometimes by ΜΙΡ in monogram. As it is scarcely possible that these two kings could have had the same mintmaster, I incline to the opinion that the monogram is *more* likely to be the name of a town than that of a man.

On the coins of the neighbouring kingdom of Parthia we have the names of at least three cities given at full length: *Katastrateia*, *Traxiane*, and *Margiane*. The last Mr. Gardner takes for the name of the province of *Margiana;* but surely it must be intended for the ancient city of Merv, which was rebuilt by Antiochus as *Antiocheia Margianè*. The names of at least three other Parthian cities are given in an abbreviated form, and not in monogram. A single monogram accompanied by the word ΠΟΛΙΣ undoubtedly refers to a city; and this example serves to strengthen the opinion that several of the other monograms found on Parthian coins may be the names of cities. Some of these monograms form combinations so simple as scarcely to admit of any other readings. Amongst these I find ΡΑ for *Rhagæ*, ΑΡΤΑ for *Artamita*,

ΧΑΡΑ for *Kharax*, ΑΠΑ for *Apamea*, ΑΝΤ for *Antiochia*, ΗΡ and ΗΡΑΚ for *Heraklea*, ΦΥΛ for *Phulake*, ΓΑ for *Gaza*, and ΑΠΟΛΛ for *Apollonia*.

The question now arises, From whence did the Parthians derive this practice of putting the names of cities on their coins? As the kings of Syria did not as a rule do so, the Parthians themselves must either have originated the practice or they must have copied it from the Bactrian Greeks. But as I have noticed a prevailing desire to trace all the coin types of the Parthians to Syrian or Bactrian types, I presume that the Parthian origin of the custom will be disputed. In any case the custom must have been familiar to the Eastern Greeks. The name of one city I have found beyond all doubt on some coins of Eukratides, namely *Karisiye-nagara*, that is the city (*nagara*) of *Karisi*. This city I take to be the same as *Kâlsi* or *Kârisi* of the Buddhist chronicles, which was the birthplace of Menander.

The practice of the Arsakidan kings was followed by the Sassanians; and on the coins of Feroz are found the names of no less than twenty-six different mint cities, accompanied by the years of the reign.

So also did the Khalifs of Baghdad give the names of their mint-cities with the Hijra dates on all their coins. Their example was followed by the Turki Sultans of Ghazni, and afterwards by the Turk and Mughal Emperors of India down to our own times.

To prevent misapprehension I may here state my views as to the information to be derived from the monograms. Such of the combinations as are simple and easily resolvable into well-known names, either in full or in part, may I think be accepted as actual names. But unless the places fulfil the condition of being within the territory held by the particular prince on whose coins they occur, they cannot be accepted. As an example of my method I will take the monogram forming **EY**, which is found on the coins of Euthydemus, Eukratides, Menander, Straton, Zöilus, Apollophanes, and Rajubul. I take this monogram to stand for Euthydemia or Sangala, a well-known city in the Panjâb, which most probably received its name from Demetrius, the son of Euthydemus, during his Eastern campaigns. That the place was certainly in the Eastern Panjâb is declared by its occurrence on the ruder coins of Straton, Zöilus, and Apollophanes, which are restricted to that district. Lastly, the monogram is common on the copper coins of Menander, who, in the Pali work named the "Questions of Milindra" is distinctly said to be the King of Sàkala.

As another example I will take the common monogram, No. 15, of the coins of the Vonones family, which I read as **KOTTOBAPA** in full. The princes of this family held Arachosia, of which the capital in the time of Isidorus was *Sigal.* As the letter *g* is very commonly elided, I think that Sigal may be read as *Siâl* or *Shâl,* a large town close to *Quetta.* As the last name is a peculiarly British rendering of *Kotta,* or "the forts," I think that Ptolemy's *Kottobara* must be simply *Kotta* or *Quetta,* with the town of *Shâl* close by to represent *Sigal.* I would remark that the same reasons which have led to the British occupation of this position must have had equal weight with the Saka Indo-Scythians when they made it their capital.

The monogram of **ΓAZAKA**, for Ghazni, No. 14, also seems unobjectionable.

Another example which I consider as almost certain is No. 3 and No. 37 monograms, which I read as

ΚΑΣΠΑΠΥΡΑ in full. This was the ancient well-known name of Multân, and it was from Multân, and not from Kashmir, that Skylax must have started. There are two objections fatal to Kashmir: 1, the city was *not* named *Kasyapapur;* and 2, no boat could descend the Jhelam or Hydaspes below Barahmula.

In the Plate of Monograms (IX.) I have included all that I could find on the coins of Moas and of the Vonones family. But I have been obliged to be content with a selection of the very numerous monograms on the coins of Azas and Azilises. Some day, perhaps, a key may be found to unlock the mystery which lies hidden in these little knots of letters.

When I made an attempt nearly twenty years ago to unravel some of the monograms on the Greek coins of Bactria and India, I stated my opinion that all the coin monograms "which are *common to a number of different princes* can only be the names of cities, and cannot possibly be the names either of magistrates or of mint-masters, or of any other functionaries."[4] Some of the numismatists of Europe, as I have already noted, seem to think that because magistrates' names are found on the coins of *Greek cities,* the same custom must have prevailed in the East with the *coins of kings.*

One example of the name of a city I can now offer which I think is not open to objection. I allude to the name of Sangala, the Shâkala or Sàkala of the Hindus. According to Ptolemy this place was also called Euthydemia (corrected from Euthymedia). At the top of the Plate I have given several different monograms of this

---

[4] *Num. Chron.*, II. Ser., viii. p. 185.

place, which seem to me to be quite satisfactory. I have marked them A, B, C, D. A is found on the coins of Euthydemus and Menander. It forms ΕΥ, which I refer to Euthydemia, as we might naturally expect to find it on the coins of Euthydemus, after whom Sangala must have received its Greek name of Euthydemia. We might also expect to find the same monogram on the coins of Menander, as in the Milinda Prasna Sâgal is said to have been the capital of *Raja Milindra. Sangala* was in the Eastern Panjâb; and we learn from Strabo that Menander had actually crossed the Hypanis or Biâs river.

B is also found on the coins of Euthydemus. It forms simply ΕΥ for Euthydemia.

C consists of two monograms which are found together on a coin of Eukratides. The upper one reads ΕΥ, as before, but the lower one gives the alternative name of ΣΑΓΓΑΛΑ in full.

D is found on the coins of no less than four kings—Straton, Zoïlus, Apollophanes, and Rajubul. It forms ΕΥ. As the coins of all the four princes on which this monogram occurs are of coarser and ruder work, and are found only in the Eastern Panjâb, I think we may admit that they were most probably struck at Euthydemia or Sangala, which was certainly the capital of that part of the country.

Of the monograms given in the Plate, Nos. 1 to 11 are found on the coins of Moa or Mauas; Nos. 12 to 19 are found on the coins of the Vonones dynasty; Nos. 21 to 49 on the coins of Azas and Azilises; and Nos. 50 to 52 on the coins of the Gondophares dynasty. No. 55 occurs on the base silver coins of Rajubul.

Monograms of Moas or Mauas.

The coins of Moas are found chiefly in the Northern Panjâb and as far south as Multân; but so far as I am aware none have yet been found either in Sindh or in the Kabul valley to the west of Peshawur. If any of these monograms represent the names of mint cities, I would suggest that No. 2, which forms **NIK**, may be *Nikaia*, the city which was built by Alexander on the site of his battle with Porus. In my "Ancient Geography of India" I have shown some good reasons for fixing the site of *Nikaia* at Mong, which is said to have derived its name from Ruja Moga.

No. 3 I would read as **ΚΑΣΠΑΠΥΡΑ**, which was the old name of Multân, and which I would therefore identify with the city of Kaspapuros, recorded by Hekatæus and Herodotus. If the monogram is intended for the name of a city, I think that my reading has a fair claim to be accepted. I am aware that the closet geographers of Europe have generally taken *Kaspapuros* for Kashmir. But I have marched along the bank of the Hydaspes after it leaves the valley as far as Muzafarabad, and I can safely assert that no boat could stem the rapids below Barahmula.

The remaining monograms of Moas I must leave unattempted. I confess, however, to a feeling of disappointment at not finding any knot of letters that might be united to form the name of Taxila.

Monograms of the Vonones Dynasty.

The coins of this family were found in Kandahar by Stacy and Hutton in 1840-41, and by Ventura and myself in the Western Panjâb. As only five specimens were got by Masson at Begrâm in a three years' collection, I conclude that these princes must have ruled over Arakhosia from Kandahar to the Indus. The metropolis of this tract of country according to Isidorus was *Sigal*, which by elision of the letter *g* I would identify with *Shál*, a large town close to Quetta. The proper name of *Quetta* is *Kotta*, which may be identified with Ptolemy's *Kottobara*. If any of the monograms on the coins of the Vonones family represent the names of cities, I should expect to find both Sigal and Kottobara tied up in some of these letter-knots. Nos. 12 to 19 are Vonones monograms.

No. 16 forms **ΣΙΓΑΛ** in full, but as it may be read in other ways I only propose *Sigal* on account of the probability of its being represented on the coins.

No. 15 I read as **ΚΟΤΤΟΒΑΡΑ** in full, and as this monogram cannot well be read in any other way, I think that there is a strong presumption in favour of its accuracy. I do not deny the possibility that *Kottobaros* might have been the name of some subordinate officer of the Vonones dynasty, and that his son might have borne the same name and have held the same office under successive rulers. But all these possibilities scarcely amount to a probability, and I must confess that I prefer the city *Kottobara*.

No. 17 offers simply **ΚΟΤΤΟ**, which I take for *Kotta* or *Quetta*, without any addition.

No. 14 I read as **ΓΑΖΑΚΑ**, or *Ghazni*, with some confidence, as I do not see that it can be read in any other way.

No. 13 may be read as **ΠΑΡΔΑΒΑΘΡΑ**, a city placed by Ptolemy on the western bank of the Indus. I presume that this must be the same place as the *Barda* of Isidorus;

but I am unable to identify it. Perhaps No. 12, which seems to be simply **B**, may be intended for *Barda*.

Another town mentioned by Isidorus is *Min*, which has been identified with Ptolemy's *Binagara* on the Indus.

Monograms of the Azas Dynasty.

The monograms of Azas and his successor Azilises are very numerous; and in the present Plate I have given a selection of those which are found on the principal coins, ranging from No. 21 to No. 49. As the successors of Moas they must have ruled over the Northern Panjâb, from Taxila to Multân.

No. 25 monogram may be read as **ΣΑΓΓΑΛΑ**, a place which was certainly within the dominions of Azas.

No. 37 is similar to No. 3 of Moas, which I have already explained as making **ΚΑΣΠΑΠΥΡΑ** in full, for the ancient city of Multân.

No. 40 may be read as **ΠΑΝΤΑΓΡΑΜΜΑ**, a town placed by Ptolemy on the Indus. It has been identified by Mr. McCrindle in his *Indian Geography of Ptolemy*, with *Panjpur*, near Embolima, because, as he says, it "agrees closely, both in its position and the signification of its name, with the Pentagramma of Ptolemy." But the true name of the place here referred to is *Panj-pîr*, or the "Five Saints" of the Muhammadans; whereas the Hindus call it *Panch-bîr*, or the "Five Heroes," and refer the name to the five Pandu brothers. This monogram might form **ΒΑΤΑΝΑΓΑΡΑ**, a name preserved by Ptolemy in the Eastern Panjâb. I would identify it with *Pathâniya*, or *Pathânkot*, one of the oldest places in the country. Its original name was *Pratisthâna*, which was shortened to *Paithâna*, or *Paithân*. It was the capital of the *Odumbaris*, of whom I possess coins as old as the time of Apollodotus.

No. 41 forms **ΒΑΡΔΑ**, which I suppose to be the same place as Ptolemy's *Pardabathra* on the Indus. As Azas seems to have outlived the last of the Vonones dynasty, he may have succeeded to some of the eastern portions of their dominions; or he may have held *Barda* during the lifetime of his contemporary *Spalirises*, as their names appear together on several of the coins.

Monograms of the Gondophares Dynasty.

The principal monogram of this family is No. 51, which forms the name of **ΓΟΝΔΟΦΑΡΑ** in full. I have no reason for supposing that he actually founded any city, but I note the fact of this possible reading as being curious, if not important.

Monogram of Rajubul.

No. 55 monogram is found on the base silver coins of Rajubul, which have been found in the Eastern Panjâb as well as at Mathura. His copper coins, with Arian legends, are found only in the Eastern Panjâb. I have therefore no hesitation in placing him at *Sangala*, as the monogram **ΕΥ** almost certainly refers to the city of *Euthydemia*, which was the Greek name of Sangala.

3. MONETARY STANDARD.

Two very marked and sudden changes took place in the weights of the gold and silver coins of N. W. India during the rule of the Greeks and Indo-Scythians. The first change took place in the weights of the Greek silver coins after the time of Eukratides. From the existing gold and silver coins of Diodotus and Euthydemus, we see that the Attic standard of weight had been preserved with a rate of 10 silver to 1 gold. The gold stater at its full weight was 134·4 grains, which at 10 rates gave the equivalent silver value at 1,344 grains. This divided by 20 gave the weight of the silver drachma as 67·2, that of the didrachma 134·4, and that of the hemidrachma as 33 6 grains. Suddenly we find that the silver coins of the sixteen kings who followed Eukratides have become heavier, the average weight of 16 didrachmas having become 146 3 grains, while that of 82 hemidrachmas had risen to 36·48 grains. As many of the latter are over 37 grains, I take this to be the full weight of the hemidrachma, while that of the didrachma must have been up to 148 grains. Now this change must represent either a rise in the value of gold or a fall in that of silver, by which the relative values of the two metals had become 11 S. = 1 G., that is, one-tenth had been added to the weight of the silver coins. Thus:—

	Grains.		Grains.	
	134·4	didrachmas	33·2	hemidrachmas
Add $\frac{1}{10}$ =	13·44	+ $\frac{1}{10}$ =	3·32	
	147·84		36·52	
or	148	new didrachmas, or	37	new hemidrachmas

This rate appears to have been maintained down to the time of the Indo-Scythian Kushâns, when the great issue of new gold coins took place and the coinage of silver ceased. Up to this time the gold money in circulation must have consisted of the staters of Alexander, Seleukus, Antiochus, Diodotus, and Euthydemus. The Saka

Scythians coined no gold, but they issued a very large amount of silver didrachmas and hemidrachmas of the same weights as those of the Greek successors of Eukratides.

We now come to the second sudden change in the weight of the new gold staters of the Kushâns, which was reduced from the full Attic standard of 134·4 grains down to something over 122 grains.

I have taken the weights of more than a hundred gold coins of the four Kushân kings, Wema Kadphises, Kanerki, Hoverki, and Vasu Deva, which give an average of 122·50 grains. But rejecting all the specimens under 123 grains, I find—

2 of Wema Kadphises	average	123·1	grs. out of	10	specimens
11 of Kanerki . .	,,	123·1	,, ,,	31	,,
25 of Hoverki . .	,,	123·4	,, ,,	125	,,
21 of Vasu Deva .	,,	123·3	,, ,,	21	,,
		492·9		187	
59 coins of four kings	,,	123·2	,,		

The fourth part of this stater would be 30·8 grains, which agrees with the existing coins, as I find that 16 quarter staters of the same four kings give an average of 30·63 grains for the quarter stater.

The actual name of these gold coins has not been discovered; but as the gold money of the Gupta kings is called *Dinâr* in several inscriptions, I have no doubt that the same name was applied to the Kushân gold coins, as they preserve the weight of the early imperial *denarii aurei* of Rome.

I would explain this change in the same manner as the other, that is, either by a rise in the value of gold or by a fall in the value of silver. As the Kushâns struck no silver money, the old silver coins of the Greeks and the Saka Scythians must have continued current; and as less gold was now given for the same quantity of silver, I conclude that the silver had fallen to 12 rates for 1 of gold. Adopting this rate for calculation, we get from the didrachma of 148 grains of silver a value of 1,480 grains of silver for the stater, which divided by 12 gives 123·33 as the weight of the gold stater, equivalent to 10 silver didrachmas of 148 grains.

The paucity of gold coins amongst the Indian Greeks may be explained by supposing that the old Persian darics had remained current down to the beginning of the Christian era, about which time the commercial intercourse between Europe and India had fallen into the hands of the Romans. The Roman empire had then advanced to the banks of the Euphrates, and as early as the reign of Claudius the Roman merchants had already taken advantage of the trade winds to make direct voyages to India from the Arabian Gulf. The trade rapidly increased in value until before the death of Pliny, A.D. 70, Rome *annually* sent to India no less a sum than fifty thousand sestertia, or about £400,000.[5] This import of specie still continued when the author of the *Periplus* visited India in A.D. 80—89, as he notes that Δηνάριον χρυσοῦ καὶ ἀργυροῦν, or both gold and silver *denarii*, were exchanged at Barygaza (or Baroch) at a profit for native money. At the same time he notes that old *drachmas*

[5] *Hist. Nat.*, XII. 41 (18). Minimâque computatione millies centena millia sestertium *annis omnibus* India et Seres, peninsulaque (Arabia) imperio nostro adimunt." The sum is about £800,000, of which in another place Pliny gives half, or quingenties HS to India. Gibbon, c. 2, values the amount at £400,000.

bearing the Greek inscriptions of Apollodotus and Menander were still current in Barygaza.[6] At other places in Southern India the principal import was great quantities of specie, *χρήματα πλεῖστα*.

These statements are specially valuable for the light which they throw upon the question of the coinage of the Kushân Indo-Scythians. Both writers were contemporary with the two great Kushân princes—Wema Kadphises and Kanishka; and there can be little doubt that a large portion of the Roman gold *denarii* imported at Barygaza must have been carried to the Panjâb, where they were recoined as *dinârs* by the Kushân princes. That the Roman gold did find its way to the north is certain, as many specimens have been extracted from Stûpas in the Kabul valley and Panjâb. But so far as I am aware very few specimens have been found elsewhere. In Southern India the Roman gold was not recoined, but remained current in company with the punch-marked silver coins. In the north the Kushâns struck no silver, and this fact is explained by the statement of the *Periplus* that the silver coins of Apollodotus and Menander were still current in his time. Along with them the tetradrachmas of Euthydemus and Eukratides must have been in common circulation, as well as the numerous hemidrachmas of the Greek princes Menander, Apollodotus, Antimachus II., and Hermæus, and the great mass of the native punch-marked silver coins.

To this influx of Roman gold I attribute the adoption of the Roman standard of 123· grains, with the name of *dinâr*, both of which continued in use for many centuries in Northern India.

---

[6] McCrindle's translation of *Periplus*, pp. 121–123.

Herr Von Sallet calls the silver coins with native legends a "reduced standard," by which I suppose him to mean that the 37 and 148 grain coins are *reduced* drachmas and tetradrachmas. Mr. Gardner, however, seems rather to look upon them as belonging to some Persian standard, with hemidrachmas of 40 grains and didrachmas of 160 grains. But I am not aware of any Persian standard comprising coins of these weights. The Persian siglos weighed upwards of 86 grains, and its double 172 grains. There are also many large silver pieces of 5 sigli, or quarter darics, which range up to 438·5 grains. My own heaviest piece weighed 433·5 grains, which would give a *siglos* of 86·6 grains. But surely the Indian Greeks and Indo-Scythians might be allowed the faculty of adjusting the weights of their coins to suit their own wants. My own opinion is that the change in the weights first of the silver coins and afterwards of the gold coins was made simply to adjust the pieces to the rate of the day.

THE INDO-SCYTHIANS.

PART I.—HISTORICAL NOTICES.

The name of Indo-Scythia is first found in Ptolemy's *Geography*, where it is confined to the provinces on both banks of the Indus, from the junction of the Kabul river down to the sea. Dionysius Periegetes uses the term "Southern Scythians," Νότιοι Σκύθαι, for the people of the provinces,[7] for which his commentator Eustathius substitutes the now well-known name of "Indo-Scythians." At the present day the name is made to include all the races of Scythian origin who held the countries lying between Persia and India for nearly nine centuries, from the occupation of Bactriana by the Sakas and Kushâns down to the conquest of Sindh and Kabul by the Arabs in the beginning of the eighth century A.D.

The countries thus occupied by the Indo-Scythians were—

I.—*Bactriana*, or the provinces lying between the river Jaxartes and the Indian Caucasus, comprising Sogdiana, Bactria, and Margiana.

II.—*Ariana*, or the provinces to the south of the Indian Caucasus, from Herat on the west to the Indus on the east, comprising Aria and Drangiana, Arakhosia and Gedrosia, with the Paropamisade of the Kabul valley.

III.—The *Panjâb*, or upper provinces of the Indus and its tributaries, from Taxila to the junction of the Five Rivers.

IV.—*Sindh*, or the lower provinces of the Indus valley, which, according to Ptolemy, included both Patalene and Syrastrene.

---

[7] V. 1088, Ινδὸν πὰρ ποταμὸν Σκύθαι ἐννάιουσιν.

The Scythians who opposed Cyrus and Alexander on the Jaxartes are described by the Greeks as Massagetæ, while their Persian neighbours knew them only as Sakas, or Sacæ.[8] Pliny says that the more ancient writers called them *Aramii*, and adds that both in their life and habits they resembled the Parthians. This is confirmed by Justin, who declares the Parthians to be only a separate branch of the Scythian family.

The country which the Scythians occupied between the Jaxartes and Oxus was known to the ancient Persians by the general name of Turân, and the name of Turanian is now applied to designate the Scythic version of the cuneiform inscriptions of Darius. All the provinces to the south of the Jaxartes belonged to the Achæmenian kings of Persia, and the Scythic version of the inscriptions must have been published for the information of the Turanian subjects of Darius. There can be no doubt therefore that the great bulk of the people on both banks of the Oxus were of Scythian origin. Thus, according to both Herodotus and Ktesias, the Parthians, Hyrkanians, and Derbikkæ, who were all of Scythian descent, were located to the south of the Oxus as early as the time of Darius. In the cuneiform inscriptions the *Umu-warka*, or *Amurgii* Scythians, are described as forming an integral part of the Persian empire; and in the time of Xerxes they furnished a contingent for the invasion of Greece. During the long Persian rule it is probable that the people of the fertile provinces of the Oxus had become more civilised than those to the north of the Jaxartes, by continued intercourse and

---

[8] Plinii, *Nat. Hist.*, vi. p. 19. In the Babylonian version of the inscriptions of Darius, *Namiri* is substituted for *Saka.* Perhaps Aramii should be *Amarii.*

frequent intermarriage with their Aryan rulers. In fact, Strabo describes the manners of the Bactrians and Sogdians as more civilised, although their mode of life was still nomadic.[9]

The language spoken by these Turanian subjects of Persia must therefore have been closely connected with that used in the cuneiform inscriptions of Darius. The names of people and of things which have come down to us show no traces of Semitic origin, but have many strong affinities with the Aryan language of India and Persia. Thus *saprakim,* "battle," must be connected with the Sanskrit *samara,* which is found in the name of *Samarkand,* while *tipi,* a "tablet," is the same as the Pali *lipi.* But the bulk of the language would appear to be different, and to have more affinity with some of the dialects of Northern India. Justin calls the language mixed Scythian and Median.[10] The following examples may be given in illustration of tbis opinion.

Amongst the Dards of the Indus the king's title is *Tham,* which is perhaps only a dialectic variety of the old Hiong-nu *Vam,* and is probably connected with the Sanskrit *dam,* the Greek δαμάζω, the Latin *dominus,* and the English *tame.* This title, I think, corresponds exactly with Justin's *Tanaus,* King of the Scythians. Herodotus mentions *Tomyris* as Queen of the Getæ, and Pliny explains *Temerinda* as "mother of the sea." By adding the feminine suffix *ere* to *tham,* we get both *Tomyris* and *Temeri,* and by adding *dá* = "water," we get *Temerindá,* as "Queen of Waters." The common terms for water amongst the aborigines of N. India are *dâ, de, di,* or *tâ, te,*

---

[9] *Geography,* xi., 11, 3.
[10] *Justin,* xli. p. 2.

ti. The longer name of *Thamimasada,* which Herodotus gives for the "King of the Sea," may perhaps be explained by the interposition of *massa*=great, thus making *Thamimasa-dâ,* or "king of the great water," or "lord of the sea."

That this word for water once prevailed over Northern India may be seen in the names of *Pad-dâ,* or Ganges, *Bahu-dâ,* or Brahmaputra, *Narma-dâ,* or Narbada, *Mana-dâ,* or Mahanadi, *Vara-dâ,* or Warda River, alias "Banyan-tree River." Other names are *Kalin-dî,* or Jumna, *Betwan-ti,* or Betwa, and *Kiyân-ti,* or Ken. I think it probable also that such names as *Charmanvati, Airâvati,* and others may have been Sanskritized from older forms in *ti.* We have an example in the *Pâra-ti,* a principal branch of the Satlej, which has no connection whatever with *Pârvati.*

The different races of Scythians which have successively appeared as conquerors in the border provinces of Persia and India are the following, in the order of their arrival:—

B.C. ? *Sakas* or *Sacæ,* the *Su* or *Sai* of the Chinese.

B.C. 163. *Kushâns,* or *Tochari,* the Great *Yue-chi* of the Chinese.

A.D. 440. *Kidaritæ,* or later Kushâns, the Little *Yue-chi* of the Chinese.

A.D. 470. *Ephthalites,* or white Huns, the *Ye-tha-i-li-to* of the Chinese.

The most detailed accounts of these different races we owe to the Chinese; but the short notices of classical authors, both Greek and Roman, are often of great value, either in confirming the Chinese accounts or in fixing the dates of important events. Generally they serve to corroborate each other, but there is a lamentable paucity of intelligible names in the Chinese records, owing chiefly to the incapacity of the Chinese syllables to express foreign names, and partly also to an absurd practice of the Chinese people in altering some of the names so as to obtain an opprobrious or derogatory meaning in Chinese. Thus the *Ta-yue-chi* meant only the "Great Lunar Race," who were not recognised by the later Chinese writers under the name of *Tu-ho-lo*, or Tochari, as described by Hwen Thsang. Similarly the ancient name of Kipin (or Kophene) was concealed under the later appellation of *Tsau-ku-ta*, and was absolutely lost under that of *Siei-iu*, which was imposed by the Empress *Wu-hen*, shortly after A.D. 684. Similarly also the *Ye-tha-i-li-to*, by having their name curtailed to *Ye-tha*, were not recognised as the Ephthalites, or White Huns, although they were both recorded to have been dominant in the same country at the same time. On the other hand the ancient name of *Hien-yun* was changed to *Hiong-nu*, or "unhappy slaves," which effectually disposes of their supposed connection with the Huns. With these preliminary remarks I will now try to put together the scattered links of Indo-Scythian history as derived from all sources.

During the sway of the Achæmenian kings the inroads of the Scythians of the Jaxartes were kept in check by the frontier satraps. After the death of Alexander the same check was maintained under the vigorous rule of Antiochus, the Governor of the Eastern Provinces, who resided at Margiané, or Merv. But about eighty years later they had already begun to give trouble to the Bactrian Greeks, and Euthydemus was allowed by Antiochus the Great to retain his kingdom, on the plea that, if he was weakened, he would not be able to withstand the Scythians. Early in the second century B.C., as related by the Chinese, the horde of the great *Yue-chi*, or *Tochari*, was driven across the Jaxartes by the Hiong-nu, and, after the loss of their king in battle, settled in Sogdiana in B.C. 163. The *Sus* or *Sais*, or the Massagetæ or Sakas of the Greeks and Persians, retired before them, and after a time the Yue-chi continued their advance into Bactria, to the south of the Oxus, of which they took possession about 130 B.C. The *Ta-hia*, or Dahæ, then retired to the west towards Margiana, while the *Su* or *Sakas* retreated to the south towards Drangiana.[11]

Mithridates I. of Parthia, who died in B.C. 135, took advantage of this period of confusion to wrest the two satrapies of Aspiones and Turiva from Eukratides, at the same time that he checked the Scythians. The position of these satrapies is unknown, but I conclude that they must have been on the west and south-west frontiers of the Bactrian kingdom, *i.e.* in Margiana and Aria, along the rivers Margus and Arius. The annexation of these provinces would have been easy, and would have brought the Parthians face to face with the retiring Saka Scythians. The victories of Mithridates would have stopped the further progress of the Dahæ, while the Sakas managed to make good their retreat into Arachosia and Drangiana. That they reached the latter province we know from the fact that after their occupation it received the name of *Sakastene* [Σακαστήνη Σάκων Σκύθων], a name which was altered to Sejistân by the mediæval writers, and is now preserved in the modern Sistân.

The Chinese fix the date of the occupation of Bactria by the Great Yue-chi or Tochari about B.C. 130, which agrees with the period of the defeat of Phraates II. of Parthia, who fell in battle with the Saka Scythians in B.C. 127 or 126. These Scythians had been engaged to

[11] Remusat, *Nouveaux Mélanges Asiatiques*, i. p. 205.

join him in his war against Antiochus, but as they arrived too late he refused to pay them, on which they invaded his territory.

His successor, Artabanus II., was killed three years later, B.C. 124-123, in battle with the Tochari. The notice of these Yue-chi is derived from the Chinese General Chang-Kian, who in B.C. 126 was sent by the Chinese Emperor Wuti to obtain their aid against the Hiong-nu. He was captured by them, but after ten years managed to escape, and returned to China in B.C. 116, having failed to induce the Yue-chi to join in a campaign against the Hiong-nu. He reported that he had found the Yue-chi in full possession of Bactriana. From another notice we learn that *about* 100 years later, or say about B.C. 16, the chief of the Kushâns conquered the other four tribes of the Yue-chi, and assumed the title of "King of the Kushâns." This chief, who was named *Khieu-tseu-kio*, has been identified with Kujula Kadphises of the coins. He crossed the Indian Caucasus and overran Pota and Kipin, and took possession of the Kabul valley. Pota has been identified by Viv. de St. Martin with *Pathánka* or *Pukhtánka*, the country of the Pathâns, while Kipin is generally admitted to be Arakhosia, which was anciently known as Kophene.

Later notices of the progress of the Sakas and Kushâns will be best kept separate. There can be no doubt that they came into conflict at an early date in the Panjâb, as that province was annexed by the Kushân King *Yun-kao-ching*, the son of Kujula, in the first century A.D., while we know from the evidence of the coins that the great Saka kings, Moas, Azas, and Azilises must have had a firm hold of it during the first century B.C.

The origin of the name of *Saká* is still uncertain. The

general opinion is in favour of the Persian *Sag*, a "dog," which is still used as a derogatory term by the Persians for their enemies. I have seen a short history of Bahâwalpur, in which the Raja of Bikaner was throughout designated as the *Sag*. But there still exists a tribe to the north-east of Ladâk who bear the name *Sok-po*, or simply *Sok* as *po* is the masculine suffix in Tibetan, *Sok-po* meaning a Sok-man, and *Sok-mo* a Sok woman. Pliny's statements that they were anciently called *Aramii* is perhaps supported by the Babylonian version of the inscriptions of Darius, in which *Namiri*, or the "hunting leopards," is substituted for *Saka*. By a slight transposition the *Aramii* would become *Amarii* or *Namiri*.

SAKAS, OR SACÆ-SCYTHIANS.

According to the Chinese accounts the *Su* or *Sai*, or *Sakas*, on being driven out of the countries on the Oxus by the *Yue-chi*, or *Tochari*, retired to the south and occupied *Kipin*, or *Kophene*, comprising Arakhosia and Drangiana. The tribes of the *Sai* then spread over the country and formed different kingdoms, and it is specially stated that all the dependencies of *Hiau-siun* and *Siun-tu* (Sindh) were inhabited by ancient tribes of the *Sai*.[12] The country which they occupied was then called *Sakastene* after them.[13] It is the Sejistân of the early Muhammadans, and the Sistân of the present day. Isidorus of Kharax

---

[12] Remusat, *Nouv. Mélanges Asiatiques*, i. p. 205. Pauthier, *Chine*, i. p. 242. A third tribe of the Sai was named *Kuen-to*. It numbered 300 families.

[13] Avienus, v. p. 1297, uses the form of *Sagam infidum*; and Orosius also uses *Sagam* as the name of the country to which St. Thomas was sent.

calls it Σακαστήνη Σάκων Σκύθων, and gives the following names of its towns: 1. Barda; 2. Min; 3. Palakenti; 4. Sigal; 5. Alexandria; 6. Alexandropolis. The fourth town *Sigal*, which is designated as *Regia Sacarum*, or the "capital of the Sakas," I would identify with *Shâl*, by the simple elision of the letter *g*. *Shâl* or *Kotta* ("the forts," vulgo *Quetta*) has always been a place of consequence. Its commanding position, on the high road from Kandahar to the Lower Indus, must have insured its occupation at a very early date. For the same reason it is now occupied by a British garrison. It is most probably the *Kottobara* of Ptolemy.

According to Stephanus of Byzantium the two cities named Arakhosia and Arakhoti, were near the country of the Massagetæ, or in other words near Sakastene, the country of the Sakas, who were of the same race as the Massagetæ.

I will now give a few notices of each of the three different provinces which the Sakas occupied: 1. Sakastene or Sejistân; 2. Sindh; 3. The Panjâb.

1.—The Sakas of Sakastene and Kipin.

Closely connected with the Su or Sakas were the *Tahia*, or *Dahæ*, who were driven out of their country by the Tochari or Kushâns at the same time. These *Dahæ* are said to have retired to the west. Now Dahæ was not a true national name, but only a term of reproach or abuse given to the nomads by their Persian and Indian neighbours. The original word in the Sanskrit, *dasyu*, "an enemy or robber," which in Persian became *dahyu*, from which the Greeks formed *Dahæ*, Δάαι, and also Δάσαι. The spoken form in India is *Dáku*, which is found in the Latin

Dacia. A similar term is still applied to the people on the east of the Caspian, whose country is now called *Dághistan* or *Dahistan*, or " Rebel-land."

Strabo couples the Dahæ with the Sacæ and Massagetæ, and adds that they were divided into three tribes—1. Parni or Aparni; 2. Xanthii or Xandii; and 3. Parii or Pissuri. As Justin[14] calls the first tribe *Spartani*, I conclude that Strabo's name must have been *Saparni*, and that these people, the worshippers of *Sapal* or Herakles, must have given their name to *Zâbulistan*, or Arakhosia and Drangiana, which is only another name for Sakastene.

The *Xanthii* are very probably the *Zâths* of the early Arab writers. As the Zâths were in Sindh to the west of the Indus, this location agrees very well with what we know of the settlement of the Sakas on the Indian frontier. In fact the Chinese expressly say that all the dependencies of *Hien-siun* and *Siun-tu* (Sindh) were occupied by ancient tribes of *Sai*, or Sakas.[15]

According to the Chinese these Saka tribes afterwards separated, and formed several distinct states under separate rulers. This statement seems to be borne out by the three distinct dynasties of kings, whose names have been preserved to us on the coins; the one proceeding from Vonones in Arakhosia, a second from Moas and Azas in the Panjâb, and a third from the Kshaharâta tribe in Sindh, to which the great Satrap Nahapâna belonged.

The Kshaharâtas would appear to have extended their territories beyond the limits of Sindh into Kachh (the *Odombeores* or *Audumbara*) and Gujarat (Surâshtra), and

---

[14] *Justin*, xli. p. 1.

[15] Remusat, *Nouv. Mélanges Asiatiques*, i. p. 206.

perhaps even to Malwa. One inscription of the Satrap Nahapâna is dated in the year 42, but unfortunately no era is mentioned. If referred to the Seleukidan century beginning in 12 B.C., the date would be 42 — 12 = 30 A.D., or just forty-eight years before the establishment of the Saka era, and the probable date of Chashtana of Ujain (Tiastanes of Ozene).

I think it probable that some reference to this southern invasion of the Sakas may be preserved in the short Sanskrit work named *Kâlakachârya Kathâ*, describing the "Inroads of the Indo-Scythians into India." This short treatise was brought to notice by Dr. Bhau Dâji, in the *Journal of the Bombay Asiatic Society*.[16] The account is as follows :—" Shortly before the Christian era the Sakas held possession of the country on the western bank of the Indus under petty chiefs called *Sâki*, who were subject to one paramount ruler named *Sâhina-sâhi*. The Sakas crossed the Indus into Sûrashtra, and advanced to Avanti-desa (Mâlwa), where they defeated Raja Gardabhilla, and took possession of Ujain. Here they remained for four years until they were driven out by Vikramâditya, son of Gardabhilla, in B.C. 57."

As the dynasty of the *Kshaharâtas* was succeeded by the new dynasty of *Chashtana* (or Tiastanes), I think it most probable that the notice by the author of the *Periplus* of Parthian rivals driving out one another must refer to these two dynasties of Scythian princes. The names of Nahapâna and Chashtan, which are certainly not Indian, seem to have some connection with the similar forms of Artapanus and Haustanes, both Parthian or Partho-Scythian names.

---

[16] *Journal*, ix. p. 139.

How firmly settled were these Sakas of Western India is most decidedly shown by some of their inscriptions which still exist in the Nâsik caves. Thus I find that the son-in-law of the Kshaharâta King Nahapâna calls himself a *Saka*. In one inscription he is designated as the *Saka Ushavadâta, the son of Dinika, and the husband of Dakshamitrâ, the daughter of Nahapâna.* None of these names are Indian, except perhaps that of Dakshamitrâ. Another inscription is dated in the year 42, on the 15th of the bright half of Chaitra. As it must precede the establishment of Chashtana in A.D. 78, I am inclined to refer the year to the Seleukidan century which began in 12 B.C., which would fix the date to B.C. 12 — 42 = A.D. 30.[17]

Two other short inscriptions record the gifts of another Saka chief named *Dâma-cheka.*[18]

The Sakas of Sejistân are repeatedly mentioned in the history of the Arsakian and Sassanian kings.

In B.C. 77 or 76, Sanatroikes obtained the throne by the aid of the Sakarauli Scythians, amongst whom he had previously sought refuge.[19]

In B.C. 33 Phraates IV. fled to the Scythians, who replaced him on the throne.

In A.D. 16 Artabanus III., with the assistance of the Dahæ and Sakæ, obtained the throne. He had previously lived amongst the Dahæ.[20]

In A.D. 40 Goterzes was similarly assisted by the Dahæ.

---

[17] See *Bombay Journal*, vii., West's Inscriptions from Nâsik, No. 14.

[18] *Ibid.*, Inscriptions Nos. 1 and 2.

[19] *Phlegon apud Photium*, quoted by Mr. Percy Gardner, and Lucian, *Macrob.* 15.

[20] Josephus, *Ant. Jud.*; Tacitus, *Ann.* ii. 3.

A.D. 230 Artaxerxes, the founder of the Sassanian monarchy, was unable to reduce the Sejistânis. According to Agathias (ii. 164), quoted by Gibbon, "the princes of Sejistân defended their independence during many years," and were not finally conquered until the reign of Varaban II., A.D. 275—292. Gibbon calls the Sejistânis "one of the most warlike nations of Upper Asia."

From this time the province of Sejistân, or Sakastene, formed one of the tributary provinces of the Sassanian empire. Accordingly in A.D. 350—357 the Sejistânis furnished a contingent to Sapor II. for the siege of Amida. They were reckoned the bravest of his troops, and they brought into the field a large body of elephants.[21]

In A.D. 650 Yezdegird, the last Sassanian king, fled from Istakhar through Kermân and Sejistân to Khorasân, and in the following year a Muhammadan army occupied Zarang, the capital of Sejistân.[22]

2.—The Sakas in Sindh.

An early notice of the Saka Scythians on the Indus is given by the author of the *Periplus*, who says that "Minnagar, the metropolis of Scythia, was in his time governed by Parthian princes, who were perpetually at strife among themselves, expelling each the other."[23] The date of the *Periplus* is not accurately known. But the mention of Zoskales (Za Hakale), King of Abyssinia, who reigned from 77 to 89 A.D., and of a King of the Nabathaians, whose kingdom was absorbed by Trajan in A.D. 105, serve to fix his date between 80 and 100 A.D. As we

---

[21] Ammian, Marcell., xix. pp. 2, 3.

[22] H. M. Elliot, *Muhammadan Hist. of India*, by Dowson, ii. p. 218.

[23] Translation by McCrindle, p. 108.

know that the Kings of Parthia proper at this time did not possess any territory even near the Indus, the so-called Parthian rulers must refer to the Indo-Scythian Sakas, who were of the same race as the Parthians.

The position of Minnagar has not been identified, but I feel nearly certain that it must have been at Brâhmanâbâd, which is one of the oldest sites in Sindh. It was the "city of Brahmans" of Alexander's historians. Its Hindu name was Brahmanawâsi, which was changed to Brâhmanâbâd by the Muhammadans, who afterwards built Mansura close to it.

As Pliny lived within a very short time of the author of *Periplus*, it is quite possible that the dynasty of Parthian kings then ruling on the lower Indus might be mentioned by him. I find the *Odombeores* or *Audumbaras*, the people of Kachh, duly recorded, and immediately preceding them are the *Varetatæ* or *Suaratarataæ*.[24] As the name has evidently been corrupted, I think it not impossible that the true reading may have been *Suaratæ*, and that they may be identified with the *Kahaharâtas* of the western cave inscriptions, of one of whose rulers, named *Nahapâna*, we possess coins as well as inscriptions. As the Kshaharâtas were certainly succeeded by another Scythian race under *Chashtan* (Tiastanes of Ptolemy), the description of Parthians expelling each other would seem to be well illustrated by the proposed identification.

There is now a gap of several centuries in the history of Sindh which is not likely ever to be filled up, as all the histories of Sindh begin with the Sahasi dynasty which ruled for one hundred and thirty-seven years preceding the accession of the Brahman Chach, that is from

---

[24] Plinii, *Nat. Hist.*, vi. p. 23.

A.D. 505 to 642. The names given in the Chachnâma are corrupt, but they are quite sufficient to prove that the kings were Scythians. All of them are named *Sâhi*, or *Sâhasi*, which is the well-known Scythian title. Five kings are mentioned, of whom the only thing related is that the fourth king was attacked and killed by Nimroz (Parvez, King of Persia) in A.D. 627. But on the authority of Kosmas the new dynasty must have been White Huns or Ephthalites. They would therefore have had no connection with the first Saka conquerors. Unfortunately no names are recorded in the histories of Sindh, but each is called simply *Rai Sâhi* or *Sâhasi*. As this seems to be only the common Scythian title of *Shâhi*, we have no means of discriminating one prince from another. I believe, however, that I have found the name of the leader in *Jibawin*, who formed the great reservoir of Suraj Kund at Multân. His name is also variously written as Jaswin, Jasur, and Jalbur, but as I possess coins bearing the names of *Jabubal* and *Jabukha*, I incline to adopt *Jabuwan* as the correct form.

The testimony of Kosmas, who actually visited the country to the west of the Indus about A.D. 530, is perhaps sufficient to show that the Scythian dynasty which ruled over Sindh from A.D. 507 to 642 must have been White Huns. As the inscription of Yasodharma, King of Mâlwa, A.D. 532, mentions that he ruled over countries which neither the Guptas nor the Hûnas had possessed, there is some difficulty as to what countries are intended. The Panjâb is most probably alluded to, as no trace of Gupta rule has yet been found there. Perhaps Sindh is also referred to, in which case the rule of the Hûnas in the time of Kosmas must have been confined to the western bank of the middle Indus. The histories of

Sindh are unanimous in claiming Mekrân as one of the provinces of the kingdom during the rule of the Sâhasi kings. I infer therefore that Yasodharma's conquests did not extend to Sindh, but may probably have included Northern Rajputâna. The mention of the overthrow of Sakas in *Ruma* (in the Salt country) by Vikramâditya about A.D. 530 must refer either to the *Sâmbhar lake* district near *Ajmer*, or to the Salt Mines in the Panjâb, and at Kâlâbagh to the west of the Indus. The latter seems the more probable, as the city of *Rhon*, Ῥῶν, is described as belonging to the Scythian Gandarike, just as Hekataeus describes *Kaspapuros*.

I annex a list of these Scythian kings of Sindh as preserved in the native histories. If their title was *Shâhi*, they would have some claim to be taken as Sakas, as the White Huns had adopted the title of *Khâkân*.

A.D.	Kings of Sindh.
505.	Dîwâîj, ? Jibawin.
533.	Siharas, Sahiras, ? Gollas of Kosmas Indicopleustes.
566.	Dîwâîj, or Rai Sâhasi, or Shâhi-shâhi.[25]
600.	Siharas, Sahiras invaded by Persians in A.D. 627, killed.
627.	Sâhasi, Rai Shâhi.
642.	Chach Brahman conquers Sindh.

The territory held by these princes extended from the frontier of Kashmir to the mouths of the Indus, and from Mekrân to the frontier of Kanauj. In A.D. 641, Hwen Thsang says that the reigning king was a *Siu-to-lo*, that is a Sudra. The names seem so much alike, Sâhasi, Sahiras, and Rai Shâhi, that I cannot help suspecting they may be only a title repeated with slight changes as Rai-Shâhi or Shâhi-Rai. Now Shâhi is a well-known Scythian

[25] H. M. Elliot, *Muh. Hist.*, i. p. 405, gives five names from the Tuhfat ul Kirâm.

title which is found on most of the Indo-Scythian coins of the Sassanian period. This is the more probable as I find mention of an ancient King of Multân named *Jibawîn*, who excavated the Suraj Kund and built a great temple containing a golden image. He may perhaps be the founder of the dynasty *Diwâij*. A more probable identification is that of *Diwâij* with the prince named *Devajari*, two of whose silver coins were found in the great Mânikyala Stûpa by General Ventura.[26] The Indian legend on these coins I read as follows.—

Sri Hitivi-cha Airân cha parameswara.
Sri Shâhi-tigin Devajâri.

The fortunate lord of India and Persia.
The fortunate valiant prince (Shâhi) Devajâri.

It will be observed that all the leading consonants *d, v, j*, occur in both names joined with a long *â*.

All the other recorded names appear to be only corruptions of the title of Shâhin Shâhi.

I am disappointed at not finding any trace of the name of Gollas in these lists of the native historians of Sindh. I am even more disappointed at the omission of all mention of Vâsu Deva, King of Multân, Uch, and Bâhmana, as declared on his coins. He was almost certainly one of the rulers of Sindh of this very dynasty, as the style of his coins shows that he belonged to the later Sassanian period.[27]

Both of the coins just noticed might perhaps be said to belong properly to Multân. But there is a large number of coins in all three metals, which bear only the title of *Sri-Shâhi*, or in some cases only *Shâhi*, which might

---

[26] See my *Archæological Report*, v. p. 121, and Pl. XXXVII.
[27] *Ibid.*

belong to the kings of Sindh, whose names have not been handed down. But as most of these anonymous coins, and as I believe that *all* of the gold ones, have been found in the Northern Panjâb or Lower Kabul valley, I am inclined rather to assign them to the Rajas of Sâkala and Gâudhâra. It is unfortunate that very few of the names have been preserved, and these mostly disguised in the strange forms of Chinese monosyllables.

Masudi records that a prince named Ranbal, who reigned in the valley of the Indus, after subjugating Eastern Persia, had "advanced to the banks of the Tigris and Euphrates."[28] This conqueror may, I think, be identified with the king who on his coins claims to be lord "both of India and of Persia" (*Sri Hitiri-cha Airân-cha parameswara*). Such an inroad might perhaps have been successful after the murder of Khusru II. in 628 A.D. This is the more probable as the ruler of Sindh had to revenge the invasion of his own country and the death of his predecessor. As Parvez had invaded Sindh by Kirmân and Mekrân, the Sindhian king would no doubt have followed the same route. I see nothing improbable in this raid, as the Persian empire never recovered its strength after the death of Parvez.

Kaikân or *Kikân*, an outlying district of Sindh on the west towards Mekran, suffered from several early invasions of the Muhammadans, who were intent upon seizing horses of a fine large breed for which the country was famous. It is the *Ki-kiamg-nu* of Hwen Thsang, who also mentions its good horses. Bilâduri calls the people *Tûrks*, by which term he probably meant Indo-Scythians. The province seems to be identical with the northern and

---

[28] Elliot's *Muham. Hist. of India*, ii. p. 418.

hilly half of Biluchistan, comprising Kilât and the country of the Brahûïs. In the Chachnâma mention is made of a high mountain called *Kaikârân*. I suspect that this name may be identified with the fort of *Kâpishkânish*, in Arakhosia, which was seized by a rebel against Darius Hystaspes. We know that the name of the town of *Kaithal* is a simple contraction of *Kapisthala* (the Kambistholi of Arrian). In the same way I think that Kâpishkânish might be contracted to *Kaikân*. Sir Henry Rawlinson thinks that the place must be looked for in the direction of Sistân, as the satrap of Arakhosia would probably have met the force advancing from Persia on the frontier of his province

3.—Sakas in the Panjâb.

There is no direct historical evidence that the Sakas ever occupied the Panjâb, but the three great kings, Moas, Azas, and Azilises, whose coins are found chiefly in the Panjâb, and very rarely to the west of the Indus, are universally accepted as Saka Scythians. They certainly preceded the Kushân Prince Kujula Kadphises and his successors, with whom they seem to nave nothing in common, whereas their connection with the Saka dynasty of Vonones and his successors is undoubted, as the name of Azas is found joined with those of Vonones and Spalirises. They agree also in having an extensive silver coinage of the same types, without a single specimen of gold,[29] while the Kushâns have an abundant gold coinage and no silver money, excepting only a solitary piece of Wema Kadphises.

---

[29] I may note here that my friend Pandit Bhagwân Lâl had a gold coin of Spalahores, but it was a forgery.

There is, however, a decided testimony of Saka occupation of some portion of Western India as late as the latter half of the fourth century in the mention by Samudra Gupta of the presents received from the Kushâns, Sakas, and Murundas: "*Daivaputra Shâhi-Shâhânu Shâhi, Saka, Murundaih.*"

Sakas are also mentioned in the beginning of the fifth century as opponents of a Vikramâditya of Mâlwa, and to them I would attribute the rude Indo-Sassanian coins which are now so abundant in Rajputâna. According to the Hindu accounts this prince conquered the Sakas in *Ruma.*[30] He is perhaps the same prince as Yasodharma, of Mr. Fleet's Mandisur inscription, who possessed countries which neither "the Gupta kings nor the Hûnas could subdue."[31] The same prince also boasts of having subdued King *Mihirakula.* As Yasodharma's inscription is dated in A.D. 532, it seems very probable that he must be the Vikramâditya of the native legend, the contemporary of Kâlidâs and Varâhamihira. But the Mihirkul whom he subdued must have been the Mihirkul, son of Toramâna of Malwa, and not the great Mihirkul, Raja of Kashmir.

It is worthy of remark also that these Saka princes, Azas and his successors, must have employed Indian servants, such as the General Aspa Varma, son of Indra Varma, as well as a son of Vijayamitra, whose name is lost on my coins. Others were no doubt only Scythian adventurers, like Jihonia and Rajubul, whose coins belong to the same period. They must have been in the service of some of the later Greek princes, and who, as their

---

[30] Bhau Daji in *Journal of Bombay Asiatic Society*, vi. p. 26.
[31] *Indian Antiq.*, xv. p. 255, Mr. Fleet's inscription.

masters' power became weaker, had gradually acquired strength, until some of them became independent. Moas, for instance, may have been a successful general under Menander and Apollodotus, and after their death a successful rebel, who wrested the Panjâb from Hermæus. The coins of Moas are found chiefly about Taxila (Shâhdheri and Mansera) and in the country between the Indus and Chenâb rivers.

Some of the later Greek princes would seem to have been driven towards the East—Artemidorus perhaps to Kashmir, and Dionysius, Zoilus, and Straton II. to Kangra.

The coins of Azas are also found chiefly in the Western Panjâb; only a few specimens are found in the lower Kabul valley. I obtained a small find from Bajâwar, but I saw twelve large pieces dug up from the inside of a temple at Shâhdheri or Taxila. Not even one was found by Masson at Begrâm, and I may say the same for Mathura, which has yielded a considerable number of the coins of Menander and Apollodotus, Antiochus II. and Straton, with a single type of the nameless king.

The find-spots of the coins of Azilises are the same as those of Azas. One large find of silver coins was made on the bank of the Jhelam river, in the hills between Barahmula and Jhelam.

The rule of Moas and his two successors may have lasted from about 100 B.C. down to the beginning of the Christian era, when the country fell into the hands of the Kushâns.

I can perhaps best illustrate my idea of what may have taken place in the Panjâb on the break up of the Greek power by referring to what actually took place in the same country after the break up of the Muhammadan empire of Delhi. All over the country the petty chiefs made themselves independent, or nearly so. Musalmân chiefs in Multân and Mamdot, Sikh chiefs in Gujrânwala, Kapurthala, Patiâla, Nabha, and Kaithal, and an Englishman, George Thomas, in Hânsi. After a time Ranjit Singh of Gujrânwâla gradually managed to overcome most of his rivals, just as I suppose Moas to have done in ancient times.

There would appear to have been several other adventurers in early days in the Panjâb, who are known to us chiefly from coins. Such are the satrap Jikonia, son of the satrap Manigul, who perhaps gave his name to Mânikyâla, and the satrap Rajubul, who almost certainly held Sangala, as his coins are found in the Eastern Panjâb, and bear the Greek monogram **EY** for Euthydemia or Sangala.

There are coins also of rajas of the same period, who must have been more or less dependent on the greater chiefs. One of these was *Dhâra Ghosha*, Raja of *Odumbara*, that is of the country of *Dameri* or *Nûrpûr*. Other chiefs are the *Kuninda* Raja Amoghabhûti, and two others named Mahadeva and Rudra Varma. All of these, by their names, must have been native Hindus.

Apparently the Sakas never held any possessions in the Kabul valley, but they probably held Ghazni, which would account for some of their coins being found about Kabul. Whatever hold they may have had on the Panjâb must have been soon lost on the conquest of the country by the Kushâns under Yun-kao-ching, in the first century A.D.

There is a curious passage in the *Mojmal ut Tawârikh*, which certainly refers to these countries on the Indus, and though the period mentioned is said to be that of

Alexander the Great, it is probable that it may preserve some distorted account of the history of the early Saka kings of Sindh, as it cannot possibly refer to the time of Alexander. The following is a brief summary of the passage.[32]

In Sindh there were three kings until the time of *Kafand*, قفند, who conquered them all. Kafand was not a Hindu. In the Chachnâma he is called *Kaid* the Hindu. Kafand sent his brother Sâmid to Mansura to expel Mahra, مهره, the Persian. Sâmid sought the assistance of *Hâl*, King of India, and Mahra fled. When Kafand died his son Ayand, ايند, succeeded him, and divided his territories into four principalities.

1. Askalandûsa, or Askalandra.
2. Zor (Alor) with Anj (? Uch).
3. Sâmid's territory (? Sâminagar, or Thatha).
4. Hindustan, Nadama, and Lohâna.

Ayand's son Râsal, راسل, succeeded him, but after a time he was expelled by a rebel. Râsal left two sons, Rowâl روال, and Barkamâris, برقماريس. The latter killed his brother, and became so powerful that all India submitted to him.

Hâl is the well-known name of Sâlivâhan, the founder of the Saka era in A.D. 78.

A similar division of the kingdom of Sindh into four principalities is given in the Chachnâma, as follows:—[33]

1. Askalandra, with Pâbiya
2. Alor (with Sewistan).
3. Brahmanâbâd.
4. Multân and Sikka.

---

[32] Elliot's *Muham. Hist.*, i. p. 108.
[33] *Ibid.*, i. p. 138.

These divisions seem to be intended for the same as those of the *Mojmal ut Tawârikh.* They were in existence during the rule of the Sâhi kings (A.D. 505—642), and were upheld by Chach, their immediate successor. Pâbiya is said to have been to the south of the Biâs River. It was therefore in the Panjâb, and consequently must have been to the north-east of Multân. I would identify it with Depâlpur, and then the strong fort of Askalandra would correspond with *Shorkot*, or Alexandreia Soriane.

The dominions of the Saka kings of Sindh are said to have included Mekrân up to the frontiers of Kirmân and Kaikân or Kikân up to the frontiers of Khorasân. Before this time Sakastene or Sistân had become tributary to the Sassanian kings of Persia, while Arakhosia or Kandahâr, the Kipin of the Chinese, would appear to have formed an independent kingdom.

About A.D. 530 Kosmas Indicoplanates travelled over the country to the west of the Indus, which was then under the rule of a king named *Gollas.* He calls the country Οὔννια, *Unnia.* Apparently at that time the name of the White Huns of Sogdiana, the opponents of the Sassanian kings, had become so well known that all peoples between India and Persia were supposed to be of the same race. At this very time also, or A.D. 550, Varâha Mihira places a tribe called *Hâra-Hauras* in the north-western Panjâb.

The coins afford but little or no assistance. According to the Chinese the people of Kipin had coins both of gold and silver, with the head of a man on one side and a horseman on the other side.[34] This description agrees only

---

[34] Remusat, *Nouv. Mélanges Asiat.*, i. p. 206.

with the coin types of Miaüs and the nameless king. But there are no gold coins of either of these kings, and only copper coins of the latter. In fact there are no known gold coins of any of the Saka kings.

I see that Wilson describes the coins of the Sakas as having a horseman on one side and a portrait or *figure of a man* on the other.[35] If this description be correct it would include all the coins of the known Saka kings of Kipin, Vonones, Spalahora, Spalgadama, and Spalirisha, as well as the Panjâb kings Moas, Azas, and Azilises.

In the Chinese notices of Kipin it is said that a king named U-to-lao was a contemporary of the Emperor Wuti (d. 87 B.C.), and that his son was driven from the throne by a rebel. This looks like a repetition of the story of Ayand and his son Râsal. But these names seem to offer no resemblance to any of the coin names of Vonones, Spalahora, Spalgadama, or Spalirisha. I suspect, however, that the rebel chief may be the king named *In-mo-fu,* who, according to the Chinese, drove U-to-lao's son from the throne and made himself King of Kipin in B.C. 49. This date is ascertained by the accession of the Emperor Hiao-yuan-to in B.C. 48, who broke off all relations with foreign countries, and would not receive In-mo-fu's embassy.

To this king I would ascribe the large silver coins (tetradrachms) with the title of *Turannountos* and the name of *Heräus* or *Miäus*. In 1861 I read the names as Heräus, but some years later, when I obtained some oboli of the same king, I adopted the reading of *Miaüs* or *Miaius*. Mr. Gardner prefers Heräus, and attributes the coins to a king

---

[35] *Ariana Antiqua*, p. 311.

of the Sakas, by reading the continuation of the legend as **ΣΑΚΑ ΚΟΙΡΑΝΟΥ**. But to this reading I strongly demur. I possess half-a-dozen tetradrachms and thirteen oboli, and on none do I find the letter **Κ** of **ΣΑΚΑ**, while on every specimen I find the addition of the letter **Β** to this word. On one of my coins the word is distinctly **ΣΑΝΑΒ**; on another specimen I find **ΣΑΝΑΟΒ**. I also find **ΚΟΡϹΑΝΟΥ** instead of **ΚΟΙΡΑΝΟΥ**, and as this is the early rendering of the tribal name of the Kushâns on the coins of Kujula Kadphises I feel inclined to adopt it, and to read the difficult word *Sanaob* as a Greek rendering of the native title of *Tsanyu* or *Chanyu*, "Son of Heaven," or king. The whole legend would then be of the paramount ruler; Miaüs (or Heräus) would therefore be a Kushân king.[36] On one of my coins I find **ΗΝΥΑΝΟΥ** instead of **ΚΟΡϹΑΝΟΥ**.

In the passage which I have quoted from the *Mojmal ut Tawârikh* the names of four kings are given as the successive rulers of Sindh. As they are specially said to be not of Indian origin there is a strong presumption that they must have been the Scythians who conquered Sindh. Their names, as already quoted, are: 1, *Kafand* or *Kid*; 2, *Ayand*; 3, *Râsal*; and 4, the two sons of the last-named, *Rowâl* and *Barkamâris*. It is curious that we possess the coins of just four princes who might possibly be identified with them were it not for the difference in the names. But it seems probable that Vonones and his relatives of the coins must have belonged to Kipin or Arachosia, while Ayand and his posterity belonged to Sindh and the Panjâb.

---

[36] Remusat, *Nouv. Mélanges Asiat.*, i. p. 207.

It is possible, however, that they may be represented by Azas and his successors, thus:—

Ayand may be Aya or Azas.
Râsal may be Ayilisha or Azilises.
The rebel might be Jihonia or Zeionises.
Rowâl might be Sapaleizes.
Barkamâris might be The Nameless King.

Should *Barkamâris* turn out to be a corrupt rendering of *Bikramâdit* this last identification might not be improbable, as several of the different types of the Nameless King have the single Arian letter *Vi* in the field. The founder of the dynasty, named *Kafand,* would then be identified with Moga or Moas.

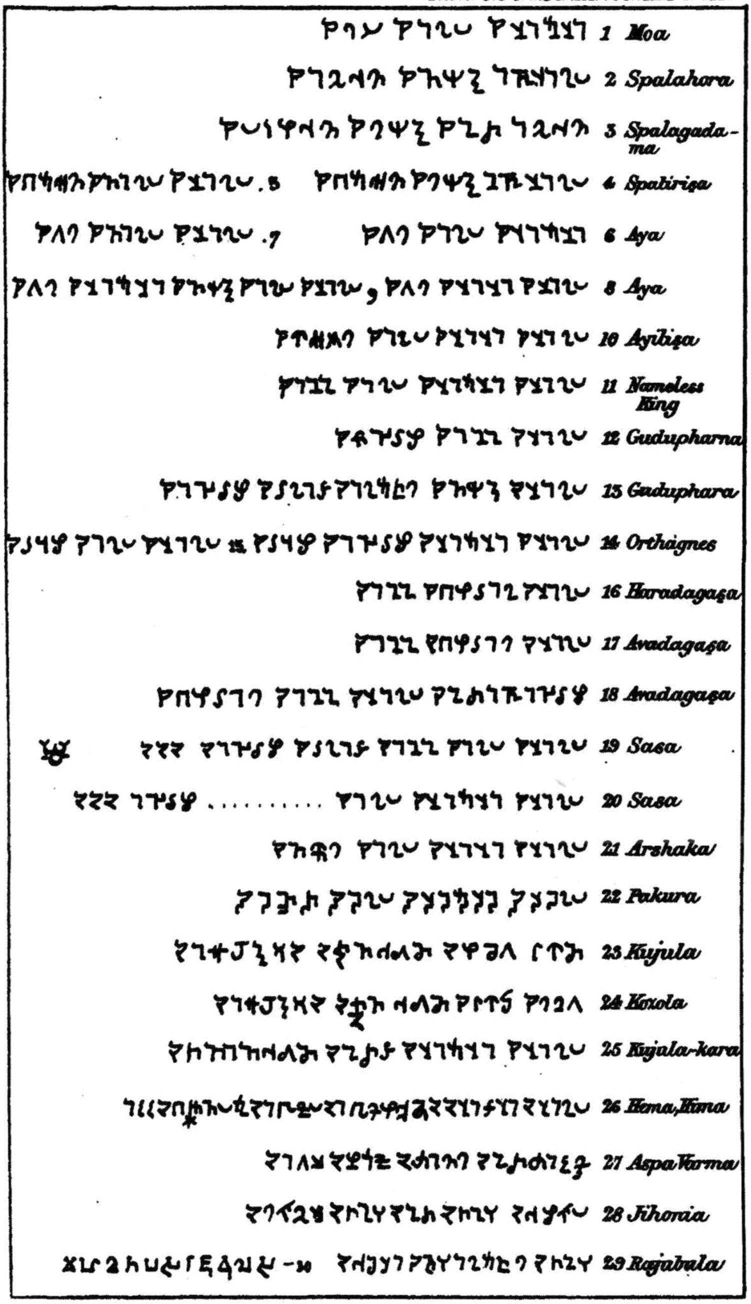

INDO-SCYTHIANS — NATIVE LEGENDS.

1. Rajatirajasa mahatasa MOASA.
2. Maharaja-bhrata dhramikasa SPALAHORASA.
3. Spalahora-putrasa dhramiasa SPALAGADAMASA.
4. Maharaja-bhrada dhramiasa SPALIRISASA.
5. Maharajasa mahatakasa SPALIRISASA.
6. Rajatirajasa mahatasa AYASA.
7. Maharajasa mahatakasa AYASA.
8. Maharajasa rajarajasa AYASA.
9. Maharajasa mahatasa dhramikasa rajatirajasa AYASA.
10. Maharajasa rajarajasa AYILISHASA.
11. Maharajasa rajatirajasa mahatasa tradatasa.
12. Maharajasa tradatasa GUDUPHARNASA.
13. Maharajasa dhramikasa apratihatasa devahadasa GUDUPHARASA.
14. Maharajasa rajatirajasa Gudupharasa GUDANASA.
15. Maharajasa mahatasa GUDANASA.
16. Maharajasa HARADAGASASA tradatasa.
17. Maharajasa AVADAGASASA tradatasa.
18. Guduphara bhrata-putrasa maharajasa tradatasa AVADAGASASA.
19. Maharajasa mahatasa tradatasa devahadasa Gudupharasa SASASA ῳ.
20. Maharajasa rajatirajasa mahatasa.
21. Maharajasa rajarajasa mahatasa ARSHAKASA.
22. Maharajasa rajatirajasa mahatasa PAKURASA.
23. Kushana yavugasa KUYULA KAPSASA sacha dharma thidasa.
24. Yauasa Khushanasa KUYULA KAPHSASA sacha dharma thidasa.
25. Maharajasa rajatirajasa devaputrasa KUYULA-KARA-KAPASA.
26. Maharajasa rajadirajasa sarvaloga-iswarasa mahiswarasa HIMA-KATHPISASA tradata.
27. Indra-varma putrasa ASPA-VARMASA strategasa jayantasa.
28. Manigulasa Chhatrapasa putrasa Chhatrapasa JIHONIASA.
29. Chhatrapasa apratihatachhakrasa RANJUBULASA.
30. Mahakhatapasa RAJUBULASA.

INDO-SCYTHIANS—NATIVE LEGENDS.

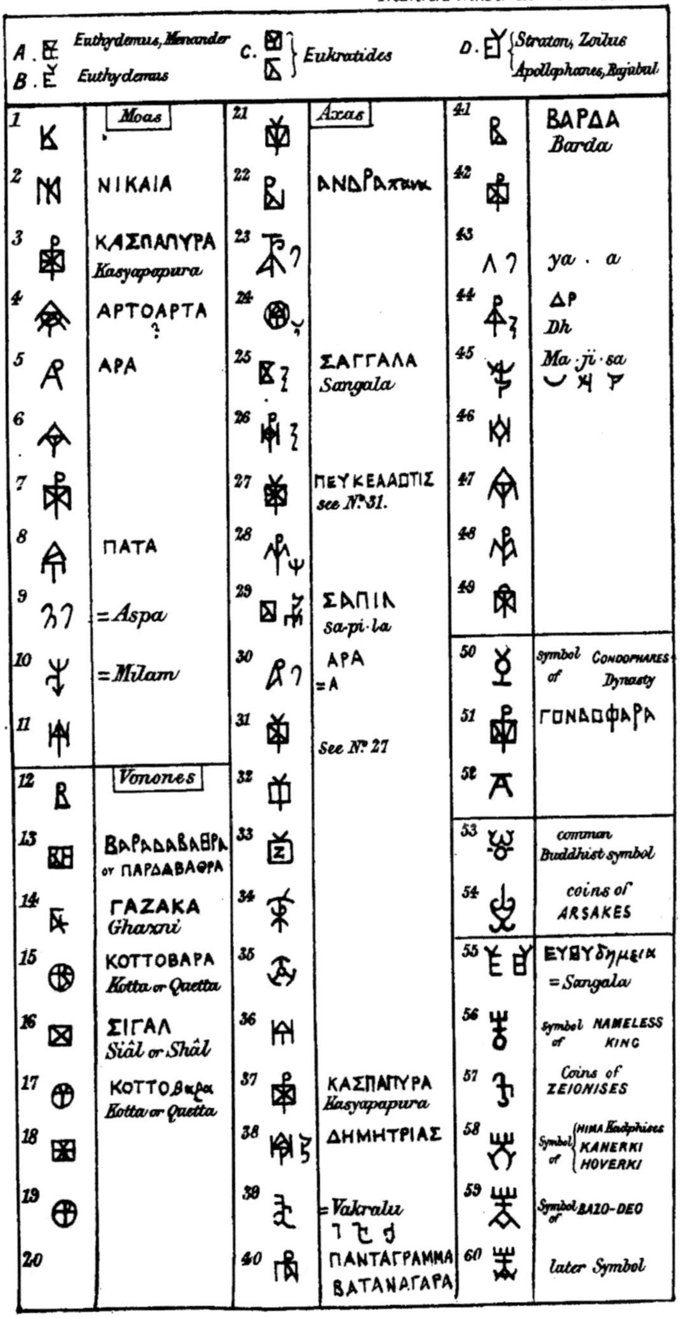

A. Euthydemus, Menander
B. Euthydemus
C. Eukratides
D. Straton, Zoilus
Apollophanes, Rajubal
Moas
1
2 ΝΙΚΑΙΑ
3 ΚΑΣΠΑΠΥΡΑ
Kasyapapura
4 ΑΡΤΟΑΡΤΑ
5 ΑΡΑ
6
7
8 ΠΑΤΑ
9 = Aspa
10 = Milam
11
Vonones
12
13 ΒΑΡΔΑΒΑΘΡΑ
or ΠΑΡΔΑΒΑΘΡΑ
14 ΓΑΖΑΚΑ
Ghazni
15 ΚΟΤΤΟΒΑΡΑ
Kotta or Quetta
16 ΣΙΓΑΛ
Siâl or Shâl
17 ΚΟΤΤΟβαρα
Kotta or Quetta
18
19
20
Axas
21
22 ΑΝΔΡαπανα
23
24
25 ΣΑΓΓΑΛΑ
Sangala
26
27 ΠΕΥΚΕΛΑΟΤΙΣ
see No. 31.
28
29 ΣΑΠΙΛ
sa·pi·la
30 ΑΡΑ
= A
31 See No. 27
32
33
34
35
36
37 ΚΑΣΠΑΠΥΡΑ
Kasyapapura
38 ΔΗΜΗΤΡΙΑΣ
39 = Vakralu
40 ΠΑΝΤΑΓΡΑΜΜΑ
ΒΑΤΑΝΑΓΑΡΑ
41 ΒΑΡΔΑ
Barda
42
43 ya · a
44 ΔΡ
Dh
45 Ma · ji · sa
46
47
48
49
50 symbol of CONDOPHARES Dynasty
51 ΓΟΝΔΟΦΑΡΑ
52
53 common Buddhist symbol
54 coins of ARSAKES
55 ΕΥΘΥδημεια
= Sangala
56 symbol of NAMELESS KING
57 Coins of ZEIONISES
58 Symbol of HIMA Kadphises
KANERKI
HOVERKI
59 Symbol of BAZO-DEO
60 later Symbol

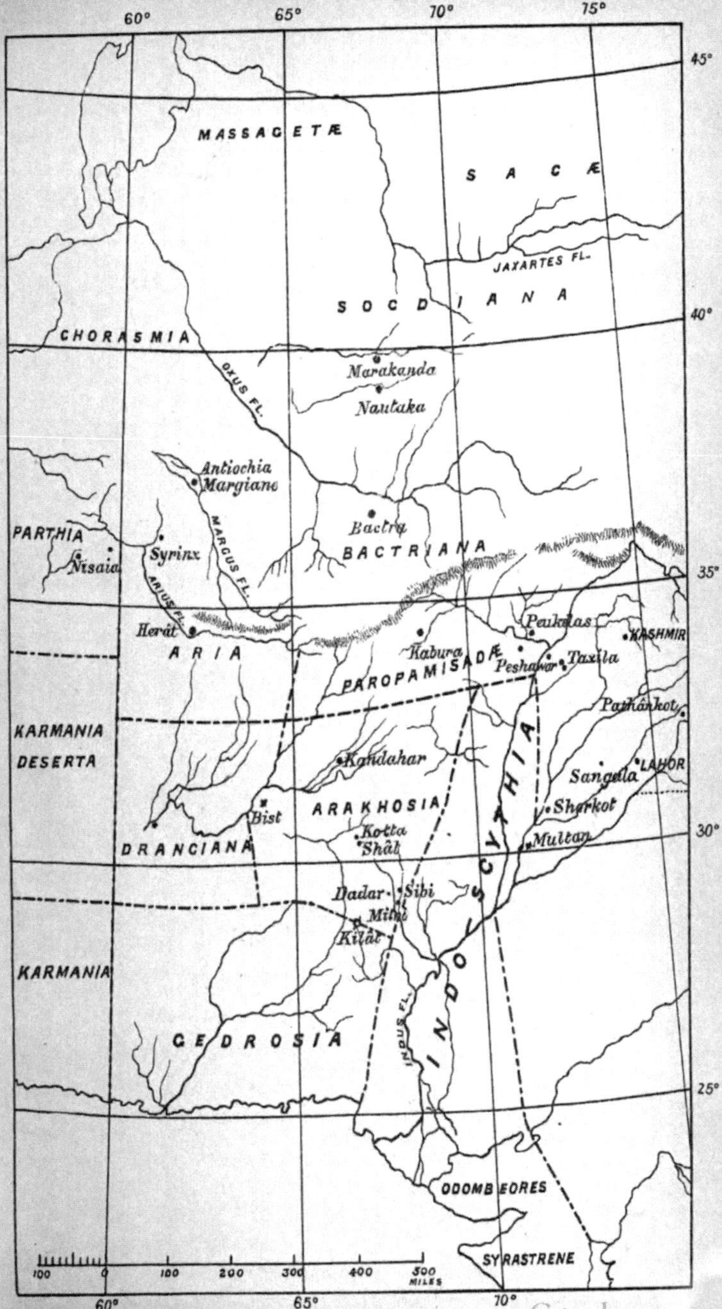

BACTRIANA, ARIANA, N. W. INDIA.

COINS OF THE

TOCHARI, KUSHÂNS,

OR

YUE-TI.

BY

MAJOR-GENERAL SIR A. CUNNINGHAM, R.E.,
K.C.I.E., C.S.I.

REPRINTED FROM THE NUMISMATIC CHRONICLE,

VOL. IX., THIRD SERIES, PAGES 268—311.

LONDON:

1889.

COINS OF THE TOCHARI, KUSHÂNS, OR YUE-TI.

According to Strabo the principal tribes of the Scythian conquerors of Bactriana were the Asii, the Pasiani, the Tochari, and the Sakarauli.[1] In the brief notices of Trogus, the Asiani and the Sarancæ are named as the conquering tribes. The first tribe, the Asiani or Pasiani of Strabo, is said to have given kings to the Tochari, and to have afterwards subdued the Sarduchæ.[2] In the first passage we may perhaps read *Saraucæ*, and in the second *Sarauchæ*, both of which might be identified with the Sakarauli or Sagaraukæ of Strabo.

As the dates of Trogus and Strabo are limited to the period between B.C. 40 and A.D. 14, the Scythian occupation of Bactriana must be assigned to the second century B.C., while the union of the five tribes and the consequent aggrandisement of the Yue-chi (or Yue-ti) under the single rule of the Asiani (or Kushâns), cannot have taken place until near the close of the first century B.C.

We derive some further information about the Scythian conquest of the provinces on the Oxus from a few brief

---

[1] *Geogr.*, xi. 8, 2.

[2] *Prolog. Trogi*, xli.—"Scythicæ gentes Sarancæ et Asiani Bactra occupavere et Sogdianos." *Prolog.*, xlii.—"Additæ res Scythicæ reges Thocarorum Asiani, interitusque Sarducharum."

notices of other Chinese writers. According to them the Great *Yue-ti* on being driven across the Jaxartes by the Hiong-nu, occupied Sogdiana in B.C. 163, at which time the king of the Yue-ti was killed, and his skull made into a drinking-cup, that was still in use one hundred and fifty years later.[3] The Yue-ti, under their widowed queen, gradually extended their dominions until they reached the south side of the Oxus, where they were found in full possession by the Chinese general Chang-Kian in B.C. 116. But their wars with the Hiong-nu were known in China before B.C. 126, when Chang-Kian's embassy was dispatched. This date is confirmed by the deaths of two Parthian kings in battle with the Scythians and Thogarii —the first, Phraates II. in B.C. 126, and the second, Artabanus in B.C. 123.

About one hundred years later, or say about 16 B.C., the chief of the Kushâns, having conquered the other four tribes of the Yue-ti, assumed the title of *King of the Kushâns,* and advancing to the south occupied *Kao-fu,* or Kabul. The name of this king was *Kieu-tsieu-khio.*[4] He must therefore be the Kujula Kadphises of the coins, on which he takes the title of king of the *Korsan,* or the *Kushâns,* as written in the native legends of his coins. At first he would appear to have reigned jointly with the Greek king Hermæus, as both of their names are found together on one very numerous series of copper-coins of the Kabul valley.

Kieu-tsieu-khio is said to have reached eighty-four years of age, and the great abundance of his coins bears ample testimony to a very long reign. He probably reigned for

---

[3] Remusat, *Nouv. Mélanges Asiat.*, i. 205.
[4] Julien's translation in *Les Huns Blancs*, p. 48.

about forty-five or fifty years, or from B.C. 16 to A.D. 35. The consolidation of the five tribes of the Yue-chi under Kujula Kadphises has been generally accepted as dating from about one hundred years after Chang-Kian's embassy, which appears to have occupied about ten years, or from B.C. 126 to 116. But M. Specht, the last translator of the Chinese accounts, fixes the date at A.D. 25.[5] But against this late date I can offer the very strong objection that in the year B.C. 2, the king of the "Great Yue-ti" is said to have sent a mission to China under *I-tsuṇ-kiu* (? Asanga) with a Buddhist book.[6] Now this king must certainly have been *Kujula*, who calls himself on his coins *Sacha-dharma-thida*, or "upholder of the true dharma." He must therefore have been a patron of Buddhism, and as he was the founder of the Kushân empire, and the immediate successor of the Greek Hermæus, he must have been the king of the Yue-ti who sent the Buddhist book to the Emperor of China in B.C. 2. His subjugation of the other four tribes of the Yue-ti, and consequent aggrandisement of the Kushân power, cannot therefore be placed later than about 10 B.C. I take his actual name to have been *Kujula*, or in Greek **ΚΟΖΟΥΛΟ** and **ΚΟΖΟΛΑ**, while *Kadaphes* or *Kadphizes* was only a title, which I believe to mean simply the "good charioteer," as I find that *Kieu-teu-fa* is so translated by D'Herbelot.[7]

Kujula was succeeded by his son *Yen-kao-ching*, or *Yun-kao-chin-tai*, who is recorded to have conquered India, where he established his generals as governors of provinces.

---

5 *Indian Antiquary*, xv. p. 19.
6 Pauthier, in *Thian-chu*, p. 14.
7 *Bibliothèque Orientale*, 8vo, iv. 62.

I would identify this king with *Wema*, or *Hema Kadphises* of the coins, who certainly reigned over the whole of the Punjâb and North-West India, as proved by the numerous find spots of his coins. As *Yun* or *Yen* is only an interchangeable pronunciation with *Wen* or *Hen*, I take this king's name to have been simply *Wen*, while *Kadphises* was his title, as in the case of his predecessor. In corroboration of this view I can point to the unique gold coin of this prince on which he is represented driving in a chariot.[8]

Now this same name of *Wen* was that of the famous progenitor of no less than ten branches of the Yue-ti, who after a lapse of six centuries claimed an uninterrupted descent from the *Shaowu Wen*. This was in A.D. 610; but only twenty years later, or in A.D. 630, Hwen Thsang found that no less than twenty-seven chiefs of the *Tu-ho-lo* or *Tochari*, called themselves kings, while they were all tributary to the great Khan of the Turks.[9] On the coins the name of this king is written OOHMO in Greek, and *Hima* in native characters.[10] The Greek seems to represent *Wemo*. One or two of the coins have *Hema* in native characters; but the common form is *Hima*. As his coins are extremely common he must have had a long reign, say of forty years, from about 35 to 75 A.D.

After him the Chinese mention king *Kia-ni-se-kia*, or Kanishka, of whom we possess several inscriptions as well as numerous coins, both in gold and copper. The name

---

[8] *Brit. Mus. Cat.* Greek and Scythic Kings, Pl. XXXII., fig. 13.

[9] Beal's *Hwen Thsang*, i. 37.

[10] The name of India is written *Hian-theu* as well as *Yin-tu*.

of Kanishka is famous in Buddhist history as a convert to Buddhism, and a great patron of Buddhist teachers. A single gold coin presents the name of ΒΟΔΔΟ, with a figure of Buddha standing in a posture well known to us from numerous statues. There are also about a dozen copper coins, which bear both standing and sitting figures of the teacher. In his inscriptions Kanishka calls himself king of the Kushâns, or Gushâns, and in the Raja Tarangini he is said to have been a *Turuskka*.[11]

No other certain names are mentioned by the Chinese writers. But in some of the early Muhammadan authors I find the names of *Bâsdeo*, *Ujen*, and *Jasand*, as successors of *Kanak* or Kanishka.[12] But according to Binakiti *Ujen* was the predecessor of *Kanak*. By reading *Wahen*, وحين, instead of وجين, I think that this king may be identified with ΟΟΗΜΟ or *Wen*. Similarly *Jasand* may be only a slight corruption of *Hasank*, or *Hushka*, while *Bâsdeo* preserves the name of *Vásu Deva* unchanged.

During the year 94 A.D., there is a notice by the Chinese that a king of the Yue-ti was taken prisoner and put to death by the Chinese.[13] As the Chinese record every present as "tribute," I think we may safely read "frontier chief" instead of "king," as at this very time Kanishka held hostages from the *tributary* Chinese Princes to the west of the Yellow River.[14]

During the period A.D. 220—280 the Yue-ti are said to

---

[11] *Raja Tarangini*, B. I., verse 170.
[12] Elliot's *Muham. Hist.*, ii. 406, and ii. 421. Haidar Razi.
[13] *Les Huns Blancs*, p. 51.
[14] Beal's *Hwen Thsang*, i. 173.

have held *Kipin* or Arachosia, *Ta-hia* or Bactria, *Kaofu* or Kabul, and *Thien-chu* or India. Their capital was *Lu-kien-shi*, or simply *Kien-shi* or *Lan-shi.* Ptolemy places the Tochari below the Zariaspæ. But the *Tochari*, or *Tushâras*, or *Tukhâras*, or *Tu-ho-lo*, then held Balkh, and were the same as the Zariaspæ. Ammianus Marcellinus makes the Tochari subject to the Bactrians,[15] by a similar mistake. At a later date, about A.D. 425 or 430, the warlike king of the Yue-ti, named *Ki-to-lo*, conquered Kabul and *Kan-to-lo*, or Gandhâra, and five districts to the north of Gandhâra.[16] While absent on this expedition the White Huns appeared on the banks of the Oxus, and he was obliged to return for the defence of his own territory; but, before leaving he installed his son in Purushapura, as King of Gandhâra, and thus established a separate dominion known to the Chinese as the kingdom of the "Little Yue-ti," or Little Kushâns.

As the White Huns managed to establish themselves to the north of the Oxus and also in Gorgo or Gurgân, the ancient Hyrkania, the power of the Kushâns was much weakened, and their dominions became limited to Balkh and Kabul. In the beginning of the sixth century the King of Kipin was at war with the King of the White Huns who held Peshawar.

Of Kujula Kadphises and Wema Kadphises the only remains are their coins, and the brief notices of the Chinese annalists. But of Kanishka and his two successors Huvishka and Vâsu Deva, we possess several inscriptions, most of which are dated, the dates ranging from the

---

[15] *Am. Marcell.*, xxiii. 6—27.
[16] Julien, in *Les Huns Blancs*, p. 44.

year 7 to 98 of some era. Several years ago I made the following remarks on this subject.[17]

"In the Indo-Scythian inscriptions the names of four different Macedonian months have been found—namely, *Panemos, Daisios, Apellaios,* and *Artemisios.* The use of these names shows incontestably that the Macedonian calendar must have been introduced in Kabul and North-West India by the Bactrian Greeks, and as the province to the west of the Indus had belonged to Seleukus I conclude that the era of the Seleukidæ must have been adopted there also. Unfortunately the year dates hitherto discovered are all small numbers, which might refer to some recently established date of the Indo-Scythians; or, as suggested by Mr. Thomas, they may possibly refer to the Seleukidan era by leaving out the hundreds, which was the common Indian mode of reckoning the *Saptârshi Kâl.* With the Indo-Scythian inscriptions, for instance, the dates of 9, 11, 18, and 28 of Kanishka, and of 33, 39, 47, and 51 of Huvishka, might either be referred to a new era, such as the Saka Kâl of 78 A.D., or to the years 9, 11, 18, &c., of the fifth Seleukidan century, by leaving out 400. In the former case the year 7 of Kanishka would be 78 + 7 = 85 A.D., while in the latter case it would be referred to the year 407 of the Seleukidan era, equal to A.D. 95-96."

As these dates are found along with the names of four Macedonian months, I feel that they should naturally be referred to the Seleukidan era. Under this view the following will be the dates of the Indo-Scythian Princes Kanishka, Huvishka, and Vâsu Deva:—

---

[17] See my *Book of Indian Eras*, p. 41.

		A. Sel.
Inscription,	Kanishka	7 = 407 — 312 = 95 and 96 A.D.
"	"	28 = 428 — 312 = 116 and 117 A.D.
"	Huvishka	33 = 433 — 312 = 121 and 122 A.D.
"	"	51 = 451 — 312 = 139 and 140 A.D.
"	Vâsu Deva	83 = 483 — 312 = 171 and 172 A.D.
"	"	98 = 498 — 312 = 186 and 187 A.D.

The accuracy of these dates has been confirmed by the discovery of gold coins of Wema Kadphises, Kanishka, and Huvishka, in the Ahinposh Stûpa (near Jalâlâbâd) along with some Roman gold coins of Domitian, Trajan, and Sabina the wife of Hadrian. As Sabina died in A.D. 137, and as there was only one coin of Huvishka amongst twenty-one specimens, the Stûpa was probably built not later than 130 A.D.

The approximate dates of the great Kushân Kings would therefore be as follows:—

B.C. 10.	Kujula Kadphises.
A.D. 35.	Wema Kadphises.
" 75.	Kanishka.
" 120.	Huvishka.
" 160.	Vâsu Deva, still reigning in A.D. 186.

The dates of the inscriptions would only be slightly altered to nine years earlier, by the adoption of the Saka Samvat, beginning with A.D. 79 = 1, as the era in which they are reckoned.

After Vâsu Deva we have no recorded names, but there are numerous gold coins of the seated *Ardokhro* type, which can only be referred to the Kushân princes who followed Vâsu Deva. They are similar to the early Gupta gold coins of Chandra Gupta and Samudra Gupta, but with the exception of a few of the earlier ones, they are much ruder in execution. The earlier specimens may date from 200 to 400, and the later specimens from 400 to 600 or 700, A.D.

There are also numerous silver coins of the Sassanian period, which must belong to Vâsu Deva's successors, besides numerous copper coins, which appear to be mere copies of the gold coins. Some of them are, indeed, ancient forgeries of the gold coins, with the gilding still clinging to the deeper parts.

At last, about A.D. 450, we find the first coins of the Little Yue-ti, with the name of their leader recorded on them, as *Kidâra Kushâna Shâhi.* These Little Yue-ti reigned over Gandhâra, and probably also over Kashmir, as I would attribute all the coins that bear the name of *Kidâra* to their descendants. The name was not dropped for many generations.

During this expedition of *Kitolo*, or *Kidâra*, the *Ye-tha-i-li-to*, or *Ephthalites*, invaded the territories on the Oxus, and Kitolo was obliged to hasten back to defend his own dominions. The Kushâns were driven to the westward, and from this time, about A.D. 470, the supreme power fell into the hands of the Ephthalites. But the mass of the population was still Kushân, and so late as A.D. 610, as I have already noted, no less than ten princes in Farghâna, Sogdiana, Naksheb, and other places to the north, claimed an unbroken descent from the *Shaowe Wen*, or King Wema Kadphises, the Kushân conqueror of India. I find a corroboration of this curious fact in the embassy of Maniach, Prince of the Sogdoites to Justin in A.D. 569. His name, ending with a guttural, proclaims him a Kushân, and the letters in the Scythian character, which he brought with him, show that he was certainly not an Ephthalite. He was, therefore, as stated by the Chinese, a Kushân prince or Shaowu, a descendant of Wen.

Ibn Khurdâdbeh speaks of a Kushân Prince of Mâwarunnahr in the ninth century; and several Kushân chiefs are mentioned in the reign of Timur. They were, of course, Muhammadans.[18]

The statement that Yenkaoching or Wema Kadphises conquered India is confirmed by numerous finds of his coins as far eastward as Gorakhpur, and Ghazipur, and the line of railway from Allahabad to Jabalpur. In all these places several hundreds of his coins have been dug up; and much-worn specimens are also procurable in all the bazars of the Gangetic Doâb.

The coins of Kanishka and Huvishka are even more common, while the later coins of Vâsu Deva are found in thousands. They are especially common round about Mathura, which was probably the head-quarters of one of the Kushân king's satraps. But the very latest of these coins are very barbarous; and, as the copper coins of the Guptas are exceedingly scarce, I conclude that the Indo-Scythian copper money remained current in India for several centuries.

During the first century of the Christian era Roman gold was brought to India in great quantities. The fact is preserved by Pliny, who states that "at the lowest reckoning, one hundred million of sesterces were annually taken from Rome to India, the Seres, and Arabia." The whole amount was upwards of £800,000.[19] In another

---

[18] Price, *Muhammadan History*, iii. 101.

[19] *Nat. Hist.* xii. 41, 18. "Minimâque computatione millies centena millia sestertium annis omnibus India et Seres peninsulaque illa (Arabia) imperio nostro adimunt." The influx of gold into India still continues, but the yearly amount is now over two millions sterling. For eighteen centuries the gold of the world has been flowing into India, from whence little or none has ever left, except with a few great plunderers.

place Pliny assigns half that sum, "quingenties H.S." for India, exclusive of Arabia. In southern India the Roman gold remained current, and is still found there in large quantities. In northern India it was recoined by the Kushân Indo-Scythians, although many specimens have been preserved in Buddhist stûpas even down to our times. In 1858 I made a record of the weights of all these Indo-Scythian gold coins within my reach, and on comparing their weights with those of the Roman gold coins, I then came to the conclusion that they might have been re-struck on Roman aurei of the first century. I refer specially to the gold coins of Wema Kadphises and Kanishka, which agree in weight with the early Imperial aurei of Tiberius and Nero.

Roman gold coins are still discovered in the Buddhist monuments of the Kabul Valley, from the time of Augustus down to the fifth century. I have had gold coins of Leo, Justin, and Anastasius sent to me several times, and twice I have obtained coins of Focas. Gold coins of Theodosius, Marcian, and Leo, were found by Masson in a stûpa, near Jalâlâbâd, on the Kabul River.

The rule of the Great Yue-ti, or Kushâns, would appear to have remained undisturbed until the invasion of the Nephthalites, or White Huns, in the fifth century. But there are notices of relations, both warlike and peaceful, with some of the earlier Sassanian kings, which must certainly refer to the Kushâns. The warlike Prince Vararanes II., having conquered the Segestanis, or Sakas of Sakastene, in A.D. 280, was still detained on his eastern frontier in A.D. 283, when the Roman Emperor Carus invaded Persia. As peace had been made with the Segestanis, the detention would have been caused by the unsettled state of the north-east frontier of Kabul, which was then held by the

Kushâns. On the death of Vararanes the throne was disputed between the brothers Narses and Hormisdas when the latter was assisted by the *Sacci* (Sakas of Segestan), and by the Gelli, who must be the same as the Gelani of a little later date. Between A.D. 301 and 309 Hormisdas II., the son of Narses, married the daughter of the king of Kabul. That the latter was a Kushân prince we learn from a gold coin of Hormisdas, which bears the well-known type of the Kushân coins of the god *Okro*, with his bull.

During the following reign of Sapor II. the relations of the Sassanian king with the princes on his eastern frontier, would appear to have been friendly for a long time. In A.D. 350 Sapor was obliged to raise the siege of Nisibis, owing to a sudden irruption of the Massagetæ—that is, of the Sakas of Sakestene or Segestan. When this disturbance was settled we find Sapor bringing to the siege of Amida, in A.D. 359, a strong contingent of the warlike Segestani, along with the forces of the Chionitæ and the Albani, commanded by their respective kings in person. Grumbates was the king of the *Chionitæ*, and his eldest son was killed at the siege. I would identify the *Chionitæ* with the Kushâns, as I take the name to be only a Greek translation of *Tushâra* or *Tukhara*, the *Tu-ho-lo* of the Chinese, and the *Tokharoi* of the classical writers—meaning "men of the snowy land." The Gelli or Gelani may perhaps be the same as the Albani, but I cannot even guess at their identification.

Little Yue-ti, or Lesser Kushâns.

The kingdom of the Little *Yue-chi*, or *Yue-ti*, was established by *Ki-to-lo*, king of the Kushâns, or Great

Yue-chi, about A.D. 425. The Chinese syllables of the king's name may be read as *Kidâra.* Now I possess three large thin silver coins of Sassanian types, each bearing, in neat Indian characters, the legend—

Kidâra Kushâna Shâ(hi),

or "*Kidâra,* king of the Kushâns." This same name of Kidâra is found also upon a great number of coins in gold and copper in the north-western Punjâb, and in Kashmir. I infer, therefore, that the descendants of *Kitolo,* or *Kidâra,* must have remained in possession of some territory on both banks of the Indus for several centuries. None of these coins have been found at Kabul, and only two were discovered by Masson, in a stûpa, near Jalâlâbâd.

I have placed the establishment of the Little Yue-ti about A.D. 425, partly because the Indian inscriptions on their coins appear to me to be not earlier than the fifth century A.D., and partly because the silver coins of *Kidâra* himself seem to be of the same age as those of Vararan V., who reigned from A.D. 420 to 440. Kitolo's conquest of Gandhâra must have preceded the irruption of the White Huns, who established themselves at Peshawar two full generations before the visit of Sung-yun in A.D. 520—or say, about 470 A.D. The pilgrim calls the reigning king a *Ye-tha*—that is, an *Ephthalite,* or "White Hun." The full Chinese name is *Ye-tha-i-li-to,* which was contracted to *Ye-tha,* just as *Fo-tho,* for Buddha, was shortened to *Fo.*

During the occupation of Gandhâra by the White Huns, I suppose that the Little Yue-ti, the descendants of *Kitolo* or *Kidâra,* may have retired to Taxila and Mânsera. I think it probable, therefore, that they are now represented by the *Gakkars*, who still hold portions of these districts to the east of the Indus. I base my supposition on the fact that the Gakkars claim descent from a hero named *Kêd*, a stranger from the Oxus, and that his descendants reigned in Kashmir for sixteen generations. These traditions accord very well with the Chinese story of the conquest of Gandhâra, by the Kushân king, *Kitolo* or *Kidara*, from the Oxus, as well as with the actual record of the name of *Kidara* on the coins of Kashmir for about four centuries.

The name of *Kitolo* is preserved by the Muhammadan historians under the form of *Kitormân*, which was the name of the *Turki* kings of Kabul, whose rule lasted down to the time of the Brahman Kallow, about A.D. 850. Alberuni says that Kanak was the last of the *Kitormân* kings, and Binâkiti says the same. Their kings also continued to use the title of *Shâhi*, which has been handed down from the time of the Great Kanishka, so that their dominion was known as the *Shâhi-râjya*. But both name and title still subsist, as the chiefs of Chitrâl, Gilgit, and Chilâs still hold the title of *Shâh-kitor*.

In fixing the date of *Kitolo* at about A.D. 425, I have been guided by the fact that he was obliged to return to his own country (Balkh) by an inroad of the White Huns (*Jwan-jwan*). Now the White Huns did not become powerful until the time of Solien Khan (A.D. 428—443). He himself was at war with Bahram Gor, the Sassanian. But his son, Chu-khân, the *Konkhas* of Priscus (A.D. 443—464) was a strong ruler, who assisted Firoz against Hormisdas, and to him I would ascribe the invasion of Kitolo's dominion. It was during his stay with the camp of Attila in A.D. 446—47, that Priscus heard of the 'Ουννοι Κιδαρίται, or Ephthalite Huns; and I would, therefore, ascribe the return of *Kitolo* to the time of *Konkhas* or *Chu-Khân*, or about A.D. 450. Kitolo then established his son in Gandhâra, and retired to his own country.

The Chinese mention that the Little Yue-ti had coins both of gold and silver, but they say nothing as to their types. To these successors of Kitolo I would ascribe most, if not all, of the gold coins that bear the name of *Kidâra* under the king's arm. The Kashmir coins of Toramâna, and his son Pravarasena, bear the same name, which I take to denote some family connection with the Kitolo kings of the Gandhâra. We know from the Raja Tarangini that Meghavâhana, the grandfather of Toramâna, had received shelter at the court of *Gopâditya*, king of Gandhâra. But there are no coins bearing this name. Unfortunately, the early history of Kashmir, which ought to have assisted us, is a confused jumble of names, of which only a few can be found on the coins. These are Hiranyakula and Mihirakula, with perhaps Gokarna, and after them, Narendraditya and Khingkila. Of the six kings of a new dynasty, not a single name agrees with the coins, and only two names of the next dynasty, Toramâna, and his son Pravarasena, are found amongst the coins. But of the succeeding dynasty of the Naga kings, established by Durlabha Vardhana, several names agree; and, as their coins still bear the name of *Kidara* under the king's arm, I look upon these kings as the last descendants of the Kushâns in Kashmir, who reigned until A.D. 855.

But the main body of the Little Yue-ti, or Lesser Kushâns, continued to hold the Kabul Valley until they were gradually driven eastward by the Muhammadans. The title of *Shâh Kitor*, which is still held by the chiefs of Chitral and Gilgit, seems to me to establish this late occupation of the Upper Kabul Valley by the Lesser Kushâns. The continued occupation by the Turki successors of Kanishka for sixty generations (? reigns) is vouched for by Alberini, who calls Mahmud's opponents, "Hindu Shâhi kings."

In A.D. 630, when Hwen Thsang visited Gandhâra, there was no king, and the country had become a dependency of Kapisa. I infer, therefore, that the Ephthalite king of Peshawar must have retired to Kabul or to Sindh, and that the Little Kushâns still held Taxila as a dependency of Kashmir. Here they would seem to have remained, while they gradually acquired possession of all the hill country between Kashmir and the Indus. I found my conclusion for this statement on the fact that most, if not all, of the gold and copper coins of this period which are found to the east of the Indus bear the royal title of Shâhi in addition to the tribal name of Kidara. The country itself is called *Shâhi-rajya*, or the "Kingdom of the Shahis," in the Raja Tarangini, while the great city of Taxila is still called *Shâh-dheri* and *Dheri-Shâhân*, or "the city of the Shâhis."

The principal occupants of this territory at the present day are the *Gakkars*, whom I take to be the actual descendants of the Little Yue-ti, or Lesser Kushâns. To establish this last position it is necessary to notice what the Gakkars say of themselves. They profess to have come from Tarân, or the country of Afrâsiyâb, under a leader named *Kîd*, or *Kaid*, several centuries before the Muhammadan invasion. If they are the descendants of the Little Yue-ti, then this leader *Kîd*, or *Kaid*, must be the *Kitolo* of the Chinese, and the *Kidara* of the coins. The earliest notice of them under their present name is due to the Muhammedans. During the campaigns of Muhammad Ghori, they were already established in their present territories. But two centuries earlier I find mention of a nameless people, who held the passes leading into Kashmir.[20] Their chief, named *Sâbli*, son of *Shâhi*, son of *Bamhi*, submitted to Mahmud, and offered his services as a guide. As not one of these names is Indian, the chief could not have been a Hindu; and as the name or title of Shâhi occurs amongst them, there can be little doubt that he and his people were Gakkars.

The Gakkars claim to have held Kashmir for sixteen generations; and if I am right in identifying them with the Little Yue-ti, or Lesser Kushâns, I think that their claim may have some foundation, as the coins of Toramâna and Pravarasena actually bear the name of Kidâra. It seems, therefore, not improbable that the princes of this family, covering seven generations, must have been very intimately connected with the Little Yue-ti. At a later date it is quite certain that the rulers of Kashmir belonged to the family of the Shâhi kings of Taxila, or from the time of Diddâ Râni in A.D. 1000, down to the Muhammadan conquest.

The name of Gakkar is said to have been derived from Gakkar Shâh, one of their kings, some centuries later than Kaid. Their original name is unknown.

Albiruni, in speaking of the Turki kings of Kabul, calls the founder of the family Barhatakin, or Barhtigin, whom I believe to be simply the fabulous *dun*-wolf Burtezena, the legendary progenitor of the Turki races. He mentions

[20] Elliot's *Muhammadan Historians*, *Utbi*, ii. 43.

Kanak as the "last of the Kitormân kings."[21] This would seem to imply that the Kitor kings had possessed Kabul; and this, indeed, seems very likely, as the reigning Prince of Kipin, in A.D. 520, was then at war with the Ephthalites of Peshawar. In another place Albiruni mentions that a genealogy of this family on a roll of silk containing sixty names was found in the fort of Nagarkot (Kangra). But while the Kitor kings were reigning at Peshawar the kings of Kabul could not have possessed Kangra. Or it may be that as the Kitor princes were the descendants of *Kitolo*, the king of the Great Yue-ti, or Kushâns, they may have reckoned their genealogy from the first Kushân king of Kabul. In this way the Kitormân kings might have reached sixty generations (or ? reigns) from 10 B.C. to 1030 A.D. or 1040 years, at an average of 17⅔ years per reign.

In A.D. 630, when Hwen Thsang was in Gandhâra, there was no king, the province having become a dependency of Kapisa. This may have happened by the extinction of the White Huns on the conquest of Gandhâra by the Kushân king of Kabul.

I think there is good reason for suspecting that the line of the Kitor kings did not end with Kanak. Albiruni mentions the names of eight kings as his successors, as follows:—

A.D.
825, *Kanak, the last Kitorman.*
1. 850, Kalar, a Brahman.
2. 860, Sâmanda,

---

[21] Reinaud, *Fragments, Arabes et Persans*, p. 149. Gibbon, *Decline and Fall*, c. 42. Elliot's *Muhammedan Historians*, ii. 18.

A.D.
3. 900, Kamalüa, a Brahman.
4. 940, Bhima, ,,
5. 950, Jayapâla (? a Kitor prince restored).
6. 1002, Anandapâla ,, ,,
7. 1021, Trilochanpâla ,, ,,
8. 1026, Bhimapâla II. ,, ,,

Of the first four of these kings we have silver coins; but there is not a single coin of any one of the last four. Kamalüa was a contemporary of Amru bin Lais, 878 to 900 A.D. Jayapâla fought with Subuktagin, and Anandapàla fought with Mahmud of Ghazni. As before stated, there are no coins of the last four princes, all of whom bear the name of Pâla, and the first is said to have been the son of Hispâl. These four kings, therefore, would seem to have no family connection with the first four. I suspect that they belong to the old Kitormân dynasty, as Anandapâl is called Shâh by Albiruni,[22] and Trilochan-pâl is called Shâhi in the Raja Tarangini. As they were not Muhammadans there was no reason for giving them this title; but as Trilochanpâl is called *Shâhi* and not *Shah*, I think it is almost certain that these last four princes must have belonged to the old Kitormân family.

I may note here that *Trilochan-pâl* is the prince whom all the Persian and Arabic writers persist in calling *Nardajan* and *Fardajan-pâl.*[23] As there are no coins of these last four princes I conclude that the very extensive mintage of Samanta Deva was found sufficient for the wants of the country.

---

[22] Sachau Albiruni, ii. 13.

[23] I made this correction as early as 1842 in my account of the Ancient Coinage of Kashmir.

Ephthalites, or White Huns.

The *Ephthalites*, or White Huns, make their first appearance in history early in the fifth century. To the industry of D'Herbelot and De Guignes we owe the collection of the various notices of Chinese authors; but our chief debt is due to Vivien de St. Martin, who, in his *Les Huns Blancs*, has added all the scattered accounts to be found in Armenian and classical writers. By the Chinese they were usually called *Jwan-jwan*, or *Jen-jen*, which is said to have a derogatory meaning in their language. Their true name of *Ephthalites* was very closely rendered by the syllables *Ye-tha-i-li-to;* but as the Chinese frequently abbreviated proper names, as *Fo* for *Fo-tho*, or Buddha, so the name of the Ephthalites was lost sight of in the contracted forms of *Ye-tha* and *Yi-ta*, which are applied to other peoples.

The earliest western notice of the White Huns is by Moses of Khorene, who mentions the *Hephthag* as one of the barbarous peoples of Scythia in the first half of the fifth century. The next notice is by the historian Priscus, who was the ambassador of Theodosius II. with Attila, in the years A.D. 445 to 447. He calls them Οὔννοι Κιδαρῖται, which appears to me to be only another name for Ephthalites, as *Hidalitæ* or *Hidarite*. In A.D. 530 they are described by Kosmas Indicopleustes as Λευκοὶ Οὔννοι, or "White Huns," and only a few years later, in A.D. 540, Procopius calls them by the same name as Ἐφθαλίτων ἔθνος, with the addition of λευκοὺς, or white. In the following century Theophanes calls the White Huns Νεφθαλίτας. Several other various spellings of the name are given by Vivien de St. Martin, as *Idalagân* by Lazarus of Parba,

Abdela by Theophylact, *Thedâl* by the Armenians, and *Haiathelah* by Firdausi and in the *Mojmal ut tawârikh*, as well as by the Sassanians.

According to Procopius the White Huns held the country to the north of the Persian dominions, with *Gorgo* as their capital, which St. Martin has identified with *Gurgân*, the chief city of ancient Hyrkania. According to Kosmas they occupied the country along the western bank of the Indus, to which he gave the name of Οὔννια, or *Unnia*, and not *Hunnia*.

From their occupation of the countries on the Oxus and the Indus, the White Huns soon came into conflict with the Persians on the west and the Indians on the east, and our knowledge of their history is chiefly due to their wars with their neighbours.

According to the Chinese, the first noted leader of the Jen-jen was *Shelun*, who reigned from A.D. 385 to 410. He dropped the native title of *tsanyu* for that of *Khakân*, which was adopted by all his successors. He was followed by three princes, of whom the last, named Tâtân, must be the *Khâkân* who fell in battle with Bahram Gor, or Vararan V., at Darband, on the Oxus, in A.D. 428. Tâtân was succeeded by his son *Solien Khan*, A.D. 428—443, who received a Chinese princess in marriage. Next came *Chu-khan*, 443—464, who was driven across the Oxus by Isdegard II. But afterwards, with his aid the Sassanian Firoz (Perozes), in 459, defeated his brother Hormisdas, and became King of Persia. Priscus calls this Ephthalite king Κούνχας, which I take to be the same as the Chinese *Chu-khan*. His successor was *Shu-lo-pu-chin*, the *Khush-Nawâz* of Sassanian history. Feroz gave his sister in marriage to the Khâkân, but his feeling of dependence so rankled in his mind that he shortly afterwards invaded the Khâkân's dominions, and was killed in battle. An ambassador from the Byzantine Emperor Zeno accompanied Feroz in this unfortunate invasion, which Gibbon, on the authority of Procopius, assigns to the year A.D. 488. But the eastern writers refer the death of Khushnawâz to 484—485. Three other princes followed, but the power of the White Huns was then declining, and no further relations with the Persian kings are recorded. The last prince, *Onowei*, was defeated in battle by *Tu-men*, the king of the Turks, who put him to death in A.D. 546. "Thus," says Gibbon, "ended the empire of the Nephthalites, or White Huns, a polite and warlike people, who had vanquished the Persian monarch, and carried their victorious arms along the banks, and perhaps to the mouth of the Indus." (*Decline and Fall*, c. 42).

The name of *Hûna* was well known to the Indians as a people on the north-west frontier. The Hûnas are not mentioned in the posthumous inscription of Samudra Gupta on the Allahabad Pillar. But as this record cannot be placed later than A.D. 380, the silence of Indian evidence is in full accord with both the Chinese and the Persian accounts, which place their first appearance in the next century. Our earliest notice of the White Huns on the Indus is due to the Chinese pilgrim, Sung-yun, who in A.D. 520 visited Gandhâra. He says that it was originally called *Ye-po-lo* (Embolina?), and adds, "this is the country that the *Yethas* (White Huns) destroyed, and afterwards set up *Laelih* to be king, since which events two generations have passed." The king was not a Buddhist, and he had been three years at war with Kipin.

If we place the reigning king's accession in A.D. 510, then the accession of Laelih may be placed two generations or about fifty years earlier, or in A D. 460—470.

The king kept 700 war elephants. This agrees with the account which Kosmas, A.D. 530, gives of King Gollas, who kept 1,000 elephants.

There is a strong temptation to identify this King Gollas with the great *Mihir-gul*, whose title of *Shâhi* proclaims him to have been a Scythian. Mr. Fleet's Mandasor Inscription of A.D. 532 mentions Mihirakula as a powerful prince, who had paid homage to the reigning king of Malwa Yasodharma. It also notes that this king possessed countries which neither the Guptas nor the *Hunâs* could subdue. From my Gwalior inscription we learn that Mihirakula's father was Toramâna, and very lately an important inscription of this Toramâna has been found in the Salt Range of the western Panjâb. As neither *Mihir-gul* nor *Toramâna* is a Hindu name, it would seem that both princes must have been Scythians. But there is nothing to show that they were Hûnas, except the fact that at this period the northern Panjâb was under the rule of the Hûnas. If we might identify Mihir-gul with Gollas, then Toramâna would be the father of the king who was reigning at Sung-yun's visit, and Laelih would be the father of Toramâna. The Western coins give the name of *Mihir-gul* with the title of *Shâhi*. The Eastern coins give *Mihir-kul* without the title.

As the date of the settlement of the White Huns in Gandhâra, and along the west bank of the Indus, corresponds with the period during which the province of Sindh, on the Lower Indus, was held by a Scythian dynasty who bore the title of Shâhi, it seems probable that the Ephthalites, as suggested by Gibbon, may have extended their conquests to the mouths of the Indus. The period of Scythian rule in Sindh lasted for 137 years, from A.D. 505 to 642. The original settlement corresponds not only with the date of Gollas on the Indus, but also with the well-ascertained period of the wide rule of Toramâna and his son Mihir Kul. The father succeeded Budha Gupta in Malwa shortly after 174 of the Gupta era, 318+175=493 A.D., while the son had already done homage to Yasodharma before A.D. 532. The great extension of the power of the White Huns may therefore be assigned to the most flourishing period of Ephthalite dominion under *Khush-Nawâz*, conqueror of Feroz of Persia, and under his son *Fukushun*, who together reigned from A.D. 464 to 508. Their rule probably lasted in the Panjâb until the close of the sixth century, as the *Hâra Hûnas* are mentioned by Varâha Mihir as a people of the North-west as late as A.D. 550. The "Western *Hûnas*" are also mentioned in the Aphsar inscription as the antagonists of Dâmodara Gupta, about A.D. 560—580. But they had disappeared as a ruling race before A.D. 530, when Hwen Thsang visited Gandhâra, as that country was then subject to the rule of Kapisa, while Taxila belonged to Kashmir.

Regarding the extension of the Ephthalite rule to Segestan I feel very sceptical. The early Muhammadan writers, who must have received all their information from the Persians, naturally described all Scythian races by the one name of Ratbil or Rantil, Zanbil or Zantil, Ratil or Abtil, &c., corrupted in a dozen different spellings. Amongst these various readings I recognise the name of the Ephthalite antagonists of the Persians. Theophylact, in the seventh century, calls them *Abdela*, and as this is the nearest form to the original Ephthalite, I conclude that the various names given to the rulers of Sejistan, Kabul, and Sindh, are simple corruptions of the one name.

The following notices of these conquerors are taken

from Elliot's *Muhammadan Historians of India*, vol. ii., pp. 417—420:—

In A.H. 22, or A.D. 643, Sejistan was taken, and shortly afterwards Mekrân and Sindh were conquered by the Muhammadans, when the king, named *Ranbil*, was killed.
In A.H. 78, or A.D. 697—98, Abdul Aziz, Governor of Sistân, invaded Kâbul, when the king, named *Zambil*, was killed.
In A.D. 775—809, the Khalifs Al Mahdi and Ar Rashid took tribute from *Ranbil*, king of Sistân.
In A.D. 813—833, the Khalif Al Mamûn took Kâbul, when the king submitted and professed Islâm.
In A.D. 869—70, Yâkub bin Lais took Kâbul from *Ranbil*, who appears to have been killed.
In A.D. 878—900, *Kamlu* was reigning at Kâbul, and was contemporary with Amru bin Lais.

But only a few years previously, in A.H. 260—61, or A.D. 873—75, coins were struck at Panjshir, in Kâbul, by Yâkub bin Lais.

With respect to the kings of Kâbul, there can be no doubt that they were not Ephthalites, as Biruni specially mentions that the rulers previous to Kamlu and his two predecessors were Turks of the family of Kanishka, which had ruled for sixty generations up to the time of Mahmûd of Ghazni.

As the White Huns were a barbarous nomad race, who were ignorant of writing, it seems probable that they may have had no coins. The pilgrim Sung-yun, who visited Gandhâra in A.D. 520, had seen the *Yetha* in their own country on the Oxus. He found them simple nomads, who practised polyandry and had no written characters. But when they were settled in Gandhâra amongst a civilised Indian population, it seems very probable that they would have struck coins in their own names, as the previous rulers had done. As they had no written characters of their own, they would of course have adopted the

Indian characters; and I am, therefore, very strongly inclined to assign the coins of *Mihir-gul* to the Ephthalite Huns of the Indus. I adopt this opinion the more readily as we learn from Sung-yun that the reigning king of Gandhâra in A.D. 520 was not a Buddhist; which agrees with the strongly pronounced Brahmanism of the coins of Mihir-gul, which display the *trisul*, or trident, as well as the standard of Siva with the humped bull, and the inscription, *jayatu Vrishi dhwaja*, "May he whose symbol is the bull (Siva) be victorious." I am inclined, therefore, to assign all the coins of this class with Brahmanical symbols, such as the conch shell of Vishnu, and the trident and humped bull of Siva, to the White Huns of the Indus.

The silence of Hwen Thsang, who twice passed through the old country of the White Huns, between A.D. 629 and 642, is a striking proof of the complete decay of their power in his time. I believe, however, that the pilgrim has actually mentioned them without recognising their name. I refer to *Hi-mo-ta-lo* on the Oxus, of which Hwen Thsang gives a translation as "under the snowy mountains." But as this meaning would give a purely Indian origin to the name as *Hima-tala*, it may be dismissed at once. I believe that the Chinese syllables simply represent the name of the Ephthalites under a slightly different form as *Hematala*, which approaches the Haiathela of Firdausi. That his *Himatala* is the *Yetha* of Sung-yun is proved by a curious custom which is mentioned by both pilgrims—that the married women wore a horn three feet long on their head-dress. As this peculiar custom is not noticed regarding any other people, I conclude with some confidence that both Yetha and Himatala are only two variant forms of the same name.

II.—Notes on the Coins.

On examining the coins of the Indo-Scythians, I observe that there are several marked differences in the money of the two great races, the Sakas and the Kushâns. The Saka coins show a decided preference for the worship of the Scythian Herakles, and offer no traces of the Persian and Indian worship of the planets and elements. The Kushâns, after the reign of their first king Kujula Kadphises, adopted the Sabeanism of Bactriana with a strong mixture of the worship of Indian gods, as shown by the use of several names of purely Indian origin.

Another striking difference between the coins of the two races is the total absence of monograms on the Kushân money, while the Saka coins are remarkable for the number of their monograms, both in Greek and in Arian characters. The coins of the Greek Hermæus are never without monograms, while those of his successor, the Kushân king Kujula Kadphises, are distinguished by their total absence.

A third difference between the two coinages is the entire want of gold money amongst the Sakas, and the same want of silver money amongst the Kushâns.

These three differences are so marked that I think they might be used as fair tests of the race of any of the kings whose nationality might otherwise be doubtful. Thus Miaüs, or Heraüs, who uses no monograms, should be a Kushân, and not a Saka, king.

The abundant use of gold by the Kushâns may, I think, be explained by the great increase of commerce which took place between Rome and India with the establishment of the Roman Empire under Augustus. During this period, as recorded by Pliny, about £400,000, or nearly half a million sterling, was the *yearly* sum paid by Rome to India.[24] What became of this gold? In Southern India it circulated unchanged with the square silver indigenous coins, but in Northern India, where the people were already familiar with the Greek coins of the Bactrian kings, the Roman gold was recoined by the Kushân princes, beginning with Hima Kadphises, who certainly reigned in the middle of the first century A.D. I came to this conclusion about thirty years ago by comparing the weights of more than a hundred Indo-Scythian gold coins with those of the early Roman Emperors.

With regard to the absence of silver coins amongst the Kushâns, I can only guess that the extensive coinages of silver money by the Greek kings were found sufficient for the wants of the people. But it still remains a mystery why the silver money was not recoined, as was done with the Roman gold. Perhaps as the hemidrachms of Antimachus, Antialkidas, Menander, and Apollodotus were familiar to the people, it was thought best not to disturb them, but to adjust the new gold coinage to the existing value of silver. Well-preserved specimens of these silver hemidrachms average 37 grains in weight, and the silver didrachms average 148 grains. If the new gold coin was equal in value to 10 didrachms and 40 hemidrachms its value in silver would have been 1,480 grains. This amount, at 12 rates of silver for 1 gold, would make the weight of the new gold coin 123·3 grains, which is, as nearly as possible, the actual weight of the Kushân gold

---

[24] *Plinii Nat. Hist.*, xii. 41. "Minimàque computatione," he says.

coins. I have taken the weights of 179 examples, which give the following results :—

19	Dinars of	Hima Kadphises	average	122·21	grains.
21	„	Kanishka	„	122·19	„
118	„	Huvishka	„	122·16	„
21	„	Vasu Deva	„	123·3	„

The later coins of Vasu Deva, which are less worn than the others, give the full weight of 123·3 grains.

The small quarter Dinârs of these four kings also average 30·8 grains, which would give a full Dinâr of 123·2 grains.

Now if these coins had been simply copied from the Roman Denarii Aurei, they would most probably have fluctuated in weight with the Roman coinage of the first and second centuries. But, on the contrary, their full weight is maintained to the last, from the earliest coins of Wema Kadphises down to the close of Vasu Deva's reign in the end of the second century A.D.

With regard to the long-continued currency of the Greek silver coins, we have the testimony of the author of the *Periplus*, who says that up to his time (80 to 100 A.D.[25]) "old drachmas bearing the Greek inscriptions of Apollodotus and Menander were still current at Barygaza." As the author was a contemporary of Kanishka, his testimony is decisive as to the continued currency of the Greek coins during the reign of the Kushân kings.

The absence of gold coins amongst the Sakas may perhaps be due to the continued circulation of the old

---

[25] He mentions *Malikhos*, king of the Nabathæans. As their kingdom was subverted by Trajan, in A.D. 105, the author of the *Periplus* cannot be placed later.

Persian Darics in Sakastene and Arakhosia. Some specimens are even now found there.

The coins offer very few examples of the Indo-Scythian speech, except in the names of the kings, as all the titles of the Saka kings are given in Greek with Indian translations. We know, however, that the language of the Sakas, or Massagetæ, was similar to that of the Parthians; and this similarity is well shown in the names of Vonones, Arsakes, Gondophares, Abdagases, and Pakores. We know also that they had a distinct dialect, as the Avesta is said to have been translated into seven different languages, amongst which were the dialects of Sejistan and Merv,[26] that is, of the Sakas of Sakastene, and the Kushâns of Merv. The only inscription of this race is a short record of Gondophares in the Indian language.

Of the Kushân dialect we have the king's names, and the royal titles of *Shaowu* or *Zâvu* ("King"), and *Raonano Rao* ("King of kings"). All the Kushân inscriptions yet found are in the Indian language. A peculiarity of the Kushân language was the fondness for the ending of proper names in *ka*. Thus we have Kanishka, Huvishka, and Kujulaka, of the coins and inscriptions, besides Jushka of the Kashmir history. At a later period we have Maniach, Prince of the Sogdoites, and during the reign of Khusru Parvez two powerful Kushân kings are mentioned under the names of Shog and Pariog.[27]

With regard to the partiality of the Scythian kings for the type of Herakles, I will now offer a few remarks which I think will be sufficient to show that the Turanian

---

[26] Hyde, *Religio Vet. Pers.*, p. 337.

[27] Prof. Rawlinson, *Seventh Ancient Monarchy*, p. 495.

races identified the Greek demigod Herakles with their own "God of the dead," named Gebeleizes and Zamolxis. Herodotus notes that the Getæ worshipped Herakles, but he does not mention his Scythian name.[28] There can be no doubt, however, that Gebeleizes, the Scythian "God of the Dead," was the same as *Sapaleizes*, whose name means "Lord of the Dead," and whose figure was copied from that of the Greek Herakles.

The earliest form of the name is the Babylonian *Iskalla*, who is also known as *Ne-uru-gal*, or "Lord of the great City" or "Kingdom of the Dead." In the curious legend of the "Descent of Ishtar into Hades," *Iskalla* is described as the god of the house where all meet, but from which none can depart; while the Queen of Hades is named *Nin-ki-gal*. She is therefore the same as the goddess *Nana*, whose image was carried off from *Erech* by Kuder-nahundi, King of Elam, in B.C. 2280.

The king's name of *Ne-uru-gal* is clearly the same as *Nergal*, who was the god of *Kutha*. In the Septuagint the god's name is written 'Εργελ, which points directly to 'Ορκος and *Orcus*, and also to *Erkle* and *Herakles*. Nergal must likewise be connected with the Sanskrit *Naraka*, "the abode of departed spirits," and therefore also with *Erech*, or *Warka*, "the burial city of the Babylonians." Another connection of the name with the dead is the Greek νέκρος, "a corpse," as well as the flower Νάρκισσος, or the "numbing," which was being plucked by Persephone at the very moment that she was seized by Hades, and carried off to become the Queen of the lower world.

In the Indian Vedas the ruler of the dead is called

---

[28] Herodot., iv. 94 and 59.

Yama, but he was also named *Vakra*, or the "cruel," which would seem to be the same name as that of the god OKPO on the Indo-Scythian coins. As King of *Naraka*, or Hades, OKPO is represented as holding a noose and a mace or club. On the coins he is further identified with HPAKIΛO or Herakles, with the club and lion's skin. On several coins OKPO is joined with the goddess NANA, which shows that these two deities were esteemed as king and queen, being the representatives of the Babylonian *Iskalla* or *Nergal*, and his queen *Nin-kigal* or *Nana*. That OKPO was the god of the dead is shown by the noose and the mace or club, both of which are lethal instruments of the Indian god Yama. As bearer of the former he is known as *Pâsa-pâni*, or "noose in hand," and as wielder of the latter he is called *danda-dhara*, or "mace-holder." A well-known title of Yama is *Chitra*, and I would suggest that the Persian name of *Sitra-takhmes* must have referred to Death's irresistible strength, its meaning being simply "strong as Chitra."

The name of *Sapal* continued in use amongst the Turanian peoples down to a very late date. Thus *Dizaboulos*, the great Khâkân of the Turks, who sent an embassy to Justinian, is called *Shapolio* by the Chinese. The Greek form of the name is due to the want of a Greek letter corresponding to *sh*, for which *Diz* was substituted. In the same way *sani*, or *shani*, the name of the planet Saturn, became *Dhizân*, from which form must have originated the Δορσάνης of Hesychius.

But the name of *Iskalla* at once suggests that of the Scythian eponymus *Skolopites*, and his people the *Skoloti*. To connect this name with *Sapalaizes*, I would refer to the Sanskrit *sava*, a corpse, and *savara*, a name of Siva, as well as to the Latin *sepelio* and *sepulcrum*. I would refer also to *Sagillus*, King of the Scythians, and to *Sigal*, the capital of the Sakastanian Sakas. The same name is found under several slight variations of spelling, of which the most notable is *Kola-xais* (or *Skola-xais*), the progenitor of the *Paralatæ* (or *Sparalatæ*), or Royal Scythians. On the coins of the Indo-Scythian Sakas we have the name of *Sapaleizes* on one side, coupled with the name of the goddess *Nanaia* on the reverse. Sapal-eizes means simply the god *Sapal*, or Herakles, whose name and worship were widely spread amongst all the Scythian races. The Indo-Scythian kings *Spalahora* and *Spalirises*, in addition to their names, offer the seated figure of Herakles on their coins. On Mount *Sambulos* (or *Sabul*, dropping the epenthetic *m*) the Parthian king Goterzes offered worship to Hercules.[29] The name of the mountain is slightly altered by Pliny to *Kambalidus*.[30]

The last reading of *Kambalidus* points to *Gebeleizes* as only a variant form of *Sapaleizes*, to which I would add that *Zamol-xis* is another variant. I think also that the *xis* of Zamol-xis and the *xais* of Skola-xais, may be simply the equivalents of *geises*, *gases*, or *geses*, and *eizes* or *ises*, which form the termination of so many Scythian names. *Xis* and *xais* might be connected with the title of *Shâhi*, which was used by the Indo-Scythians both on coins and inscriptions. *Gases* and *eises* are found in Abdagases, Bolagases, Monneses, &c., and may possibly have some connection with the Sanscrit *isa*, or "lord," as in *Vagises*.

In further connection with the dead we have the form of Σαυλῶη, which was the name of the place which held the tombs of the Parthian kings. And this form leads

[29] *Taciti Annal.*, xii. 13.
[30] *Plinii Nat. Hist.*, vi. 31.

to *Shaul* or *Sheol*, the Hebrew name of Hades. *Bet-saloë* also was the name of a place at *Kutha*, in Persia, which was noted for the worship of *Nergal*, or Hercules.

This widely-spread use of names connected with *Sapal*, or Heracles, seems to point to an early period in the world's history, when the worship of the God of the Dead had extended from the eastern shores of the Caspian to the banks of the Danube. And this extent of the Scythian territories was in fact claimed by the envoys of the Massagetæ when they met Alexander on the banks of the Jaxartes, "ultra Tanaim usque ad Thraciam colimus."[31]

In the following account I have divided the coins of the Indo-Scythians into several different classes, which correspond with the several different periods of their history.

Class A.—*Rude Imitations of Greek Coins*, from first occupation in B.C. 163, down to establishment of Kushâns in 116 B.C.

Class B.—*Coins of the Sakas or Sacæ-Scythians* in Arakhosia and India, from B.C. 116 to 16.

Class C.—*Coins of the Great Yue-chi, or Kushâns*, in Kabul and N.W. India, from B.C. 16 to A.D. 200.

Class D.—*Coins of the Later Kushâns* in Kabul and N.W. India, after A.D. 200.

Class E.—*Coins of the Little Yue-chi, or Lesser Kushâns*, in Peshâwar and N.W. Panjâb, after A.D. 430.

Class F.—Coins of the Ephthalites, or White Huns, on the Indus, in A.D. 480 to 600.

Class A.—Rude Imitations of Greek Coins.

Class A includes imitations of the small silver coins of Alexander the Great, and of the larger silver pieces of

[31] Curtius, *Vit. Alex.*, vii. 8, 30.

Seleukus I. and Antiochus I. of Syria, and of the Bactrian kings Euthydemus, Demetrius, Eukratides, and Heliokles. These Bactrian imitations are by far the most numerous, and more especially those of Euthydemus in silver, and of Heliokles in copper. On some of the imitations of Antiochus and Euthydemus there are native characters in addition to the corrupt Greek names of the imitated coins. These native legends have not yet been read. They may be only transliterations of the Greek names, but Mr. Thomas's attempts to read them as such were not successful. The characters appear to me to be similar to those on the coins of the Arsakian kings of Parthia.

On the imitation of the tetradrachms of Eukratides I find the detached Greek letters NA. I have a cast of a true tetradrachm with the same letters, and there is a true coin of the same type in the British Museum. If these letters are intended for a date, they would represent 51, or, with the centurial figure added, they would represent 151 of the Seleukidan era, equivalent to B.C. 161, which corresponds with the early part of the reign of Eukratides.

The small silver oboli are simple copies of the coins of Eukratides, including even the monogram.

One of the coins having the name of Heliokles, with the figure of Zeus, is also a simple copy both of the obverse and reverse. But the other coin with the horse on the reverse is perhaps original, although the horse may have been copied from the square copper coins of Hermæus.

All these rude imitations of the Greek coins I attribute to the early Indo-Scythians who conquered the countries on the Oxus. Only a few stray specimens are found in the Kabul valley, and none in the Panjâb. The types are nearly all taken from the coins of the Greek kings who ruled in Bactria, the few exceptions being copied from the money of Mithridates I. of Parthia. The Scythian archer, on the imitation coins of Antiochus, is probably original.

It is not easy to fix a date for the issue of these coins, but I am inclined to think that none of them can be earlier than B.C. 163, when the *Yue-chi*, being driven to the south of the Jaxartes by the Hiong-nu, pushed the Sakas to the south and west. The Bactrian Greeks then retired to the south of the Oxus, and, after some time, continued their retreat to the south of the Indian Caucasus, and left the whole of Bactriana in the hands of the Scythians. These coins I believe to have been issued chiefly by the Sakas; but until we can read the names recorded on some of them in native characters it seems useless to hazard any speculations about their issue. This rude coinage probably continued down to about B.C. 16, when the Kushân conqueror Kujula Kadphises imposed his name on the reverse of the copper coins of Hermæus.

The coins of *Hurkodes* are the only Scythian pieces that offer purely native types not borrowed from the Greeks. If I am right in identifying the hero figured on the reverse as the representative of the mythical leader of the Turki races, *Burtechino* or *Bertezina*, then Hurkodes must have belonged to the great horde of the Yue-ti; but to which of the five divisions there is nothing to show. The latter part of the name recalls the Thracian Kotys—of which Miltokuthes seems to be a compound form. But it is more probable that the Scythian name of *Hurkodes* may be a compound of *Hurk*, "the wolf," which is found in *Hyrkania*, and that Hurkodes is only a variant rendering of *Bertechino*, or *Bertezina*, or *Barhatigin*, the hero of the Turkish race. The armed figure on the reverse would then be the God of War, who was specially worshipped by the Scythians. The legend of *Ardethrou* would then be equivalent to *Raorethro* of the coins of Huvishka—that is, the god *Ares*, or *Athro*. According to Abu Rihan's account, *Barhatigin* preceded *Kanak* or *Kanishka*. There are two distinct kinds of his coins—one with the war god on the reverse and the other with the fore part of a horse bridled. On the former the inscriptions are always in Greek letters; on the latter they are sometimes Greek on the obverse and Parthian on the reverse, or Parthian on both sides. The Greek inscription on the obverse is always **YPKWΔOY**, and the corresponding Parthian inscription I read as *Karatakin*, or *Garatagin*. The Parthian inscription on the reverse I have not succeeding in reading. Mr. Thomas read it as *Kuât*.

The Greek legend of **MAKAPOY APΔHΘPOY**, which accompanies the divine figure on the reverse of the large coins, I take to mean simply "Ardethra of Makar," taking *Makar* to be the same as *Bakar* of the following legend, preserved by Biruni.[32] "Kabul was formerly governed by princes of the Turkish race, and the first of them, named Barhtigin, dwelt when he arrived at Kabul in a cave (named *Bakar*)." After remaining in the cave for some time without food, "Barhtigin came all of a sudden out of the cave . . . clothed as a Turk, *with a tunic, cap, boots, and armed from head to foot*." A similar story was told of Bertezena, the first leader of the Turks. But Bertezena, or Burtechino, is clearly the same name as Barhtigin, and I have no doubt that the divine figure on these coins is intended for the legendary leader of the

---

[32] Elliot's *Muh. Hist.*, ii. 9. On the later coins **MAKAPoY** is changed to **OAKAPo**, which is an equally correct rendering of *Bakar*.

Turks, armed from head to foot, just as he was said to have issued from the cave.

The date of the coins of Hurkodes cannot be placed earlier than the first century, owing to the late shape of the *omega*, ω. Raoul Rochette suggested that they might "have been struck by some of the barbarous tribes upon the borders of the Caspian, from whence they seem to have been brought."

Smardates and Rangodeme.—This curious coin presents two heads; that of a king on the obverse, and of a queen on the reverse. I have two other specimens of the same types, but in very bad order. I read the two names as ΤΑΝΛΙ ϹΜΑΡΔΑΤΗϹ and ΚΥΡΙΑ ΡΑΓ-ΓΟΔΗΜΗ, or King Smardates, and Queen Rangodeme. I take the king's name to be Smardates preceded by the title of *Tanli*, which I refer to the Scythian *Tham*, or "king." *Tanli* or *Tanais* may be compared with Justin's Scythian King *Tanaus*. The queen's name I take to be Rangodeme, and the term *Kuria* to be the title of "queen." We know from Herodotus that the Scythian Apollo was called ΟΙΤΟΣΥΡΟΣ, but from an inscription we learn that the full form was ΟΙΤΟΣΚΥΡΟΣ, while the moon was called ΣΕΛΟΙΤΟΣΚΥΡΑ. The terms *skuros* and *skura* would thus seem to mean simply "god and goddess," or king and queen. By dropping the initial Σ in both we get *kuros* and *kura*.

There is nothing except the rude workmanship and the round form of the sigma, Ϲ, to declare the age of these coins. My three specimens were obtained at different times, and they are the only specimens that I have seen during fifty years of collecting. My impression is that they belong to the country on the Oxus, and that their style is due to Parthian rather than to Indo-Grecian influence.

III.—DESCRIPTIVE LIST OF THE COINS.

Rude Imitations of Greek Coins.

Pl.	No.	Inches.		Grains.	
					Imitations of Alexander.
	—	0·6	Æ	40	Rude copy of silver drachma. Barbarous head covered with lion's skin to r. *Rev.*—Figure seated on chair, with bird on outstretched r. hand, copy of Zeus Aetophorus. These pieces are small and thin, and are very common.
					Imitation of Seleukus I.
I.	1	1·05	Æ	244	Rude copy of silver tetradrachm. Barbarous head to l., covered with lion's skin. *Rev.*—Zeus Aetophorus seated in chair. Corrupt Greek legend, ΣCΛCTK [for ΣΕΛΕΥΚ*ου*]. Under the seat the letters ΔΙ, and beneath them Π.
					Imitations of Antiochus I.
I.	2	0·6	Æ	46	Rude copy of silver drachma. Helmeted head with cheek-piece, to r. *Rev.*—Victory placing wreath on trophy. ANTIoXo.
I.	3	0·7	Æ	51	Rude copy of silver drachma. Diademed head of king to l., with moustaches. Native legend of five letters behind head.

III.—DESCRIPTIVE LIST OF THE COINS—*continued.*

Pl.	No.	Inches.		Grains.	
					Rev.—Scythian archer standing. Greek legend, **ΒΔCΙΝΕΠ —CANTI · X · Y.** N.B. There are rude copies of this coin without Greek letters. The shape of the Greek *sigma* betrays a late date.
I.	4	0·5	Æ	28	Rude copy of silver drachma. Diademed head of king to l., with moustaches. Native legend behind the head, as in No. 3. *Rev.*—Horse's head to l., with the Greek letter **K.** N.B. These coins are very rare, but there are numbers of very rude copies in two different sizes.
					IMITATIONS OF EUTHYDEMUS.
I.	5	1·05	Æ	175	Rude copy of silver tetradrachm. Rude diademed head of king to r. *Rev.*—Herakles seated on rock to l., club resting on knee. Legend of seven native letters behind, and corrupt Greek legend to l. **EVoYΛHM.** N.B. There are several gradations in the state of corruption of these coins. The earliest bear Greek legends only, as Ariana Ant: I. 5., the letters being only slightly altered. In the second stage the Greek letters are corrupt and imperfect. A third class have mixed legends of rude Greek and native

I.	6	1·05	Æ	137	letters. The fourth and latest are extremely rude, and bear native characters only: Ariana Antiqua, I. 9. I have given the inscribed reverse and form of these rude pieces, No. 6 of the Plate. Both Mr. Thomas and myself have attempted to read the legend, but without much success. The letters appear to be Parthian.
					Imitations of Eukratides.
I.	7	1·1	Æ	212	Rude copy of silver tetradrachm. Helmeted head of king to r. *Rev.*—The Dioskuri mounted, to r. Corrupt Greek legend, **ΙΛΣΙΛΕΠΣ ΜΕΓΛ●Υ ΕΥΚΙΛΤΔΥ**. In the field to r. the detached letters **ΝΑ**. N.B. There is a genuine tetradrachm with these two letters in the British Museum, and I possess a cast of a similar coin.
I.	8	0·4	Æ	9	Rude copy of silver obolus. Helmeted head of king to r. *Rev.*—Caps and palms of the Dioskuri. Greek legend, **ΒΑΣΙΛΕΠΕ ΕΥΚΡΑΤΔοΥ** (*sic*). Greek monogram in field forming **ΑΝΤΙ**.
I.	9	0·45	Æ	9	Rude copy of silver obolus. Helmeted head of king to r. *Rev.*—Caps and palms of the Dioskuri. Greek legend, **ΛΙΑΚΟ ΚΟΖΟΥΛΟ**. Greek mon. in field.

III.—DESCRIPTIVE LIST OF THE COINS—*continued.*

Pl.	No.	Inches.		Grains.	
					N.B. *Liaka Kujulaka*, as we learn from a copperplate inscrip- found at Shah-dheri (Taxila), was a satrap in the W. Punjâb. The record is dated in the year 78 of the era of the great king *Moga*. If this king is the same as Moas of the coins, the inscription must belong to the latter half of the 1st century B.C. The satrap Kusulaka is also mentioned in the great Satrap inscription from Mathura, with the title of *Maha Chhatrapa*.
					IMITATIONS OF HELIOKLES.
I.	10	1 15	Æ	233	Rude copy of silver tetradrachm. Large head, diademed to r. *Rev.*—Zeus standing to front, with spear and thunderbolt. Corrupt Greek legend on three sides, ΒΑCΙΛΕΛC ΔΙΙΑΙΥ ΗΑΙΙΕΥC, for ΒΑΣΙΛΕΠ≤ ΔΙ-ΚΑΙοΥ ΗΛΙοΚΛΕοΥΣ. N.B. There are small coins of the same types and legends, weighing 57 grains.
I.	11	1·1	Æ	228	Rude copy of silver tetradrachm. Large rude head, diademed to r., as in No. 10. *Rev.*—Horse stepping to l., as on coins of Mithridates I. of Parthia. Corrupt Greek legend, as on No. 10.

					N.B. There are also small coins of this type. On some specimens the *omikrons* are not omitted, but are represented by simple small dots.
					NATIVE TYPES.
I.	12	0·6	Æ	25	Horse stepping to the r., as on the last. *Rev.*—Feathered arrow, surrounded by a wreath.
I.	13	0·5	Æ	17	Rude head to l., with native legend. *Rev.*—Pallas armed to front, with native legend. [*Brit. Mus. Cat.*, xxiv. 16.]
I.	14	0·55	Æ	39	Very rude head of king to r. *Rev.*—Rude figure of Herakles with club. Greek legend in late letters, ΦϹΕΙΓΑ ΧΑΡΙϹ.
					HURKODES. [*Brit. Mus. Cat.*, xxiv. 8.]
	15	0·65	Æ	44	Silver coin, drachma size (slightly broken). Bearded head of king to r. ΥΡΚШΔΟΥ. *Rev.*—Armed figure to front, flames rising from shoulders, spear in r. hand. ΜΑΚΑΡΟΥ ΑΡΔΗΘΡΟΥ. N.B.—On later specimens. ΟΑΚΑΡΟ ΟΡΔΗΟΡΟ.
	16	0·5	Æ	12	King's head to r. with long pointed beard. Native legend of six letters behind head.

III.—DESCRIPTIVE LIST OF THE COINS—*continued.*

Pl.	No.	Inches.		Grains.	
					Rev.—Half horse, bridled to r. Native legend of five letters above. N.B. These horse coins are of three kinds :— 1. With Greek name of Hurkodes on both sides. 2. With Greek name on obv. and native legend on rev. 3. With native legend on both sides.
					SMARDATES OR MARDATES.
I.	17	0·7	Æ	54	King with crested helmet to r. ΤΑΝΛΙ ϹΜΑΡΔΑΤΗϹ. *Rev.*—Head of queen to r., covered with veil, holding flower in r. hand. ΡΑΓΓΟΔΗΜΗ ΚΥΡΙΑ. N.B. I take *kuria* to be the royal title of queen, and *Rangodeme* to be her name. *Eme* is, in fact, the feminine suffix of the Mongols.

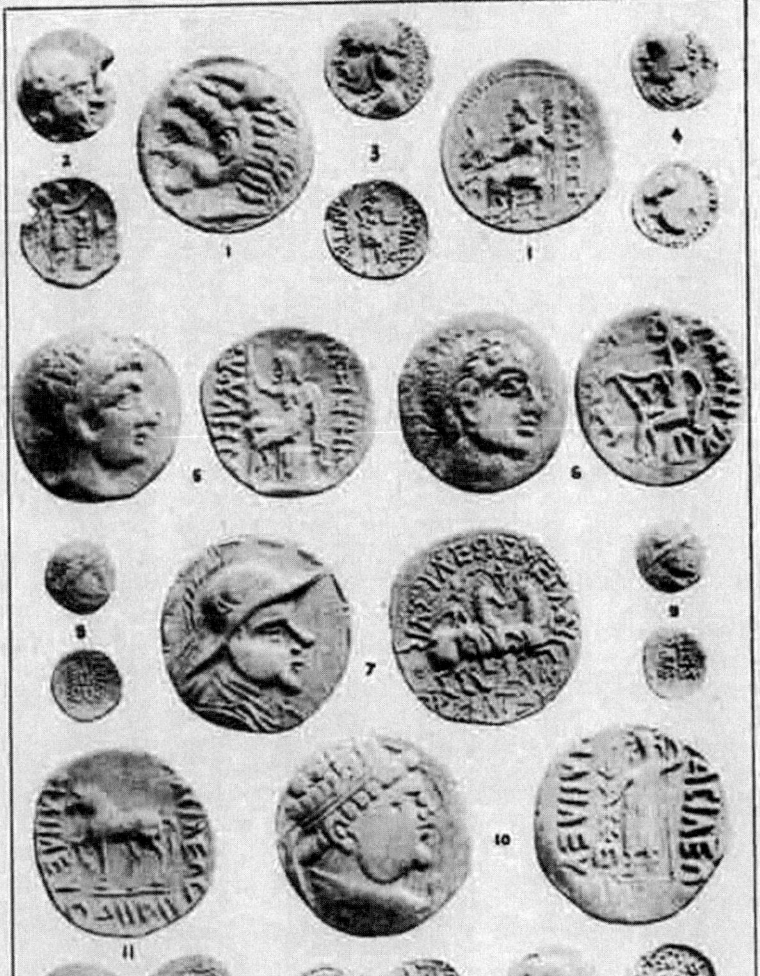

INDO- SCYTHIANS - SAKAS. Pl. I

COINS OF THE SAKAS.

PART II.

BY

Major-General Sir A. CUNNINGHAM, R.E., K.C.I.E., C.S.I.

REPRINTED FROM THE NUMISMATIC CHRONICLE,

Vol X., Third Series, Pages 103—172.

LONDON:

1890.

COINS OF THE SAKAS.

Class B.

Coins of the Sakas or Sacæ-Scythians.

Class B includes all the coins which bear names either of Parthian origin, or of kindred forms, beginning with Moas and Vonones and ending with Pakores. There appear to be at least three distinct families of these Princes, the two earlier ones of Moas and Vonones being contemporary, while that of Gondophares was some time later. All the coins of this class have on their reverse literal translations in the Indian Pali language and in Arian characters of the Greek legends of the obverse.

Coins of MOAS.—The earliest coins of the Sakas or Sacæ-Scythians are certainly those of *Moa*, or *Mauas*, as his name is written in Greek characters. This name is found only in Western Asia in the compounds Moagetes and Moaphernes, but I have failed to find the meaning of it. Arrian mentions a king of the Sakas, named *Mabakes*, who joined Darius Codomannus. His name might also be read as *Mauakes*. A coin of Moagetes, tyrant of Kibyra, was published by Pellerin, with a monogram forming ΜΟΑΓ. Moaphernes was the uncle of Strabo's mother, and was a person of some consequence during the reign of Mithridates of Pontus.[1] If the full name of this king was Moga, as I originally suggested in my reading of the copper-plate inscription of King Moga, it is quite possible that the old town of Mong, in the Panjâb, may have derived its name from him as *Mogapura*, which would soon have been curtailed and nasalized into Mong, after the usual Panjâb fashion. It is certain at least that the coins of Moas are found only in the Panjâb, not a single specimen, to my knowledge, having been found in the Kabul valley. The first coins of this prince were obtained by Ventura in the Panjâb, and the whole of my own collection, now numbering over two hundred specimens of more than twenty different types, was gathered in the same country. His silver coins have been found at the old town of Mansera, sixteen miles to the north of Abbottabad, and about eighty miles to the north of Rawul Pindi.

By what route Moas and his followers reached the Panjâb is not clear; but I feel quite certain that they could not have come through Kashmir by the Karakoram Pass, as suggested by Professor Gardner, as that pass, instead of being open all the year round, is closed during winter, and could *never* be traversed by an army, even in summer. My own opinion is that the first bands of Scythians, the Sakas, came from the Oxus, as stated by the Chinese. They first occupied Sakastene, or Arachosia and Drangiana, but soon spread themselves over the country to the eastward, where they gradually got possession of the valley of the Indus, including both the Panjâb and Sindh. In fact, the Chinese authorities distinctly say that the Sakas, after their retirement to the south, formed several separate states.[2] The bolder and more adven-

[1] *Strabon. Geogr.* xi., 2, 18, and xii. 3, 33.

[2] Remusat, *Nouv. Mélanges Asiatiques*, i. 205.

turous spirits might have pushed ahead, and overrun the Panjâb up to the foot of the Kashmir hills within a couple of years, just as in after years was actually done by the Brahman Chach, as well as by the first Muhammadan conqueror, Muhammad Kâsim. I see no necessity for supposing that Moas and Azas came through Kashmir. Bâber and all previous invaders came from the west.

The Indian dominion of Moas seems to be plainly indicated by the Indian types of many of his coins. Thus, there are 4 with an elephant, 1 with an elephant's head, 4 with a river deity—which can only be the Indus, and 3 with a humped bull, or altogether eleven types referring directly to India out of the twenty-two types already known.

In later times we know that Husâm-ud-din Ewaz had already made himself the independent ruler of Bengal within twenty years of the occupation of Delhi by Kutb-ud-din Aibak. We have only to suppose that Moas was the leader of the Sakas about B.C. 120, and that he himself pushed forward from Sakastene to India, leaving Vonones in command behind him. Then, about 100 B.C., Vonones may either have rebelled, or have been installed by Moas himself as king of Sakastene, while Moas himself was content with his Indian dominions.

Some supposition of this kind is perhaps required to account for the names of Vonones and Azas appearing on the same coin. On the death of Moas the vacant throne may have been claimed by Vonones, and the claim could have been adjusted by admitting the equal authority of Azas. Both chiefs called themselves "King of Kings."

The type of Poseidon trampling upon a river-god would seem, as suggested by Raoul Rochette, to point to a successful passage of the Indus. On one coin Poseidon, with trident in hand, is represented trampling the river-god with his foot, while he levels a thunderbolt against a small figure which is clinging to an *aplustre*, or raised "poop-ornament" of a boat. On another coin the same figure is apparently seeking protection from a tall female figure, which perhaps represents India. On another rare coin Zeus is seen seated, with the hasta pura in his left hand, and with right hand extended towards a small female figure surrounded by foliage, which I take to be a personification of India. This identification seems to be confirmed by the presence of the humped bull and the elephant on other coins.

It is worthy of note that on all the large coins of Moas the native legend is limited to the simple title of *Rajadiraja* as the translation of ΒΑΣΙΛΕΩΣ ΒΑΣΙΛΕΩΝ, while the coins of all his successors take the fuller and loftier title of *Maharajadiraja*. On the large coins with the elephant's head the only legend is in Greek, ΒΑΣΙΛΕΩΣ ΜΑΥΟΥ. But in this instance the coin is probably an early one, as it is a simple copy of a coin of Demetrius. The small copper coins bear the simple title of *Maharajasa Moasa*.

The find spots of the coins of Moas and the Eastern Sakas are restricted to the Panjâb, so far as my experience extends. A few specimens of Azas have been obtained round about Peshawur and in the Swât valley. I saw twelve of his coins extracted from beneath the statue platform of an ancient temple at *Shâh-dheri* or Taxila.[3]

Coins of VONONES.—The coins of Vonones and his family come chiefly from the ancient Arachosia, or Kandahar and Ghazni. Some have also been found in Sistân,

[3] *Archæological Survey of India*, v. 72.

the ancient Drangiana. A few have been obtained at Kabul, but as not even a single specimen was got at Begram by Masson during his three years' collection, it seems almost certain that Vonones could not have ruled there. For a similar reason the family of Vonones could not have ruled for any time in the Panjâb, as their coins are very rarely found there. In fact, the Panjâb must have been held by Azas and his successors, whose coins are very numerous all over the northern districts.

It seems strange that no coins of Vonones himself have been found, his name being restricted to the obverses of the coins of Azas,[4] Spalahores, and Spalgadames. I think it probable that he was the great chief of the Saka horde, after the death of Moas, and that he must have remained in Sakastene, while his relatives and generals had possession of the eastern countries, Kandahar, Sindh, and the Panjâb.

I note that the silver coins of the two branches of the Sakas in Kandahar and the Panjâb bear the same type of the king on horseback, but their copper money has little in common. The type of the horseman was first introduced by Moas, and its general adoption by both branches seems to point to a community of race. Politically they were certainly connected, as Azas acknowledged the supremacy of Vonones, and afterwards of Spalirises, by placing their names on the obverse of his coins. On the first he adopts the simple title of Rajadiraja, which was used by Moas, while he gives the title of **ΒΑΣΙΛΕΩΣ**

---

[4] When E. Thomas stated that I had discovered a coin with the joint names of Azas and Vonones (Prinsep's *Ant.* ii., 203) he forgot that the coin was in the Stacy collection and that he had catalogued it himself (*Bengal Asiat. Soc. Journal*, 1858, p. 252).

ΒΑΣΙΛΕΩΝ to Vonones. On the other coins he adopts an equal title with that of Spalirises.

Spalahora does not take the royal title of *Basileus.* He is simply the king's brother, and was no doubt the governor of a province with the title of Maharaja. His son *Spalyadames* also does not take the royal title, but calls himself simply the son of Spalahora. *Spalirises,* therefore, would appear to have been the *King* who succeeded Vonones. At first he calls himself the king's brother, and has the simple title of ΒΑΣΙΛΕΩΣ. But afterwards as king he becomes ΒΑϹΙΛΕѠΝ ΒΑϹΙΛΕѠϹ. With Azas he calls himself ΒΑϹΙΛΕѠϹ ΜΕΓΑΛΟΥ, while Azas has the titles of *Maharajasa Mahatakasa.* At the same time the types of this coin are copies of one of the finest coins of Moas, while the monogram is the same, forming ΝΙΚ [No. 2], although it does not appear to have been used by Azas himself.

There is a peculiarity in the Greek spelling of the name of Spalirises that requires special notice. On a few specimens it is written ΙΠΑΛΙΡΙϹΟΥ, as if the first letter was an imperfect square *s.* But the usual form is, ΡΠΑΛΙ-ΡΙϹΟΥ, *Rpalirisou.* As the initial letter in the native legend is undoubtedly *ṣp,* the Persian form of the Indian *ṣw,* I take the character to be formed of the palatal sibilant Π *ṣ* with ⊦ *p* joined on the right, thus making *ṣp.* As this *ṣ* is frequently pronounced as *sh,* the initial *rho,* Ρ, of the Greek rendering must be taken to represent the palatal sibilant, thus making the initial syllable *ṣpa,* as in the Persian *aṣpa.* Now we know that the regular sibilant *sh* in the names of Kanishka, Huvishka, and Kushân is represented by a peculiar form of the Greek *rho,* thus Þ, with the perpendicular stroke elongated upwards. This peculiar use of *rho* to represent *sh* I pointed out in 1872, when I suggested that it was in accordance with a well-known usage of the Turki dialects, which changes an initial *s* or *z* to *r*.[5] The lengthening of the perpendicular stroke I was of course aware of, but I then considered it as only an abnormal variation. From these coins of Spalirises it would seem that the attempt to represent *sh* or the palatal sibilant *ṣ* by a Greek *rho*, was made upwards of a century before the time of Kanishka. The square sigma Ꮯ is used for the name of Spalahora, ꞆΠΑΛΥΡΙΟꞆ, and the round sigma C in the name of Sapaleizes, CΑΠΑΛΕΙΖΗC.

It is difficult with our present scanty information to assign, with any degree of certainty, the countries over which the family of Vonones reigned. The facts recorded by Masson would seem to exclude them from the Kabul valley, as only two coins of Spalahores and three of Spalirises were found at Begrâm during three years' search. A good number of specimens were obtained by Colonel Stacy and Captain Hutton at Kandahar, and I have picked up a few in the Panjâb. The Ventura collection, also made in the Panjâb, contained only four specimens of this family.[6] I am inclined to place them at the Saka capital of *Sigal*, which I would identify with *Shâl* or *Kotta* (*vulgo* Quetta), the *Kottabara* of Ptolemy. Their dominions would have embraced the Kandahar valley, and perhaps also Ghazni, while the Kabul valley was still held by some of the later Greeks.

Coins of AZAS.—The numerous silver coins of Azas, with but one exception, present the king on horseback on the obverse, with only the slight difference that on some

---

[5] *Num. Chron.*, 2nd Series, xii., 181. Dr. Stein's paper on this subject was not published until 1887, or fifteen years later. His Zoroastrian readings I will discuss hereafter.

[6] Thomas, *Prinsep.*, Plate XV., Figs. 5, 6, 9 and 10.

pieces the king bears a couched lance, while on others he carries a whip, and has a bow case behind him. These two varieties are given in Plate V., marked A and B.

This type of the king on horseback seems to distinguish all the Saka princes from the Kushâns. Moas has only two horseman coins of copper, but the horseman is by far the commonest type on all the coins of his successors Azas and Azilises. It is also the common type on most of the coins of Vonones and his relatives Spalahora, Spalgadama, and Spalirises. And at a still later date it was adopted by Gondophares and the members of his family Abdagases and Sasan. Lastly, it forms the type of at least nine-tenths of the money of the Nameless King.

Masson has recorded the important fact that not a single coin of Azas was obtained from the ruined city of Begrâm, to the north of Kabul. But his money is very plentiful in the Western Panjâb, where Ventura made a large collection, and where I have since obtained a great number of all types and sizes. I believe, therefore, that Moas and his successors, Azas and Azilises, must have ruled over the Western Panjâb, with their capital at Taxila, from about 100 to 20 B.C. During this time the Eastern Panjâb was certainly held by some of the later Greeks, with their capital at Sangala. These Greeks would include Zoilus, Dionysius, Straton II, and Apollophanes.

The Satraps, whose coins have been found in considerable numbers, such as Zeionises or Jihonisa, and Aspa Varma, must have been governors under Azas and Azilises. Of Aspa Varma we are quite certain, as he calls himself on his coins the General [*stratega*] of Azas.

Miaüs or Heraüs.

The nationality of Miaüs (or Heräus) and of the Nameless King is unsettled. I have placed their coins along with those of the Sakas, or Sacæ, chiefly on account of the horseman type, which is common to all the known Saka kings of the families of Moas and Vonones. For the same reason I look upon Gondophares and his relatives Abdagases and Sasan as later Sakas.

The coins of Miaüs (or Heräus, as read by Mr. Gardner) are altogether exceptional, as they consist chiefly of tetradrachms and oboli, of which no other examples have been found amongst the money of the Saka princes. I think it probable that Miaüs, or *Miaius* (as his name is also written), may be the interloper *Yin-mo-fu*, or *In-mo-fu*, to whom the Chinese attribute the conquest of Kipin in B.C. 49. The name on the coins is variously written, and may be read as **MAOY** and **HIAOY** on the tetradrachms, and as **MIAOYC** and **MIAIOYC** on the oboli. The name is preceded by the title of **TYPANNOYNTOΣ** on the large coins, and followed by **ΣANAB** or **ΣANAOB KOPCANOY**, while the oboli omit the two titles, and read simply **MIAOY KOPCANOY**.

Mr. Percy Gardner[7] reads the name of the king as Heraüs, or **HPAOY**, just as I did myself when I got the first tetradrachm some twenty-five years ago. But after finding the oboli I gave up that reading for **MIAOY**. Mr. Gardner reads the whole legend as **TYPANNOYNTOΣ HPAOY ΣAKA KOIPANOY**. But he has omitted the letter **B** at the end of **ΣAKA** (or **ΣANA**),

---

[7] *Brit. Mus. Catalogue of Greek and Scythian Coins*, Introd., p. xlvii.

which is found on all the eight or ten tetradrachms that I have seen, and is quite distinct on the British Museum coin. He also points out that the third letter of the word read as ΣANAB is not found like the other N's on the coin, but like a retrograde И. But I may refer him to his own note at the foot of the same page, where the same retrograde form is found in the word read by him as KOIPANoY, but which should therefore be KOIPA-KoY. M. Tiesenhausen's coin, he admits, seems to read, ΣANAB, and I may add that on one of my tetradrachms the N is properly formed, reading ΣANAOB. I may mention also that on one specimen all the N's of *Turannountos* and *Koiranou* are retrograde.

Heraüs, according to Mr. Gardner, thus becomes a King of the Sakas; but according to my reading of the last two words ΣANAB (or ΣANAOB) KOPCANOY, he must have been the king (*Sanaob* or *tsanyu*) of the *Korsâns* or *Kushâns*. We know that on all the coins of Kujula Kadphizes the name of his tribe *Kushâna* in the native legend, is rendered as KOPCAN in the Greek legend. We know also that *Tsanyu* or *chanyu* was a royal title. As an interloping conqueror Miaüs may have been a Kushân, who made a temporary conquest of Kipin. All that the Chinese authors say of *Yin-mo-fu* or *In-mo-fu*, is that he was the son of the King of *Yung-Khiu*, and that he attacked and killed the son of *U-theu-lao*, King of Kipin, and took possession of his throne in B.C. 49.[8] As *U-theu-lao*, the father, was a contemporary of *Wu-ti* of the Han dynasty, who died in B.C. 87, his son would have succeeded him about 70 B.C., and this date would agree very well with the date of his supplanter

[8] Remusat, *Nouv. Melanges Asiatiques*, i. 207.

Yin-mo-fu, who sent an embassy to the Emperor *Hiao-yuan-ti* in B.C. 49.

Now the coins of Miaüs (or Heraüs) certainly belong to about the same period. The tetradrachms use the correct form of the sigma, Σ, as on the coins of Hermæus and Kujula Kadphizes, while on the coins of Kujula alone, and on those of Kadaphes, the round sigma, C, is used. Miaüs must therefore have preceded the final settlement of the Kushâns under Kujula in the latter half of the first century B.C. That he was a contemporary of Kujula is rendered nearly certain by the discovery of one of his oboli by Masson in the Kotpur Stûpa No. 2 along with ten copper coins bearing the joint names of Hermæus and Kujula Kadphizes.[9] There was also included a clay seal with the "standing figure of an armed prince" holding a spear and shield. An engraving of this seal is given by Wilson in Pl. IV., Fig. 6, of the *Relics of Masson's Topes*. It agrees with the armed soldiers on some rare coins of the Kushân Prince Kujula Kadphizes, of which two specimens are shown in the accompanying plates. All the evidence therefore is strongly in favour of my conclusion that Miaüs was a contemporary of Kujula. I may add the fact that both princes use the form of KϿPCAN for the name of their tribe.

Another point in favour of the identification of Miaüs with *In-mo-fu* is the fact, also recorded by the Chinese, that the gold and silver money of *Kipin* bore on one side the figure of a horseman, and on the other side the head of a man.[10] Now, there are only two kings in the whole

[9] Wilson, *Aziana Antiqua*, p. 66, describes it as a small piece of silver, with one side worn smooth. I examined the coin myself in 1867 in the Masson collection in the India Office, and recognised it as an obolus of Miaüs.

[10] Remusat, *Nouv. Mélanges Asiatiques* i., 206.

series whose money corresponds with this description. These two are Miaüs and the Nameless King. But as no silver money of the latter has yet been found, the description agrees only with that of Miaüs.

The Greek title ΣANAB or ΣANACB may perhaps be intended for the Scythian title of *tsanyu,* which is a contraction of *Tsemli-kuthu-tanju,* or "Heaven's-son-great," of which only the first and last syllables are preserved in the Scythian title. The meaning of this title is exactly the same as that of the Chinese *Tien-tse,* or "Son of Heaven." In the Indian inscriptions of the Kushân Princes Kanishka and his successors Huvishka and Vasu Deva the same title is given to them in its Indian form of *Deva-putra,* or "God's-son." I therefore read ΣANAB KOPCANOY as *tsânav-korsanou,* the exact equivalent of *Deva putra Kushâna.* In support of this reading I am now able to refer to a duplicate copper coin of Miaüs, on which one half of the Arian legend is quite legible. Under the king's bust I read *Maharaja,* the equivalent of TYPANNCYNTOΣ, and on the right hand I read *Deva-putra ku,* the rest being illegible. All the left half of the legend is lost. But the title of *Devaputra,* which was peculiar to the Kushân kings, coupled with the reading of KOPCANOY, seems to me to offer a very strong proof that Miaüs was not a *Saka* king. I take him to have been the chief of the *Kushân* tribe of the Great Yueti, and I think also that he may possibly have been the father, as well as the predecessor, of Kujula Kadphizes, who united the five tribes of the Great Yueti, and conquered the last Greek Prince Hermæus.

Coins of the NAMELESS KING.—The immediate successor of Miaüs was most probably the Nameless King, who gives only the titles of BACIΛEYC BACIΛEωN

ΣΩΤΗΡ ΜΕΓΑΣ. His coins are exceedingly common all over the Panjâb, as well as in Kandahar, and in the Kabul valley. They are of several types, but not one of them gives even a single letter of any name. The inscription is simply ΒΑΣΙΛΕΥΣ ΒΑΣΙΛΕΩΝ ΣΩΤΗΡ ΜΕΓΑΣ. All of them have a three-pronged symbol, which was apparently the peculiar symbol of this prince. On two of my coins the symbol has four prongs, owing perhaps to a blunder of the die-cutter. On the helmeted and bilingual coins, and also on the small Ardokhro coins, there is a single Arian letter, +ւ, *Vi*, which may possibly be the initial of the king's name, perhaps of Vikramâditya, whose date, as well as I am able to judge, must have coincided with that of this nameless prince. His rule must have been very extensive, as well as very long, as his coins are found as far eastward as Mathura.

I have sometimes thought that this nameless prince with the initial Vi might be identified with one of the early Kushân kings, by supposing that these coins without name might be the money of his different satraps in the conquered provinces, while the gold and copper coins, which bear the names of the Kushân kings themselves, would have been the coinage of the Kabul valley. The syllable Vi would thus stand for the initial of *Vima* or *Vikramadita.* I have already noticed that both sets of coins have the inscription in the nominative case, ΒΑΣΙΛΕΥΣ ΒΑΣΙΛΕΩΝ. The sceptre carried in front of the face is also a peculiarity of the Kushân king's coinage.

The want of monograms which distinguishes the coins of the Nameless King from those of the Partho-Scythian dynasties of Moas, Vonones, and Gondophares, would seem to connect him with the Kushâns. The bust also does the same. But the horseman is the favourite type of the Saka kings.

The coins of the Nameless King are found in copper only. His Mathura coins were a local coinage, which is not met with elsewhere. As Mathura certainly belonged to the early Kushân kings this local coinage must have been issued with their authority.

I have already pointed out the possibility that Vonones and the *Saka* kings may be alluded to in the traditional account of the early rulers of Sindh preserved by Rashid-ud-din.[11] Their names are.—1. *Kafand*, the founder, who was not a Hindu; 2. *Ayand;* 3. *Râsal*; and 4. *Roâl*, and his brother, 5. *Barkamâris.*

1. *Kafand*, who sent his brother *Sâmid* against *Mahra*, the Persian, to expel him from Sindh. By a very slight change of *r* to *w* the name of *Mahra* may be read as *Mahwa*, which would correspond exactly with the Greek *Maua*. As Vonones and Mauas would appear to have been contemporaries, the former ruling in Arakhosia, the latter in the Panjâb, I think that the identification of *Mauas* with *Mahra*, the antagonist of Kafand, is not an improbable one. The name of Kafand might even be a possible alteration of *Wanûm*, or Vonones.

2. *Ayand* I would identify with Azas, whose name is written *Aya* in the native legends of his coins. He was a powerful king, who divided his dominions into four separate governments. This would agree with the known facts of the reign of Azas, who certainly confided one province to his general, *Aspa Varma*, and most probably a second to the satrap *Zeionises*, whose coins are copied from those of his supposed suzerain. Azas was also a contemporary of Vonones, as both names are found on a rare coin of early date copied from Moas.

---

[11] H. M. Elliot's *Muham. Historians of India*, i. 108.

3. *Râsal* I would identify with *Azilises*. He is said to have lost part of his kingdom to a rebel. This rebel, I have already suggested in another place, might have been Miaüs (or Heraüs).

4. *Roâl* I would identify with *Sapaleizes*, as the reign of each was a short one.

5. *Barkamâris*, his younger brother, might be the *Nameless King*, whose coins are very numerous. All India is said to have submitted to him. For "all India" we must read the countries on both banks of the Indus, now known as Afghanistan and the Panjâb.

Dynasty of Gondophares.

There are four members of the dynasty of Gondophares, who are united by a common symbol, as well as by an acknowledgment of relationship. The symbol may be described as a variant form of the caduceus of the planet Mercury. If I am right, its use would be very appropriate on the coins of Gondophares, as I take his name to be one of the Indian titles of the god of the wind, as *Gandha-vâha*, or in Persian *Gonda-bara*, or the "Scent-bearer."

The names of these princes are Abdagases, the nephew of the founder, Orthagnes, and Sasa. With them must be classed Arsakes and Pakores, and perhaps Sanabares. I possess also four coins of this Partho-Scythian class, with a king's bust and Victory, which, as the portraits differ from those of the known kings, must belong to other princes of the same dynasty. Unfortunately the legends are too much injured to be deciphered.

The date of *Gondophares* is very clearly defined by his coins, which are certainly *later* than those of the dynasties of Vonones and Azas, and earlier than those of Kanishka —that is, they are later than B.C. 50, and earlier than

A.D. 78. This date is corroborated by the legendary account of the visit of St. Thomas to King Gundofores, to which I was the first to draw attention in 1854.[12]

The *Legenda Aurea* says that Gundofores, King of Upper India (*Indiam superiorem*), sent an official (*præpositus*) named Abbanes, to obtain a skilful architect. St. Thomas accompanied Abbanes to India, where he is said to have converted the king himself, as well as his brother *Gad*, and his sister's son, *Labdanes.*[13] Another version says that *Migdonia*, the queen's sister, was converted, on which account St. Thomas was put to death.[14] Lastly Leucius, in the Apocryphal Acts, states that the Apostle was sold as a slave to King Gundophores, after which he went to the country of *Meodeus*, where he was eventually put to death.[15]

An inscription of *Gadaphara*, or Gondophares, found at Takht-i-Bahi, to the north-east of Peshawur, is dated in the 26th year of his reign. There is also a date of Samvat 103, as I read it. The numeral for 100 is certain, and as this is followed by three upright strokes, the whole date would appear to be 103. The era, however, is quite unknown. If referred to the Vikramâditya Samvat it would be 103 — 57 = 46 A.D. This date would place the beginning of the reign of Gondophares in 46 — 25 = 21 A.D., and, as his coins are very numerous, he must have had a long reign, perhaps thirty or forty years, or down to A.D. 50 or 60. The reading of the name of Gadaphara in

---

[12] *Journal Bengal Asiat. Soc.*, 1854—"Coins of Indian Buddhist Satraps."

[13] *See* Thomas, *Prinsep*. ii. 214—Gutschmid quoted by Oldenberg in *Ind. Antiq.* ix. 262.

[14] Turner, *Anglo-Saxons*, ii. 147, and Mrs. Jameson's *Sacred and Legendary Art*, i. 225.

[15] Sir Henry Yule, *Cathay*, ii. 376.

the Takht-i-Bahi inscription is thought to be doubtful by those who have not seen the stone. I have examined the inscription many times, and I reassert that the reading of the name is most certainly *Gadaphara*, the separation in the middle of the name being simply due to an original fault in the stone. I may note here that there are many similar faults in the great *Kâlsi* inscription of Asoka.

Abdagases is a known Parthian name, as that of one of the nobles who dethroned Artabanus in A.D. 35. He was then an old man of great power and influence, but the active rebellion was carried on by his son Sinnakes. As the dates correspond, it seems to me quite possible that this Abdagases may have been the father of Gondophares, as well as of Sinnakes, and that the son of Sinnakes may have been named after his grandfather, Abdagases. This would make our Abdagases the brother's son of Gondophares, as stated on his coins. The discovery of a silver coin of Gondophares, of Parthian type, with the title of Autokrator, is greatly in favour of my conjecture that he must have belonged to a powerful Parthian family, such as that of Abdagases, the noble who assisted in the dethronement of Artabanus. I may note that I have possessed two silver coins of Artabanus, countermarked with the peculiar symbol of Gondophares.

The coins of Abdagases, like those of his uncle, are of two distinct classes, namely, *bust* coins and *horseman* coins. The latter alone give the family relationship of *bhrâta-putra*, or brother's son, while the former bear the simple titles of BACIΛEωC CωTHPOC. Perhaps the horse-man coins may belong to a period of dependency during the lifetime of his uncle, while the bust coins may be assigned to his independent sovereignty. His name is written in Arian character *Avadagasa*.

A few rare specimens of the bust type bear the somewhat similar name of *Hardagases*, in Greek ΑΡΔΑΓΑCοΥ, and in Arian letters *Hardagasa*. The Greek Ρ and the Arian initial H are quite distinct; but as I have not seen more than four specimens, I am inclined to look upon them as exceptional variations, more particularly as the Arian legend may be preferably read as *Haradagasa*. In this case the Greek Ρ would be only an incomplete Β.

The coins of *Sasan*, as I have ventured to call the king whose name in the native character, if indeed it be a name, is written *Sasasa*, are not uncommon. They are of two types, each bearing a horseman on the obverse, and a figure of Zeus on the reverse. On one class Zeus simply extends his right hand; on the other he holds out a figure of Victory. On both the name of *Gadaphara* occurs in the native legend. On the first kind the name of *Gadaphara* is preceded by a title which I read as *Devahadasa*, or *Devatrada*—the letter *d* is certain. It seems to be a title of Gondophares, as it is found on his square coins. I have suggested *Deva-hridya* as a possible reading, after the manner of *Diotrophes* and *Theotropos*. On the Greek side I have not, amongst hundreds of specimens, been able to make out any name. I have found ΑCοΥ on one coin and ΑCΗC on another. The native name is written with three similar letters, *Sasasa*, of which the last is simply the genitive case. I have sometimes thought that *Sasasa* might be a colloquial form of *Swasriyasa*, or the "sister's-son" of Gondophares. *Sasi*, however, is found in several native names, as Sisenes, Sisimithres, Sisikoptos, Sisugambis, and others. Sasan, or Sassan as it is also written, was an undoubted Persian name. Two or three of this name are mentioned amongst the ancestors of Ardashir, of whom one at least was as old as the date of Gondophares. In the St. Thomas legend *Labdanes* is said to have been the sister's son of Gondofores.

The coins of *Orthagnes* are of two classes, each bearing a bust and a figure of Victory, but with different legends. One has the simple titles of ΒΑCΙΛΕωC ΜΕΓΑΛοΥ, while the other has ΒΑCΙΛΕΥC ΒΑCΙΛΕωΝ ΜΕΓΑC ΟΡΘΑΓΝΗC. The native legends also differ, the former being a mere copy of the Greek, while the latter introduces the name of Gudaphara immediately before the king's own name. The four letters forming the name seem to read *Gurdanasa*, or simply *Gadanasa*. Gurdana occurs in the name of *Gurdanaspa*. *Orthagnes* would have been pronounced *Orthanes* (Strabo), and I would compare it also with Ordones and Bardanes. I consider the name of Orthagnes to be the true form of the later *Orlagno*, which is found on the coins of the Kushân king, Kanishka. According to Dr. Stein this name (ΟΡΛΑΓΝΟ) "was first recognised by Benfey as *Verethraghna*, the Iranian war-god."[16] The king's name of ΟΡΘΑΓΝΗC shows that the other form is corrupt, and that we should rather read ΟΡΔΑΓΝΟ. *Verethraghna* is the old Avestic form of the name, which became *Varahrân* in Pahlavi, and Bahrâm in modern Persian. Dr. Haug[17] compares the old form with the Vedic *Vritrahâ*, which was one of the titles of Indra, as the "killer of enemies." An older Indian form was probably *Vritraghan*, in which the *g* of *Orthagnes* and *Orlagno* is preserved. The old form of *ghan* is seen also in *Amitra-ghâta*, which has the same meaning of "enemy killer." I would further compare the name with the Latin *Feretrius*, which was an old title of Jupiter.

As the name of Orthagnes is written in Arian characters

---

[16] *Babylonian and Oriental Record*, i. 159.
[17] Haug, *Essays on the Parsis*, by West, p. 213.

as *Gurdana* or *Gadana*, beginning with the letter G, it seems not improbable that he is the king's brother mentioned in the legend of St. Thomas under the name of *Gad*.

The coins of *Arsakes* are extremely rare. Dr. von Sallet has published a square copper piece copied from the money of Moas, but without any native legend. The Greek legend is incomplete ΒΑCΙΛΕѠC ΘΕΟΥ . . CΑΚΟΥ. The name might therefore be either Basakes or Masakes; but as Arsakes is known from other coins of a different type it seems a preferable reading. The types of this square coin would point to some connection with the earlier dynasty of Moas, but as the types of the larger coins are like those of the Gondophares family it seems more probable that Arsakes belonged to the later dynasty. The use of the round sigma, C, on three of his four known coins, shows conclusively that he must have been later than Moas and Azas. He takes the title of ΒΑCΙΛΕΥΟΝΤΟC ΒΑCΙΛΕѠΝ, which is also found on some coins of Abdagases. The types are the king on horseback, with Zeus carrying a figure of Victory. He uses a symbol peculiar to himself. None of his coins have been found in the Panjâb.

The coins of *Pakores* come from Kandahar and the countries to the west of Bhakar, on the Indus. They follow the types of Orthagnes with a bust of the king and a figure of Victory. The native characters are peculiar in having an angular foot-stroke. The name of the king is written *Pakurasa*.

The great power of Gondophares is proved by the wide extent of country over which his coins are found. In 1840—41 both Colonel Stacy and Captain Hutton obtained them in Kandahar and Sistan, whilst I have found them all over the Panjâb, from the hills down to Multan.

Masson obtained only fifty-five specimens from Begrâm during his three years' collection, but he found none in the Kabul Stûpas, and only four specimens in those near Jalalabad, where they were in company with numerous coins of Kujula Kadphises and a few of the Nameless King. I conclude, therefore, that he was a contemporary of Kujula, who must have held the Kabul valley, while Gondophares ruled over Kandahar and Sistan in the west, and over Sindh and the Panjâb in the east. After his death, about A.D. 50 or 60, the Panjâb was wrested from his successors by *Yen-kao-ching*, or Wema Kadphises, the Kushân conqueror of North-west India.

SAKA SATRAPS.

I have kept the coins of the Saka satraps apart from those of the kings, as I felt uncertain where to place them. That they belong to the period of Saka rule is clearly shown by their types, which are chiefly copied from the coins of Azas.

But a most decisive proof of their Saka nationality is found in the Arian Pali inscriptions of a pillar capital which was found at Mathura about twenty years ago by my lamented friend, Pandit Bhagwân Lâl. The principal inscription records the erection of a Stûpa for the relics of Buddha by the Queen Nandasriyâ in the time of the great Satrap *Rajul* (Rajubul of the coins) and of the Yuva Raja Kharadost, who also bore the title of Satrap. Mention is made of Prince *Tulama*, the son of Kharadost, and also of the Satrap *Sudâs*, the son of Rajul. A separate inscription on the same capital records the name of the great Satrap *Kusulaa*, who is almost certainly the Satrap named *Liaka-kusulaka* in the Taxila copper plate.[18] In both

[18] *Bengal Asiat. Soc. Journal*, 1863, and *Royal Asiat. Soc. Journal*, vol. xx., p. 230—for translation by Professor Dowson.

inscriptions the title of *patika* is added to his name. A silver obolus of this Satrap, copied from the well-known oboli of Eukratides, is shown in Plate I., Fig. 8. On the same capital with these Satrap names there is a short record which proves that all of them must have been *Sakas*. The words are *sarva Sakastâna puyae*, "for the merit of all the people of Sakastân," that is of the country occupied by the *Sakas*. The name of the city of Taxila is also found on the capital. At this time, therefore, the Indian territory of the Sakas must have extended from the Indus to Mathura, and from Kashmir to Sindh.

The Taxila copperplate inscription of *Liaka-Kusulaka* is dated in the year 78 of the great king *Moga*. As the number 78 is too high for a single reign the date must refer to the era of Moga, and if, as I suggested in 1863, he is the same as King *Moa*, or *Mauas*, of the coins, who was certainly one of the leaders of the *Sakas*, the establishment of the era may be referred to their conquest of the provinces on the Indus. As this event cannot be placed later than B.C. 120 the date of Liaka-Kusulaka would fall about 40 B.C., or rather more than half-a-century before the conquest of the Panjâb by the Kushân king, Wema Kadphises.

But we learn further from this Mathura inscription that most, if not all, of the *Saka* Satraps had embraced Buddhism. I had previously discovered the *Stûpa* of the Satrap *Jihonisa*, or Zeionises, at Manikyâla, and now we learn that the whole family of the great Satrap *Rajubul* had founded a *Stûpa* at Mathura to contain some relics of Buddha. There is nothing, however, to show whether the great *Saka* kings themselves, Mauas, Azas, and Azilises, had also become Buddhists. Their coins show no traces of Buddhism. On the contrary they show the marked devotion of the Saka Scythians to the worship of the club-hero *Sapal*, or Herakles, the *Gebeleizes* of Herodotus, and the *Sapaleizes* of our coins.

The worship of the club-god was indigenous in the Panjâb, as we learn from Q. Curtius that a statue of Herakles was carried in front of the army of Porus when he advanced against Alexander. Strabo also says that the people in the hills of India worshipped Bacchus, while the people of the plains worshipped Herakles.[19] The worship of Bacchus appears to me to have been founded on a mistake. According to Khares of Mytilene, one of the companions of Alexander, the actual *name* of the god was Σοροάδειος, that is, *Sûrya Deva* or the "sun-god." The name of *Sûrya*, or *Sûrah*, the sun, must have been confounded with *sŭra*, wine, as Khares gives its translation as οἰνοποιός, or "wine-maker." We know from Philostratus that there was a temple of the sun at Taxila, and from Plutarch, *de Fluviis*, that there was another on the Hydaspes, to which the elephant of Porus ascended on the advance of Alexander. The Indian Herakles is called *Dorsanes* by Hesychius. Arrian also says that the Suraseni called him *Gêgenês*, or "indigenous,"[20] and Diodorus states that he was born in India.[21]

JIHONISA OR ZEIONISES.

As the coins of Zeionises or Jihonisa are of superior execution, I would assign him to an early date during the reign of Azas, or about 80 B.C. I take him to have been the Satrap of Taxila, as I found one of his coins in a Stûpa at Manikyâla, along with a relic casket marked

---

[19] *Geogr.* xv. 1, 88.
[20] *India*, viii. p. 4.
[21] *Hist.* ii. p. 24.

with the Arian letter 𐨗 (J) on each of its three pieces.[22] The coins give the name of his father *Manigul*, and as he is also called a satrap, I think it probable that *Manikyâla* may have received its name from him. The coins of Jihonisa are found chiefly in the north-west Panjâb. The silver pieces are rare, but the copper coins are common. The name of Manigul is decidedly like that of a later prince Mihirgul.

Aspavarma, Son of Indravarma.

The coins of this chief certainly belong to the reign of Azas, as the name of the king is found in the Greek legend of the obverse, while the striker of the coin calls himself *Strategasa* (Στρατηγὸς) in the Arian legend of the reverse. Both the name and the title were first read by myself. I see that Dr. Von Sallet proposes to read *Aspa-bati*, while Dr. Oldenberg prefers *Aspa-pati*. But I most decidedly demur to both of these readings. The compound letter which I have read as *rm* in conjunction is simply formed by lengthening the right limb of the crescent-shaped *m*, across which is placed the letter *r*. The correctness of the attribution is proved by its use in the well-known word *Dharma*, on the coins of Kadaphes. Exactly the same process is followed in the formation of *rv* in *Sarva*, and of *ry* in *achârya*, and of *rkhe* in *Arkhebiyasa* (Arkhebios), and of *rt* in *Artemidorasa* (Artemidorus). The coins of Aspa Varma are common. They are found all over the Panjâb, but chiefly in the north-west. The legends are neatly but rather stiffly executed. No specimens were found at Begrâm by Masson, which tallies exactly with the absence of the coins of Azas himself at the same old site.

[22] *Archæol. Survey of India*, vol. ii., Pl. LXV.

SON OF VIJAYA-MITRA.

There are some rare coins of the same types as the last, which bear the names of other native chiefs. Nos. 7 and 8 of the Plate give the father's name in *Vijaya-mitra-putrasa*, or "Vijaya-mitra's son;" but I can only trace the beginning of the satrap's own name as *Ati* or *Atri*. The coins can be distinguished at once by the presence of a *star* on the right, and of a Buddhist symbol on the left.

KHARAMOSTIS, SON OF ARTAÜS.

The coins of the satrap Kharamostis are very rare. They are all square, and bear types of the horseman and lion as on some of the coins of Azas and Azilises. The specimen No. 9 gives the Greek legend complete—

ΧΑΡΑΜΩϹΤΕΙ ϹΑΤΡΑΠΕΙ ΑΡΤΑΟΥ.

The native legend is generally incomplete, and has not yet been read satisfactorily. I make out with some hesitation—

Khara[m]ostasa Artasa chhatrapasa putrasa.

The father's name would appear to be simply *Arta* in the native legend, and *Artaüs* in the Greek legend. The coins are found only in the North-west Panjâb. They are very rare, as I have seen only seven specimens in fifty years. I had one in 1841, which was engraved in my unpublished plates. But he must have been a chief of some note, as his name occurs three times in the great satrap inscription from Mathura, which is now in the British Museum.

In line 4 on top he is called *Khara ostara Yuva Rajna.*

In line 1 of No. 3 he is called *Khara osta Yuva Raja.*

In right corner of No. 4 he is called *Kharda asa Chhatrevasa.*

Here we see that he bears the title of *Yuva-raja*, or "Sub-raja," which was generally given to the heir-apparent. In one only is he called satrap in the peculiar local form of *Chhatrava* for *Chhatrapa*, a peculiarity which is seen also in the word *thuva*, for *thupa*, the Pali form of Stûpa. The same peculiarity still exists in the use of *wind* for *pind* in Rai-wind, near Lahore.

Râjubula.

The coins of this satrap were first made known by myself in 1854[23] from a hoard of base silver pieces found at Mathura. Since then I have received several small copper coins of similar types and legends from the Eastern Panjâb, besides a few copper specimens from Mathura of pure Indian types, with Indian Pali legends. On these last the inscription is simply *Mahakhatapasa Râjubulasa*, "of the great Satrap Râjubula." In the Greek legends of the billon coins he takes the title of "King of kings,"

BACIΛЄI BACIΛЄѠC CѠTHPoC PAZIBA,

but in the Arian legends of the reverse he is called simply Satrap, with the additional title of "invincible with the discus,"

Apratichakrasa Chhatrapasa Ranjubulasa.

Several of these billon coins have the Greek monogram No. 55, forming **EY**, which I take to represent Euthydemia or Sangala, as on the coins of Zoilus and others, from which his types are copied. From the find-spots of his coins, I conclude that Râjubul must have held the East Panjâb and North-west India as far eastward as Mathura. In the great satrap inscription from Mathura his name is shortened to *Rajula* in two different places.

---

[23] *Journal Bengal Asiat. Soc.* p. 679.

An imperfect inscription which I found at a well near Mathura gives the full name in Indian Pali letters as *Râjubula*.[24] I take him to have been the independent ruler of North-west India just before the conquest of Wema Kadphises early in the first century A.D.

SAUDÂSA.

Râjubula was succeeded by his son *Saudâsa*, of whom both coins and inscriptions have been found at Mathura. On his coins he is called *Mahakhatapasa putasa Khatapasa Saudâsasa*, or simply "Satrap" and not "great Satrap," like his father Râjubul. I had already proposed this connection with Râjubul, which has since been confirmed by the discovery of the great Satrap inscription at Mathura in which he is called

Mahachhatravasa Rajulasa-putra Sudâsa chhatrava,

that is, "the great satrap Rajula's son Saudâsa the satrap." As none of his coins have been found in the East Panjâb, I conclude that his rule was limited to the districts around Mathura during the rule of the great Kushân conqueror Wema Kadphises.

---

[24] *Archæological Survey of India*, vol. xx. p. 49.

COINS OF THE SAKAS.

*The numbers marked * are not figured on the Plates.*

Pl.	No.	Form.	Inches.	Metal.	Grains.	
						MOA OR MAUAS. SILVER COINS.
II.	1	○	1·05	Æ	141	[Duplicate Bodleian Library. Weight 121 grains.] *King radiate*, standing *in Biga* to r., holding spear in r. hand. Driver in front of King. ΒΑΣΙΛΕΩΣ ΒΑΣΙΛΕΩΝ ΜΕΓΑΛοΥ ΜΑΥοΥ. *Zeus* to front seated in chair, r. hand extended to r., holding hasta pura in l. hand. *Rajatirajasa mahatasa Moasa.* No. 1, mon. to l.
	2	○	0·65	Æ	32	[Duplicate Brit. Mus. Weight 87·6 grains.] Same types and legends, and mon., as No. 1.
	3	□	0·60	Æ	31	Same types and legends as No. 2; mon. E.
	4	○	1·05	Æ	149	[*Brit. Mus. Cat.*, xvi. 2.] *Zeus* standing l., holding hasta pura in l. hand, r. extended. Legend as on No. 2. *Victory* to r., with wreath and palm. Legend as on No. 1. No. 2 and 3 mon.
	5	○	0·65	Æ	36	Same types and legends as on No. 4. Mon. No. 3.

COPPER COINS.

II.	6	○	1·2	Æ	155	[*Brit. Mus. Cat.*, xvi. 1.] *Elephant's head*, with upraised trunk and bell. *Rev.—Caduceus.* **ΒΑΣΙΛΕΩΣ ΜΑΥοΥ.** No. 2 mon.
	7	○	1·2	Æ	175	[*Brit. Mus. Cat.*, xvi. 3, unique.] *King on horseback* to r., whip and couched lance. Greek legend, as on No. 1. No. 4 mon. *Rev.—Standing female*, turreted crown and wheel. Arian legend, as on No. 1, and field Arian letters *dami*.
	8	○	1·00	Æ	133	[*Brit. Mus. Cat.*, xvi. 4.] *Artemis radiate* running to r., flowing drapery, chiton and boots. Greek legend, as on No. 1. *Rev.—Humped Indian bull* to l. No. 5 mon. Arian legend, as on No. 1.
	9	○	1·05	Æ	128	[*Brit. Mus. Cat.*, xvi. 5.] *Herakles* standing to front; club on l. shoulder. Greek legend, as on No. 1. *Rev.—Maneless Indian lion* to l. No. 2 mon. Arian legend, as on No. 1.
	10	□	0·9	Æ	128	[*Brit. Mus. Cat.*, xvi. 6.] *King on horseback* to r., with whip and couched lance. Greek legend, as on No. 1. No. 6 mon.

COINS OF THE SAKAS—*continued.*

Pl.	No.	Form.	Inches.	Metal.	Grains.	
						Rev.—*Pallas* with spear and shield running to r. Arian legend, as on No. 1. In field, Arian letters *dami*. [*Brit. Mus. Cat.*, xvi. 7.]
II.	11	□	0·85	Æ	171	*King on horseback* to r., with whip and couched lance. *Rev.*—*Victory* to l., with palm and wreath. Greek legend, as on No. 1. No. 3 mon.; also No. 8. [*Brit. Mus. Cat.*, xvi. 8.]
	12	□	0·9	Æ	168	*Draped female* to front, with crescent on head, and sceptre in l. hand. A six-pointed star on each side. Greek legend, as on No. 1. *Rev.*—*Winged Victory* to l., with wreath and palm. Arian legend, as on No. 1. In field, Σ and A.
	13	□	0·9	Æ	145	*Male figure to front*, with elephant goad over l. shoulder. Greek legend, as on No. 1. *Rev.*—*Harpy* with outspread wings (?) Arian legend, as on No. 1. Mon. No. 2. [*Brit. Mus. Cat.*, xvii. 7.]
	14	□	0·55	Æ	35	*Apollo* standing to front, arrow in r. hand, holding bow with r. ΒΑΣΙΛΕΩΣ ΜΑΥΟΥ as on No. 6. Mon. M.

						Rev.—*Tripod* in beaded square. Arian legend *Mahārājasa Moasa.*
	14A*	□	0·5	Æ	29	Same types and legends as No. 14. [*Brit. Mus. Cat.*, No. 28.]
	15	□	0·8	Æ	66	*Horse* to r., trotting. ΒΑΣΙΛΕΩΣ ΜΑΥοΥ. *Rev.*—*Bow in bow-case.* Mon. No. 2. Arian legend, *Mahārājasa Moasa.* [*Brit. Mus. Cat.*, xvii. 6.]
III.	16	□	1·0	Æ	143	*Elephant* walking to r., holding wreath in upraised trunk. Greek legend, as on No. 1. *Rev.*—*Indian humped bull* to r. Mon. No. 3. Arian legend, as on No. 1. [*Brit. Mus. Cat.*, xvii. 5.]
	17	□	0·95	Æ	139	*Elephant running* to r., holding wreath in upraised trunk. Greek legend, as on No. 1. *Rev.*—*King seated* on raised cushion. Mon. No. 3. Arian legend, as on No. 1.
	18	□	0·85	Æ	98	*Elephant walking* to r., with trunk touching the ground. Greek legend as on No. 1. (Corner broken off.) *Rev.*—*Humped Indian bull.* Mon. No. 3. Arian legend, as on No. 1. [*Brit. Mus. Cat.*, xvii. 3.]
	19	□	1·1	Æ	165	*Male figure standing* to front, holding club in r. hand and a peculiar headed sceptre in l. hand. Greek legend, as on No. 1. Mon. No. 6.

COINS OF THE SAKAS—*continued.*

Pl.	No.	Form.	Inches.	Metal.	Grains.	
						Rev.—*Standing female* to r., with flying drapery, holding out a long fillet. Arian letters *Dami.* Arian legend, as on No. 1. N.B. As the mon. on the obverse can be read as ΔAMI in exact agreement with the two Arian letters, I conclude that this is the true reading of the monogram.
III.	20	□	0·8	Æ	141	[*Brit. Mus. Cat.*, xvii. 4.] *Male figure* standing to r., r. hand extended, sceptre in l. hand. Greek legend, as on No. 1. *Rev.*—*Male figure* standing to front, with petasus on head. Arian legend, as on No. 1. Mon. No. 8.
	21	□	0·95	Æ	144	[*Brit. Mus. Cat.*, xvi. 9.] *Zeus seated* on throne; sceptre in l. hand; r. hand extended to small female figure surrounded by rays (?). Greek legend, as on No. 1. *Rev.*—*Female standing* to front, head turreted, sceptre in l. hand, and veil held out by r. hand. Mon. No. 8.
	22	□	1·05	Æ	186	[*Brit. Mus. Cat.*, xvii. 1.] *Poseidon standing* to front, holding trident in l. hand, and

					trampling on a river-god with r. foot. Greek legend, as on No. 1. *Rev.*—*Female figure* standing to front between two vines which she grasps with her hands. Arian legend, as on No. 1. Mon. Nos. 5, 8, 1.
23	□	0·85	Æ	122	[*Brit. Mus. Cat.*, xvii. 2.] *Poseidon to front*, holding trident in r. hand, and hurling thunderbolt with l. hand at a small figure, which clasps an aplustre, or poop ornament of a boat. His r. foot is trampling on a river-god. Greek legend, as on No. 1. *Rev.*—*Female standing* between two vines, as on No. 22. Arian legend, as on No. 1—Arian mon. No. 9, *aspa*. A second has *a* only.
24	□	0·85	Æ	129	*Poseidon*, as on No. 23. Mon. No. 10, of Arian letters, forming *melam* or *milam*. Greek legend, as No. 1. *Rev.*—*Female standing* to front, grasping vine with l. hand, and extending r. hand to small figure advancing with outstretched arms on left. Arian mon. *pri*. Arian legend, as on No. 1.
25	□	0·85	Æ	—	*Poseidon standing* to front. L. hand holding trident, r. hand extended; apparently trampling on river-god. (Coin broken off.) Greek legend, as on No. 1.

COINS OF THE SAKAS—*continued.*

Pl.	No.	Form.	Inches.	Metal.	Grains.	
						Rev.—*Female standing* to front, between two vines (?). Arian legend, as on No. 1.
III.	26	□	0·5	Æ	28	Same as last on both sides. [*Brit. Mus. Cat.*, No. 14, p. 70.]
	27*	□	1·1	Æ	153	*Zeus on throne*, holding Victory in r. hand. Before him forepart of elephant with upraised trunk. Greek legend, as No. 1. *Rev.*—*Herakles standing* to front, in l. hand club and lion's skin, in r. hand wreath, with which he is crowning himself. Arian legend, as on No. 1.
						VONONES AND SPALAHORES.
IV.	1	○	1·0	AR	152	[*Brit. Mus. Cat.*, xxi. 7.] *King on horseback* to r. with couched lance. **ΒΑΣΙΛΕΩΣ ΒΑΣΙΛΕΩΝ ΜΕΓΑΛΟΥ ΟΝΩΝΟΥ.** *Rev.*—*Zeus laureate*, standing to front, spear in l. hand, thunderbolt in r. hand. Arian legend, *Mahârâja bhrâta dhramikasa Spalahorasa.* Mon. No. 12.
	2	○	0·6	AR	87	[*Brit. Mus. Cat.*, xxi. 8.] Same types and legend as No. 1. Mon. Nos. 12, 13, and 14.

3	□	0·8	Æ	125	[*Brit. Mus. Cat.*, xxi. 9.] *Herakles standing* to front, in l. hand club and lion's skin, in r. hand wreath, with which he is crowning himself. Greek legend as on No. 1. *Rev.*—*Pallas standing* to l., with helmet, spear, and shield, r. hand extended. Arian legend, as on No. 1. Mon. Nos. 12 and 13.
3A*	□	0·7	Æ	64	N.B. A half coin of same types and legends.
					VONONES AND SPALGADAMES.
4	○	1·0	Ꞧ	136	*King on horseback*, to r. with couched lance. **ΒΑΣΙΛΕΩΣ ΒΑΣΙΛΕΩΝ ΜΕΓΑΛοΥ οΝΩΝοΥ.** *Rev.*—*Zeus laureate*, standing to front, spear in l. hand, thunderbolt in r. hand. Arian legend, *Spalahora putrasa dhramiasa Spalagadamasa.* Mon. No. 51.
5	○	0·6	Ꞧ	87	[*Brit. Mus. Cat.*, xxi. 10.] Types and legends as on No. 4. Mon. No. 15.
6	□	0·85	Æ	91	[*Brit. Mus. Cat.*, xxi. 11.] *Herakles standing*, club and lion's skin in l. hand, wreath in r. hand, with which he is crowning himself. Legend as on No. 4. *Rev.*—*Pallas standing*, as on No. 3. Mon. No. 15. Arian legend, as in No. 4.

COINS OF THE SAKAS—*continued.*

Pl.	No.	Form.	Inches.	Metal.	Grains.	
						SPALAHORES AND SPALGADAMES.
IV.	7	□	0·85	Æ	122	[*Brit. Mus. Cat.*, xxi. 12.] *King on horseback*, to r. **ϹΠΑΛΥΡΙϽϹ ΔΙΚΑΙΟΥ ΑΔΕΛΦΟΥ ΤΟΥ ΒΑϹΙΛΕωϹ.** *Rev.*—*Herakles seated* on rock, in l. hand club, resting on knee. Arian legend, *Spalahora putrasa dhramiasa Spalagadamasa.* Mon. Nos. 15, 16.
						VONONES AND AZAS.
	8	○	1·00	Æ	—	Collection of Bengal Asiatic Society. See *Journal*, 1858, p. 252. *Herakles standing* to front, l. hand holding club, r. hand on hip. **ΒΑΣΙΛΕΩΣ ΒΑΣΙΛΕΩΝ ΜΕΓΑΛοΥ οΝΩΝοΥ.** *Rev.*—*Maneless lion* walking to l. Mon. No. 2. Arian legend, *Rajâdirajasa mahatasa Ayasa.*
						SPALIRISES.
	9	○	0·65	AR	85	[*Brit. Mus. Cat.*, xxii. 1.] *King on horseback* to r., with couched lance. **ΒΑϹΙΛΕωϹ ΑΔΕΛΦοΥ ϹΠΑΛΙΡΙϹοΥ.**

No.	Shape	Size	Metal	Weight	Description
					Rev.—*Zeus standing* with spear and thunderbolt. Mon. No. 16. Arian legend, *Mahârâja bhrâta dhramıasa Spalirisasa.*
					[*Brit. Mus. Cat.*, xxii. 2.]
10	□	0·90	Æ	128	*King walking* to l., with battle-axe and bow. ΒΑϹΙΛΕѠΝ ΒΑϹΙΛΕѠϹ ΜΕΓΑΛ□Υ ϹΠΑΛΙ-ΡΙϹ□Υ.
					Rev.—*Zeus on throne*, r. hand extended, l. hand holding sceptre. Arian legend, *Mahârâjasa mahatakasa Spalirisasa.* Mon. No. 17.
					Spalirises and Azas.
11	○	0·9	AR	139	*King on horseback* to r., with couched lance. ΒΑϹΙΛΕѠϹ ΜΕΓΑΛΟΥ ΡΠΑΛΙΡΙϹΟΥ.
					Rev.—*Zeus standing*, sceptre in l. hand, thunderbolt in r. Arian legend, *Mahârâjasa mahatakasa Ayasa.* Mon. No. 18.
					[*Brit. Mus. Cat.*, xxii. 3.]
12	○	0·65	AR	37	The same types and legend as No. 11. Same mon.
					[*Brit. Mus. Cat.*, xxii. 4.]
13	○	1·0	Æ	117	*King on horseback* to r. Same legend as No. 11.
					Rev.—*Strung bow and arrow.* Mon. No. 19. Arian legend, same as No. 11.

COINS OF THE SAKAS—*continued.*

Pl.	No.	Form.	Inches.	Metal.	Grains.	AZAS. SILVER COINS.
V.	1	○	1·1	Æ	139	*King on horseback* to r., with couched lance. Type A. **ΒΑΣΙΛΕΩΣ ΒΑΣΙΛΕΩΝ ΜΕΓΑΛoΥ ΑΖoΥ.** Arian letter *pri* under horse. *Rev.*—*Winged figure of Victory* to l., with palm-branch and wreath. Mon. No. 21, with Arian letter *so*. Arian legend, *Mahárájasa rajarajasa Mahatasa Ayasa.* [*Brit. Mus. Cat.*, xviii. 12.]
	2	○	0·75	Æ	34·5	*Zeus standing* to l., sceptre in l. hand, r. hand extended. Greek legend, as on No. 1. *Rev.*—*Winged figure of Victory* to r., holding wreath and palm. Arian legend, as on No. 1. Mon. No. 22.
	3	○	1·05	Æ	145	*King on horseback*, with couched lance. Type A. Greek legend, as on No. 1. Arian letter under horse. *Rev.*—*Zeus laureated standing* to front, with sceptre in l. hand, and thunderbolt upraised in r. hand. Arian legend, as on No. 1. Mon. No. 23, with Arian letter *a*. [*Brit. Mus. Cat.*, xvii. 2.]
	3A	○	0·6	Æ	33	Same types, legends, and mon. as No. 3.

	4	O	0·95	Æ	150	[*Brit. Mus. Cat.*, xvii. 9.] *King on horseback* to r., with couched lance. Type A. Greek legend, as on No. 1. *Rev.*—*Zeus laureated standing* to front, sceptre in l. hand, thunderbolt in extended r. hand. Arian legend, as on No. 1. Mon. No. 25, with Arian letter *dhra*.
	4A	O	0·75	Æ	85	Same types and legend as on No. 4. Mon. No. 25, with Arian letter *ṅa*.
	5	O	1·05	Æ	142	[*Brit. Mus. Cat.*, xvii. 8.] *King on horseback*, with couched lance. Type A. Greek legend, as on No. 1. Arian letter *pri* under horse. *Rev.*—*Zeus radiated* to l., sceptre in l. hand, r. hand extended. Arian legend, as on No. 1. Mon. No. 24, with Arian letter *man*. N.B. This reverse is the same as the obverse of No. 2.
	6	O	0·95	Æ	152	[*Brit. Mus. Cat.*, xvii. 12.] *King on horseback*, with whip and bow. Type B. Greek legend, as on No. 1. Arian letter *de* before horse. *Rev.*—*Zeus standing* to l., sceptre in l. hand, Victory in extended r. hand. Mon. No. 26, with Arian letter *dhra*. Arian legend, as on No. 1.

COINS OF THE SAKAS—*continued.*

Pl.	No.	Form.	Inches.	Metal.	Grains.	
V.	6A	○	0·65	Æ	36	(Same types and legends as No. 6.) Mon. No. 26, with Arian letter *sa*.
	7	○	1·0	Æ	149	*King on horseback*, with whip and bow. Type B. Greek legend, as on No. 1. Arian letter *pra* before horse. *Rev.*—*Poseidon with trident* walking to r., r. hand extended. In field mon. No. 27, with Arian letter *si*. Arian legend, as on No. 1.
						[*Brit. Mus. Cat.*, xviii. 10.]
	8	○	1·00	Æ	138	*King on horseback*, with couched lance. Type A. Greek legend, as on No. 1. *Rev.*—*Female figure* to l., carrying palm on l. shoulder, and uncertain object in r. hand. Mon. No. 28. Arian legend, as on No. 1. N.B. It seems very doubtful for whom this female figure is intended. H. H. Wilson calls her Victory, while Professor Percy Gardner suggests a city. I incline to Demeter, or Fortune (*Tyche*). The date-palm is a good symbol of productiveness, quite equal to the cornucopiæ.
	8A	○	0·60	Æ	35	Same types and legends as No. 8. Mon. No. 31.

9	○	1·00	Æ	145	[*Brit. Mus. Cat.*, xviii. 4.] *King on horseback*, with whip and bow. Type B. Under horse, Arian letter *lu*. *Rev.—Pallas to front*, spear and shield in l. hand, r. hand raised to head. Mon. No. 29, with Arian mon. *sasi*. Arian legend, as on No. 1.*
9A	○	0·70	Æ	36	Same types and legends as No. 9. Mon. No. 23.
10	○	1·05	Æ	143	*King on horseback* to r., with whip and bow. Type B. To r., Arian letter *ga*. Greek legend, as on No. 1. *Rev.—Pallas standing* to l., shield on l. shoulder, r. hand extended. Arian legend, as on No. 1. Mon. No. 23.
10A	○	0·70	Æ	33·5	[*Brit. Mus. Cat.*, xviii. 6.] Same type, legends, and mon. as No. 10.
11	○	1·05	Æ	141	[*Brit. Mus. Cat.*, xviii. 2.] *King on horseback* to r., with couched lance. Type A. Greek legend, as on No. 1. *Rev.—Pallas* to l., shield on l. arm, and thunderbolt in raised r. hand. Mon. No. 23, with Arian *a*. Arian legend, as on No. 1.
11A	○	0·70	Æ	35·5	Same types and legends and mon. as No. 11.
12	○	1·00	Æ	143	[*Brit. Mus. Cat.*, xviii. 8.] *King on horseback*, with whip and bow. Type B. Greek

* See Plate XIII for statue of Athene from Peshawar.

COINS OF THE SAKAS—*continued.*

Pl.	No.	Form.	Inches.	Metal.	Grains.	
						legend, as on No. 1. Arian letter *ph* in front of horse. *Rev.—Pallas* to r., holding spear and shield with l. hand, and extending r. hand. Mon. Nos. 29, 33; also No. 31, with Arian *si*. Arian legend, as on No. 1.
V.	12A	○	0·65	AR	37·5	Same types, legends, and mon. as No. 12.
	13	○	1·00	AR	136	*King on horseback*, with whip and bow. Type B. Greek legend as on No. 1. Arian letter *ka*. *Rev.—Pallas* to r., carrying shield with l. hand, and holding with r. hand spear behind her. Mon. Nos. 32, 33. Arian legend, as on No. 1.
						COPPER COINS.
VI.	1	□	1·10	Æ	172	[*Brit Mus. Cat.*, xix. 10.] *Poseidon* to front, holding trident in l. hand, and trampling on river-god with right foot. **ΒΑΣΙΛΕΩΣ ΒΑΣΙΛΕΩΝ ΜΕΓΑΛΟΥ ΑΖΟΥ.** *Rev.—Female standing* between two vines, which she clasps one in each hand. Mon. No. 21. Arian legend, *Maharâjasa rajarajasa mahatasa Ayasa*.

2	□	1·00	Æ	205	[*Brit. Mus. Cat.*, xix. 9.] *King riding two-humped camel* to r., with whip in r. hand and bow behind. Greek legend, as on No. 1. *Rev.*—*Humped Indian bull* to r. Mon. No. 25. Arian legend, as on No. 1.
3	□	0·90	Æ	187	[*Brit. Mus. Cat.*, xix. 8.] *King on horseback* to r., with couched lance. Greek legend, as on No. 1. *Rev.*—*Humped Indian bull* to r. Mon. No. 23. Arian legend, as on No. 1.
3A*	○	1·20	Æ	320	Same types, legends, and mon. as No. 3.
3B*	□	0·50	Æ	18	Same types as No. 3. ΒΑΣΙΛΕΩΣ ΜΕΓΑΛοΥ ΑΖοΥ. *Rev.*—Same as No. 3. Arian legend, *Maharájasa mahatasa Ayasa.*
4	○	0·80	Æ	145	[*Brit. Mus. Cat.*, xx. 1.] *King on horseback*, triform symbol, No. 35. ΒΑCΙΛΕѠΝ ΒΑCΙΛΕѠC ΜΕΓΑΛ□Υ ΑΖ□Υ. *Rev.*—*Female standing* to front, l. hand holding cornucopia; r. hand stretched out. Complex Arian monogram forming *Shegasha*, No. 34, with *kha.* Arian legend, *Maharájasa mahatasa dhramikasa Rajadirajasa Ayasa.*
5	○	0·80	Æ	151	*King on horseback*, jumbled Greek inscription.

COINS OF THE SAKAS—*continued.*

Pl.	No.	Form.	Inches.	Metal.	Grains.	
						Rev.—*Pallas* armed to r. Arian legend, *Maharájasa Rajadirajasa mahatasa Ayasa.* In field, No. 28 mon., with Arian letter *bu*, and Buddhist symbol.
VI.	6	□	0·85	Æ	110	*King on horseback* to r. ΒΑΣΙΛΕΩΣ ΒΑΣΙΛΕΩΝ ΜΕΓΑΛΟΥ ΑΖΟΥ. *Rev.*—*Herakles* sitting on rock, l. hand resting on rock, r. hand holding club on knee. Mon. No. 31. Arian legend, *Maharájasa mahatasa Ayasa.* N.B. Two specimens agree in omitting *rajarajasa.*
	7	□	0·8	Æ	84	*Male figure* standing; in l. hand elephant goad, r. hand extended. Greek legend, as on No. 1. *Rev.*—*Lion* to r., with forepaw raised. Arian legend, as on No. 1.
	8*	○	0·75	Æ	77	[*Brit. Mus. Cat.*, xix. 8.] *Hermes* to l., holding caduceus in l. hand, r. hand extended. Greek legend, as on No. 1. Mon. No. 36. *Rev.*—*Demeter* to l., r. hand extended; cornucopiæ in l. hand. Arian legend, as on No. 1. Mon. No. 37, with Arian *ba.*

9	○	1·10	Æ	170	[*Brit. Mus. Cat.*, xix. 1.] *King squatted on cushion* looking to l., whip in r. hand, and holding sceptre in l. hand across his knees. Blundered Greek legend, intended for No. 1. In field, Arian *gha*. N.B. This is the only specimen out of several hundreds on which the whip is in the right hand. *Rev.*—*Hermes* to front, l. hand carrying caduceus, r. hand extended. Mon. No. 87, with Arian **B** and *ta*. Others have Mon. No. 87, with *sam*. Arian legend, as on No. 1.
9A*	○	0·80	Æ	97	Same types and legends as No. 8.
9B*	○	0·50	Æ	21	Same types and legends as No. 8.
10	○	1·10	Æ	204	[*Brit. Mus. Cat.*, xix. 2.] *Demeter seated on throne*, r. hand extended, l. hand holding cornucopiæ. Greek legend, as on No. 1. *Rev.*—*Hermes* to front, r. hand extended, caduceus in l. hand. Arian legend, as on No. 1. Mon. No. 29, with Arian *sasi*. N.B. Many coins of this type have been struck upon the elephant coins of Azas. I possess one with half of the elephant visible, and with half Greek, half Arian, legends on both sides.
11	○	0·60	Æ	33	[*Brit. Mus. Cat.*, xix. 4.] *Lion* to r. Greek legend, as on No. 1.

COINS OF THE SAKAS—*continued.*

Pl.	No.	Form.	Inches.	Metal.	Grains.	
						Rev.—*Demeter* to l., cornucopiæ in l. hand, r. extended. Arian legend, as on No. 1. Mon. 37, with *bu.*
VI.	12	○	1·00	Æ	213	[*Brit. Mus. Cat.*, xix. 7.] *Indian elephant* to r. Greek legend, as on No. 1. *Rev.*—*Humped Indian bull* to r. Mon. 23 and 28. Arian legend, as on No. 1.
	12A*	○	0·60	Æ	31	Same types and legends as No. 11.
	12B*	□	0·90	Æ	109	Same types and legends as No. 11.
	12C*	□	0·45	Æ	24	[*Brit. Mus. Cat.*, xix. 12.] Same types as No. 11. Greek legend, ΒΑΣΙΛΕΩΣ ΜΕΓΑΛΟΥ ΑΖΟΥ. Arian legend, *Mahārājasa mahatasa Ayasa.*
	13	○	0·90	Æ	153	[*Brit. Mus. Cat.*, xix. 5.] *Female figure* to front, naked to waist, l. hand on hip, r. hand raised to head. Greek legend as on No. 1. Mon. 39 and 40. *Rev.*—*Humped bull.* Arian legend, as on No. 1.
	14	○	1·05	Æ	220	[*Brit. Mus. Cat.*, xix. 6.] *Humped Indian bull* to r. Mon. 29. Greek legend, as on No. 1.

						Rev.—*Maneless Indian lion* to r. Mon. Arian *sasi*. Arian legend, as on No. 1.
	14A*	○	0·85	Æ	115	Types and legends as No. 13. *Obv*. Mon. 33; *Rev*. Mon. 32.
	14B*	○	0·60	Æ	45	Same types and legends as No. 13.
	14C*	□	0·70	Æ	65	Same types and legends as No. 13.
	15	□	0·90	Æ	138	[*Brit. Mus. Cat.*, xix. 11.]
						Herakles to front, club and lion's skin on l. arm, r. hand raised to crown himself. Greek legend, as on No. 1. Mon.
						Rev.—*Horse* to r. Arian legend, as on No. 1. Mon. Arian *mi*.
						AZILISES.
						SILVER COINS.
VII.	A 1	○	—	Æ	—	These two coins bear the joint names of Azas and Azilises. A I., in the French collection, gives the name and titles of Azas on the Greek obverse, and the name and titles of Azilises on the Arian reverse. A II., in my own collection, reverses this order, the name of Azilises being on the Greek side, and that of Azas on the Arian side. The type of the obverse A is the king on horseback.
	A 2	○	—	Æ	140	
	B	○	1·00	Æ	150	*King on horseback*, with whip and bow, with couched lance. Type B.

COINS OF THE SAKAS—*continued.*

Pl.	No.	Form.	Inches.	Metal.	Grains.	
VII.	1	○	1·00	Æ	137	*King on horseback*, with couched lance. Type A. ΒΑΣΙΛΕΩΣ ΒΑΣΙΛΕΩΝ ΜΕΓΑΛΟΥ ΑΖΟΥ. *Rev.*—*Pallas armed* to l., shield on l. arm; thunderbolt in upraised r. hand ready to hurl. Arian legend, *Mahārājasa rajarajasa mahatasa Ayilisasa.* Mon. No. 23, with *a*. [*Brit. Mus. Cat.*, xx. 4.]
	1A	○	0·65	Æ	35	Same types, legends, and monogram as on No. 1.
	2	○	2·00	Æ	149·5	*King on horseback*, with whip and bow. Type B. Mon. No. 42. *Rev.*—*Zeus diademed* and bearded to r., carrying sceptre in l. hand, and in r. hand a small uncertain object. Mon. No. 43. Arian legend, as on No. 1.
	2A	○	0·70	Æ	35	Same types, legends, and mons. as No. 2.
	3	○	1·00	Æ	148	*King on horseback* to r., with whip and bow. Type B. Greek legend, as on No. 1. Mon. No. 42. *Rev.*—The Indian goddess *Lakshmi* standing to front on a lotus flower, from which two stalks spring to the r. and l., each supporting a small elephant, which pours water on the head of the goddess. Arian legend, as on No. 1. Mon. No. 43.

4	○	1·00	Æ	139	[*Brit. Mus. Cat.*, xx. 9.] *King on horseback*, with couched lance. Type A. Greek legend, as on No. 1. *Rev.*—*Goddess* to l., with filleted palm in l. hand, and uncertain object in r. hand. In field to r. Arian letter *sam*; to l. Mon. No. 44, with Arian letter *dhra*. Arian legend, as on No. 1.
4A	○	0·70	Æ	36	[*Brit. Mus. Cat.*, xx. 11.] *Types and leg nds* as on No. 4. Mon. 28, with *na*.
5	○	1·05	Æ	146	[*Brit. Mus. Cat.*, xx. 7.] *King on horseback* to r., with whip and bow. Type B. Mon. No. 38. Greek legend, as on No. 1. *Rev.*—*One of the Dioskuri* to front, with sword and spear. Arian legend, as No. 1. Mon. No. 45, Arian *mis*.
5A	○	0·65	Æ	35	[*Brit. Mus. Cat.*, xx. 8.] *Types and legends* as No. 5. Mon. No. 38.
6	○	1·00	Æ	150·5	[*Brit. Mus. Cat.*, xx. 5.] *King on horseback*, with whip and bow. Type B. Greek legend, as on No. 1. Mon. No. 46. *Rev.*—The *Dioskuri dismounted* to front, each with Phrygian cap, spear, and sword. Arian legend, as on No. 1.

COINS OF THE SAKAS—*continued.*

Pl.	No.	Form.	Inches.	Metal.	Grains.	
VII.	6A	○	0·65	Æ	34·5	[*Brit. Mus. Cat.*, xx. 6.] *Types and legends* as No. 6. Mon. 46 (No. 6 mons.).
	7	○	1·10	Æ	150	*King on horseback*, with whip and bow. Type B. Greek legend, as on No. 1. Mon. No. 48.
						Rev.—*Two figures*, male and female, standing to front, male figure apparently Zeus, as on No. 2, with sceptre and small uncertain object in r. hand. The female, with turreted head-dress and wreath, represents a city. Arian mons. *spila* and *pa*. Arian legend, as on No. 1.
	7A	○	0·70	Æ	35	*Same types*, legends, and mon. as No. 7.
	8	○	1·05	Æ	147	*Zeus* to l., with sceptre in l. hand, and Victory with wreath and palm in r. hand. Greek legend, as on No. 1. Mon. No. 49.
						Rev.—*Mounted Dioskuri*, with palms, charging to r. Arian legend, as No. 1. Arian letters *pan* and *na*.
	8A*	○	0·65	Æ	35	*Types*, *legends*, and mon. as on No. 8.
	9	○	0·65	Æ	36	*Zeus* seated on throne to r., holding small figure of Victory with wreath in r. hand. Mon. No. 47 to r. Greek legend, as No. 1.
						Rev.—*Mounted Dioskuri*, with palms, charging to r. as on No. 8.

VIII.	1	□	0·90	Æ	157	COPPER COINS. [*Brit. Mus. Cat.*, xxi. 3.] *King on horseback* to r., with couched lance. **ΒΑCΙΛΕΩΣ ΒΑΣΙΛΕΩΝ ΜΕΓΑΛοΥ ΑΖΙΛΙΣοΥ.** *Rev.—Humped bull* to l. In field **Σ** and Arian *sa*. Arian legend, *Mahârâjasa mahatasa Ayilisasa.*
	2	□	0·85		88	[*Brit. Mus. Cat.*, xxi. 2.] *King on horseback* to r. Greek legend, as on No. 1. *Rev.—Elephant* to r. Mon. No. 31, with Arian *si*. Arian legend, *Mahârâjasa mahatasa Ayilisasa.*
	3	□	0·80	Æ	122	[*Brit. Mus Cat.*, xxi. 1.] *King on horseback* to r. Greek legend, as on No. 1. *Rev.—Herakles seated* on rock to l., club in r. hand, resting on knee, l. hand on rock. Mon. No. 31. *Arian legend, Mahârâjasa mahatasa Ayilisasa.*
	3A	□	1·00	Æ	112	N.B. One specimen has been struck on a coin of Spalirises, as shown by part of Greek legend **ΕωΝ ΒΑCΙΛΕωC**, and part of Arian legend *Mahatakasa* still remaining. Both of these forms are peculiar to the coins of Spalirises.
	4	□	1·00	Æ	152	*Elephant moving* to r. Greek legend, as on No. 1. *Rev.—Humped Indian bull* to r. Arian legend, as No. 1.
	5	□	0·85	Æ	152	*Herakles standing* to front, holding club in l. hand, and wreath in r. hand. Jumbled Greek legend.

COINS OF THE SAKAS—*continued.*

Pl.	No.	Form.	Inches.	Metal.	Grains.	
						Rev.—*Humped Indian bull* to l. Mon. No. 29. Arian legend imperfect ——— *sa mahatasa* ——.
VIII.	6	□	0·85	Æ	113	*Female figure* with turreted head-dress seated on throne to r. ΒΑΣΙΛΕΩΣ ΒΑΣΙΛΕΩΝ Μ———.
						Rev.—*Male figure* to front, carrying club in l. hand, and Victory in r. hand. Arian *ra* in field. Arian legend, as on No. 1.
	7	□	0·60	Æ	39	*Male figure* to r., carrying club and Victory. Arian legend, as No. 1. Mon. No. 47.
						Rev.—*Female figure*, with flowing garments, to front. Arian legend imperfect, *harajasa*.
	8	□	1·00	Æ	187	[*Brit. Mus. Cat.*, xxi. 4.] *King helmeted* standing to r., with spear and shield in l. hand, and right hand extended. Greek legend, as on No. 1.
						Rev.—*Female figure* to r., holding out wreath in r. hand. Arian legend, as on No. 1.
	9	□	0·90	Æ	72	[*Brit. Mus. Cat.*, xxi. 6.] *Male figure* to front, carrying two indistinct objects on l. shoulder, r. hand extended. Mon. No. 38. Greek legend, as on No. 1.

						Rev.—*Lion* to r., with r. forepaw raised. Arian legend, as on No. 1.
	10	□	0·95	Æ	140	[*Brit. Mus. Cat.*, xxi. 5.]
						Herakles to front, in l. hand club and lion's skin, r. hand extended. Greek legend, as on No. 1. Mon. No. 38.
						Rev.—*Horse to r.* Arian legend, as in No. 1. Arian mon. over horse, No. 45.
						HERAÜS OR MIAÜS.
IX.	1	○	1·05	AR	215	[*See Brit. Mus. Cat.*, xxiv. 7.]
	1A	○	1·15	AR	237	Bare diademed *bust of king* to r., in circle of fillets.
		○	1·30	AR	206	*Rev.*—*King on horseback* to r., Victory flying behind to crown him.
		○	1·20	AR	240	Upper legend, ΤΥΙΑΝΝ□ΝΤ□Σ ΗΙΑ⊏Υ.
		○	1·15	AR	233	Lower legend, ΣΑΝΑΒ Κ⊐ΡΕΑΝ□Υ.
						N.B. Mr. Gardner reads ΣΑΚΑ Κ□ΙΡΑΝ□Υ, which leaves the final letter **B** unaccounted for.
	2	○	0·45	AR	11	Same head as on No. 1.
						Rev.—*Male figure* standing to r. ΜΙΑΙ⊐Υ Κ□ΡΕΑΝ⊏Υ.
	2A	○	0·45	AR	11	Similar to No. 2.
	2B*	○	0·45	AR	11	Same types as No. 1. ΗΙΑ⊐Υ Κ⊐ΙΡΑΝ⊐.
	2C*	○	0·45	AR	11	Same as No. 2B.

COINS OF THE SAKAS—*continued.*

Pl.	No.	Form.	Inches.	Metal.	Grains.	
IX.	3	○	0·90	Æ	150	*King's head*, as on No. 1, with Arian legend. *Rev.—King on horseback*, with Victory flying behind. ΤΥΡΑΝΝΟ . . . . . ΚϹ ΡϹΑΝ. N.B. The name of this king is uncertain. In 1861, when I got his first coin, I read the name as Heraüs, just as Mr. Percy Gardner still reads it; but some years afterwards, on obtaining other specimens, and more particularly a number of oboli, it seemed to me that Miaüs would be a preferable reading. Some of the oboli insert an *i* after *a*, thus making either ΗΡΑΙΟϹ or ΜΙΑΙΟϹ. If the copper coin had been in better preservation we should, no doubt, have got the reading in the Arian legend. I have discussed the name and position of this king in another place.
						NAMELESS KING.
	4	○	0·90	Æ	195	[*Brit. Mus. Cat.*, xxiv. 6.] *Bust of king* to l., with crested helmet, holding a lance upright in r. hand, surrounded by circle of fillets. Behind head three-pronged symbol, No. 56, and in front the Arian letter *Vi*.

						Rev.—*King on horseback* to r., with r. hand raised. In front the same three-pronged symbol, ΒΑϹΙΛЄΥϹ ΒΑϹΙΛΕΥωΝ ϹωΤΗΡ ΜΕΓΑϹ. [*Brit. Mus. Cat.*, xxiv. 1.]
	5	○	0·70	Æ	152	*King on horseback* to r., as on No. 4, with same symbol. *Rev.*—*Zeus* to r., with sceptre. To r., round vessel with plant; to l., Arian letter *Vi.* Arian legend, *Mahârâjasa rajatirajasa mahatasa tradatasa.*
	5A	○	0·5	Æ	30	*Same types*, legends, and symbols as No. 5. [*Brit. Mus. Cat.*, xxiv. 2.]
	6	○	0·75	Æ	140	*Radiated* and *diademed bust of king* to r., holding lance upright in r. hand. Four-pronged symbol behind head. *Rev.*—*King on horseback* to r., uncertain object in r. hand. Four-pronged symbol in front. Greek legend, as on No. 4. (These coins usually have the three-pronged symbol.)
	6A	○	0·55	Æ	31	Same types and legends, as No. 6. [*Brit. Mus. Cat.*, xxiv. 5.]
	7	○	0·65	Æ	66	*Diademed bust of king* to r. Three-pronged symbol to r. *Rev.*—*Zeus standing*, with spear and thunderbolt, as on the coins of Heliokles. Greek mon. forming ΠΛ. Greek legend, as on No. 4. N.B. These coins are commonly found at Mathura.

COINS OF THE SAKAS—*continued.*

Pl.	No.	Form.	Inches.	Metal.	Grains.	
IX.	8	○	0·45	Æ	25	*Figure standing* to front, like **ΟΚΡΟ** with trident and club Three-pronged symbol, and Arian letter *Vi*. *Rev.*—*Female figure* to r., holding cornucopiæ like **ΑΡΔΟΧΡΟ**. Buddhist symbol and pot of flowers.
						SAPALEIZES.
	9	○	0·6	AR	26	[*Brit. Mus. Cat.*, xxiv. 14, 15.] *Helmeted head* of king to r. **ϹΑΠΑΛΕΙΖΗϹ**. *Rev.*—*Maneless Indian lion* to r. On each side Greek legend, **ΝΑΝΑΙΑ**.
						GONDOPHARES. SILVER COIN.
X.	1*	○	0·75	AR	58	[*Brit. Mus. Cat.*, xxxii. 10] at Berlin. *Bust of King* to l., diademed and bearded with Arsakidan tiara. *Rev.*—*King seated on throne* to r. Victory behind crowning him. **ΒΑϹΙΛΕΩϹ ΒΑϹΙΛΕΩΝ ΜΕΓϹ ΥΝΔΟΦΕΡΗϹ ΑΥΤ□ΚΡΑΤ□**.

COPPER COINS.

2	□	0·70	Æ	88	[*Brit. Mus. Cat.*, xxii. 12.] *King on horseback* to l., receiving wreath from Victory. Greek legend incomplete on the few known specimens. **ΦΑΡ⊐Υ ΕΓΑΛ□Υ Γ□ΝΔΑ.** *Rev.—The Gondopharian Symbol* ☿. Arian legend in small letters incomplete, the missing portion supplied in brackets [*Maharájasa rajadirajasa mahatasa*] *dhramikasa apratihatasa devahadasa Gondopharasa.* In field to r. and l., Arian letters *san* and *bre*.	
3	○	1·0	Æ	125	*Bare diademed head of King* to l. Corrupt and imperfect Greek legend, **ΒΑΣΙΛΕ——ΙΝΔΥ ΦΡΡ·Υ.** *Rev.—Winged Victory* to r., with palm and wreath. Arian legend in rude letters not read, but seems to be, *Maharájasa rajadirajasa mahatasa Gudupharasa.* N.B. On all my three specimens the sigma is of the early form.	
4	○	0·95	Æ	138	[*Brit. Mus. Cat.*, xx. 11.] *Bust of King* to r., diademed and bearded. **ΒΑCΙΛΕΩC CΩΤΗΡΟC ΥΝΔ⊐ΦΕΡΡ⊐Υ.**	

COINS OF THE SAKAS—*continued.*

Pl.	No.	Form.	Inches.	Metal.	Grains.	
						Rev.—*Winged Victory* to r., with wreath and palm. Arian legend, *Mahardjasa tradatasa Gondopharnasa.* N.B. The compound letter *rn*, in the latter half of the name, is quite distinct. It is formed of the common *n* with *r* placed across it. All my specimens of this type have this form, and so has the British Museum specimen above quoted. [*Brit. Mus. Cat.*, xxii. 7.]
X.	5	○	0·45	Æ	37	*Bearded head* to r. Rude Greek legend. *Rev.*—*Pallas* with shield and thunderbolt. Arian legend, completed from several specimens: *Mahârâjasa tradatasa Gondopharasa.* In field, Arian letters *ho* and *stra.* [*Brit. Mus. Cat.*, xxii. 8], Billon.
	6	○	0·95	Æ	145	*King on horseback* to l., with r. hand stretched in front. Victory flying behind with wreath to crown him. ΒΑϹΙΛΕѠϹ ΒΑϹΙΛΕѠΝ ΜΕΓΑΛΟΥ ΥΝΔΟΦΕΡΡοΥ. In field to l., the Gondopharian symbol No. 50.

						Rev.—*Poseidon* to front, with trident and palm. Arian legend, *Mahardjasa rajarajasa tradatasa Devahada Gandapharasa.* In field to l. a symbol like the figure 6; to r. the Arian letter *gu*.
	7	O	0·85	Æ	125	[*Brit. Mus. Cat.*, xxii. 7], Billon. *King on horseback* to r., with r. hand raised. Greek legend, as on No. 6; to r. Gondopharian symbol No. 50. *Rev.*—*Pallas* to r., with spear; r. hand to front. Arian legend, *Maharajasa mahatasa Gudupharasa.* In field to r. No. 27 mon., and to l. Arian mon.
	8	O	0·8	Æ	151	[*Brit. Mus. Cat.*, xxii. 5.] *King on horseback*, as on No. 7. Greek legend and symbol, the same as No. 7. *Rev.*—*Zeus* to r., sceptre in l. hand, r. hand stretched out. Arian legend, as on No. 7. In field to l. mon. No. 27, and to r. Arian letters *phre* and *bu*.
	9	O	0·8	Æ	148	[*Brit. Mus. Cat.*, xxii. 9], Billon. *King on horseback*, with symbol and legend as No. 7. *Rev.*—*Poseidon* standing to front, holding trident in l. hand, and r. hand extended to l. Arian legend,

COINS OF THE SAKAS—*continued.*

Pl.	No.	Form.	Inches.	Metal.	Grains.	
						Maharaja Rajaraja mahata dhramia Devahada Gondopharasa. In field to l. No. 51 mon., and to r. Arian mon. *dacha.*
X.	10	○	0·8	Æ	105	[*Brit. Mus. Cat.*, xxii. 10.] *King seated* on chair to r., back of chair surmounted by two Gondopharian symbols. ΒΑCΙΛ . . . . *Rev.*—*Winged Victory* to r., with wreath and palm. . . . ΥΥΝΛΟΦΙΟΥΝ . . . In field to r. Φ.
	11	○	0·75	Æ	115	*King seated* on throne half turned to r.; Gondopharian symbol. Legend nearly all lost. ΒΑCΙΛ faintly traceable. *Rev.*—*Male figure* to front. Mon. No. 27 to l., with Greek Β and Arian *r* to r. Legend lost.
						ORTHAGNES.
	12	○	0·95	Æ	122	[*Brit. Mus. Cat.*, xxxiii. 9.] *Bust of King* to l., bearded and diademed. ΒΑCΙΛΕΥC ΒΑCΙΛΕΩΝ ΜΕΓΑC ΟΡΘΑΓΝΗC. *Rev.*—*Winged Victory* to r., with wreath and palm. Arian legend, *Maharajasa rajatirajasa Gandapharasa Gudranasa* (?).

	No.	Shape	Size	Metal	Weight	Description
	13	O	0·85	Æ	121	*Diademed bust of King* to l. Greek legend incomplete. . . . ΜΕΓΑΛοΥ ΟΡΘΑ . . . *Rev.*—*Winged Victory*, with wreath and palm to l. Arian legend incomplete: *mahatasa Gudranasa* (?). N.B. The exact form of the name is doubtful. I believe it to be the same as the ΟΡΛΑΓΝΟ of the gold coins of Kanishka, and also as the *Orthanes* of Strabo. This form would easily pass into Gurdanes, a name which is preserved in Gurdanaspes, a general in the service of Khusru Parvez.
						SANABARES.
	14	O	0·75	Æ	58	[*Brit. Mus. Cat.*, xxiii. 10.] *Bust of King*, diademed and bearded to r. Behind the head the Parthian letters *sa*. *Rev.*—*The King seated* and holding a bow, as on the Parthian coins. Greek legend, ΒΑϹΙΛΕΥϹ ΜΕΓΑϹ ϹΑΝΑΒΑ. Above, ΓΙΤ; to r. mon. No. 52.
	15	O	0·85	Æ	110	[*Brit. Mus. Cat.*, xxiii. 12.] *Bust of King* to r., diademed and bearded. ΒΑΣΙΛΕΥΣ ΒασιλεΩΝ. *Rev.*—*Winged Victory* to r., with wreath. . . . ϹΑΝΑΒΑΡοΥ.

COINS OF THE SAKAS—*continued.*

Pl.	No.	Form.	Inches.	Metal.	Grains.	
						HARDAGASES OR ABDAGASES. N.B. The bust coins bearing these two names are so exactly alike in types and general appearance, that the slight difference in the spelling may be quite accidental. But as there is a difference in the Arian reading as well as in the Greek reading, I have thought best to give both names.
XI.	1 2	○	0·9	Æ	130	[*Brit. Mus. Cat.*, xxiii. 1.] *Bust of King*, bearded and diademed to r. ΒΑCΙΛΕѠC CѠΤΗΡΟC ΑΡΔΑΓΑCΟΥ. *Rev.*—*Winged Victory* to r., with wreath and palm. Arian legend, *Maharâjasa tradatasa Haradagasasa.* In this legend the initial letter of the name is *h*, of the same form as *h* in *maharaja.* It has a foot turn to the right, quite different from the initial letter in Abdagases. Were it not for the Greek ΑΡΔΑ, I should be ready to accept the Arian legend as representing an aspirated form of the name as Habdagases.

3	○	0·9	Æ	141	Diademed and bearded *head of King* to r. **BACILEωC CωTHPoC ABΔAΓACoY.** *Rev.*—*Winged Victory* to r., with palm and wreath. Arian legend, *Mahârâjasa Avadayasasa trâdatasa.*
4	○	0·8	Æ	125	Same types and legends as No. 3, but both types to l.
					[*Brit. Mus. Cat.*, xxiii. 3.]
5	○	0·85	Æ	139	*King on horseback* to r. Gondopharian symbol in front. **ΒΑϹΙΛΕΥΟΝΤΟϹ ΥΝΔΙΦΕΡΟ ΑΔΕΛΦΙΔΕωϹ.** *Rev.*—*Zeus standing* to r., with sceptre. Arian legend, *Gandaphara bhrata putrasa maharâjasa tradatasa Avadagasasa.* Various Arian monograms. N.B. One coin has **ΓΟΝΔΟΦΑΡΑ** on Greek side.
6	○	0·85	Æ	152	*King on horseback* to l. Gondopharian symbol in front. **ΒΑΣΙΛΕΥΟΝΤΟΣ ΒΑΣΙΛΕΩΝ ΑΒΔΑΓΑΣΟΥ.** *Rev.*—*Zeus standing* to front, holding Victory in r. hand. Arian legend, as on No. 5. Mon. No. 27, with **B** and Arian *va.*
7*	○	0·85	Æ	—	*King on horseback* to r. Greek legend incomplete. **ΒΑϹΙΛΕΥ□ΝΤ□Ϲ . .** *Rev.*—*Zeus holding out figure of Victory.* Arian legend incomplete, *Maharâjasa*——A(vadagasasa). In field to r., **B** and Arian *va.*

COINS OF THE SAKAS—*continued.*

Pl.	No.	Form.	Inches.	Metal.	Grains.	
						SASAN. The coins of this king, which are no longer rare, are found in company with those of Abdagases, which they closely resemble, both in types and legends. The name of the king I have read provisionally as Sasan. On the Greek side I have not been able to get more than the termination in ACOY; but on the Arian side the name is complete and distinct as *Sasasa*, which would give *Sasa* in Arian and *Sases* in Greek. His connection with the family of Gondophares is shown by his use of the family symbol.
XI.	8	○	0·80	Æ	158	*King on horseback* to r., with Gondopharian symbol. Greek legend jumbled—ΛΙΙΛΩΙΝΝΙΣΙΙΙVΙV. *Rev.—Zeus* to r., with r. hand extended. Arian legend, *Maharâjasa mahatasa tradatasa Devahadasa Gadapharasa Sasasa.* In field to l., Buddhist symbol, No. 53; to r., Arian letters *va* and *pa.*
	8A*	○	0·5	Æ	33	Same types and legends as No. 8.
	9	○	0·85	Æ	150	*King on horseback* to r., with Gondopharian symbol. Greek legend, BACIΛEYO . . . . . ACOY.

No.	Shape	Size	Metal	Weight	Description
					Rev.—*Zeus standing to front* holding out Victory in r. hand. Arian legend, *Maharájasa rajatirajasa mahatasa dhramikasa Gudapharasa Sasasa,* In field to l., mon. No. 27; and to r., Greek **B**, with Arian *ra.* **ARSAKES.** [*Brit. Mus. Cat.*, xxxii. 12.]
10*	□	0·7	Æ	—	*Horse* to r. Mon. No. 5, forming ΑΡ. ΒΑϹΙΛΕѠϹ ΘΕοΥ ΑΡϹΑΚοΥ. *Rev.*—*Bow-case with bow,* surrounded by a square of astragalus beads. N.B. As both of the types of this coin are found in the Parthian series, and as it wants the Arian legend, I incline to refer it to Parthia.
11	○	0·9	Æ	—	*King on horseback* to r. . ΒΑϹΙΛΕΥοΝΤοϹ ΒΑϹΙΛΕѠΝ ΔΙΚΑΙοΥ ΑΡϹΑΚοΥ. (coin stolen). *Rev.*—Type obliterated. Arian legend, *Maharájasa rajarajasa Mahatasa Arshakasa tradatasa.*
12	○	0·9	Æ	122	*King on horseback* to r. Arian letter *ga.* ΒΑΣΙΛΕΥοΝΤοΣ ΒΑΣΙΛΕΩΝ (δικαι)ΟΥ ΑΡΣΑΚοΥ. *Rev.*—*Zeus* to l., holding figure of Victory. Mon. No. 37 to l.; symbol No. 54 to r. Arian legend, *Maharájasa rajarajasa* . . . Arsha (kasa).

COINS OF THE SAKAS—*continued.*

Pl.	No.	Form.	Inches.	Metal.	Grains.	
						PAKORES.
XI.	13	○	0·85	Æ	122	*Bust of king*, diademed and bearded, to l. ΒΑCΙΛΕΥC ΒΑCΙΛΕωΝ ΜΕΓΑC ΠΑΚοΡΗC. *Rev.*—*Winged Victory* to r., holding out wreath. Arian legend, *Maharajasa rajatirajasa mahatasa Pakurasa*. Various Arian letters in field. N.B. The Arian characters have a foot stroke turned to the left.
						SATRAPS. JIHONISA OR ZEIONISES. [*Brit. Mus. Cat.*, xxiii. 4.]
XII.	1	○	1·05	AR	152	*Satrap on horseback* to r., with whip and bow. ΑΝΝΙΓΛοΥ ΥΙΙΥ ΣΑΤΡΑΠΕΙ ΖΕΙωΝΙCΟΥ. Buddhist symbol in field to r. *Rev.*—*King standing* on l., facing a female figure, who is crowning him with a wreath. This figure has a modius on her head, and a cornucopiæ on her l. arm, and is most probably intended for a city. In field to r. and l., Arian letters. Arian legend, *Manigulasa Chhatrapasa putrasa Chhatrapasa Jihonisasa*. N.B. From the legend we learn that the Satrap *Jihonisa* was the son [*putra*] of the Satrap *Manigula*.

No.	Shape	Size	Metal	Weight	Description
2*	○	0·55	AR	35	*Similar types and legends* to No. 1. E. C. Bayley.
3*	○	1·05	AR	—	[*Brit. Mus. Cat.*, xxxii. 11.] *King on horseback*, with Greek legend, as No. 1. *Rev.*—*Satrap standing* to front, on l. Victory, and on r. a male figure, both crowning the king. Arian legend, as on No. 1.
4	○	1·00	Æ	126	[*Brit. Mus. Cat.*, xxiii. 5.] *Humped Indian bull* to r. Various letters to r., *sa*, *pu*, and on one coin Buddhist symbol over bull. Greek legend, as on No. 1. *Rev.*—*Maneless Indian lion* to r. Two Arian letters, as on the silver coins. Arian legend, *Manigula-putrasa Chhatrapasa Jihonisasa.*
4A	○	0·60	Æ	31	*Same types and legends* as No. 4.
5	□	0·85	Æ	—	[Thomas's *Prinsep*, Pl. xlii. 8, p. 211.] *Elephant* to r. Greek legend, corrupt and imperfect. CΕΙωΝΙΙ . . . . ΗΙοΑ. *Rev.*—*Humped Indian bull to l.* Arian legend, *Jihonisasa Manigula putrasa Chhatrapa* (*sa*). N.B. I possess two casts of a second specimen.
					ASPA-VARMA.
6	○	0·85	Æ	155	[*Brit. Mus. Cat.*, xx. 2.] *King on horseback* to r., with whip and bow Arian mon. *Aya.*

COINS OF THE SAKAS—*continued.*

Pl.	No.	Form.	Inches.	Metal.	Grains.	
						ΒΑΣΙΛΕΩΣ ΒΑΣΙΛΕΩΝ ΜΕΓΑΛoΥ ΑΖoΥ. *Rev.*—*Pallas armed* to r., spear and shield in l. hand, r. hand stretched out. Star and Buddhist symbol to l. Mon. No. 28 to r. Arian legend, *Indra Varma putrasa Aspa Varma Strategasa jayatasa.*
						VIJAYA-MITRA'S SON.
XII.	7	○	0·8	Æ	149	*Horseman* to r. Jumbled Greek legend.
	8	○	0·8	Æ	144	ΙΟϹΙΛϹΙΙΝΕΙΠ. *Rev.*—*Pallas armed*, as on No. 6, with same mon., star, and symbol. Arian legend imperfect. 7. *Vijaya mitra putrasa* . . . . (Aditi ?) 8. *Vijaya mitra putrasa* . . . *sasa Maharajasa.* N.B. Until the discovery of some new specimens, the son's name will remain very doubtful.
						KHARAMOSTIS. [*Brit. Mus. Cat.*, xxiii. 6.]
	9	□	0·75	Æ	84	*Horseman* to r., with couched lance. Arian letters *sa.*
	10	□	0·8	Æ	80	ΧΑΡΑΗѠϹΤΕΙ ϹΑΤΡΑΠΕΙ ΑΡΤΑΟΥ.
	11	□	0·9	Æ	96	*Rev.*—*Maneless Indian lion* to r. Arian mon. above. Arian legend, *Chhatrapasa Kharamastasa Artasa putrasa.*

					N.B. In the great inscription of the Satraps found at Mathura, the name of this Chief occurs three times:— 1. *Kharaostasa Yuva rajna.* 2. *Kharaosto Yuva raya.* 3. *Khardasa Chhatravasa.* The reading of the name is, therefore, still uncertain. The use of initial *O* in the middle of the name is peculiar.
					RÂJABULA.
12	O	0·6	Æ	38	[*Brit. Mus. Cat.*, xv. 11.] *Diademed bust of king* to r. **BACIΛEI BACIΛωC CωTHPOG PAIY.** *Pallas armed* with shield and thunderbolt Arian legend, *Apratihatachakrasa chhatrapasa Rajabulasa.* In field Arian letters *a* and *ga*.
13	O	0·55	Æ	36·8	[*Brit. Mus. Cat.*, xv. 12.] *Bust of king*, as on No. 12, but ruder. Corrupt Greek legend. *Rev.—Pallas armed* to l. Arian legend shortened to *Apratichakrasa Chhatrapasa Rajabulasa.* Arian letters *ha* and *sti*. On some the Greek mon. No. 55, forming **EY**.
14*	O	0·5	Æ	34	*Bust as on No.* 13, with corrupt Greek legend.

COINS OF THE SAKAS—*continued.*

Pl.	No.	Form.	Inches.	Metal.	Grains.	
						Rev.—*Pallas armed* to l. Arian legend, *Maha Chhatrapasa apraticharkrasa Rajabulasa.* Various Arian letters in field. N.B. These copper coins found in E. Panjâb and to east of Satlej River.
XII.	15*	○	0·7	Æ	93	*Figure standing* between tree and snake. Indian Pali legend, *Mahakhatapasa Rajubulasa.* *Rev.*—*Figure being anointed* by two elephants. N.B. In the great Satrap inscription from Mathura, where all these coins were found, this chief's name is thus shortened—*Mahachatravasa Rajulasa.* [Thomas's *Prinsep*, Pl. xliv. 21.]
	16	○	0·65	Æ	51	*Figure standing* between trident, and snake held in r. hand. Indian Pali legend, *Mahakhatapasa putasa khatapasa Saudâsasa.* Swastika beneath figure. *Rev.*—*Lakshmi* being anointed by two elephants. N.B. These coins of *Saudâsa* are found at Mathura, where also I got a long inscription bearing his name. In the great Satrap inscription he is said to be the son of the Satrap Rajula, a relationship which I had previously suggested.

MOA or MAUAS

INDO-SCYTHIANS. SAKAS. PLATE II.

Num. Chron. Ser. III Vol. X Pl. VI

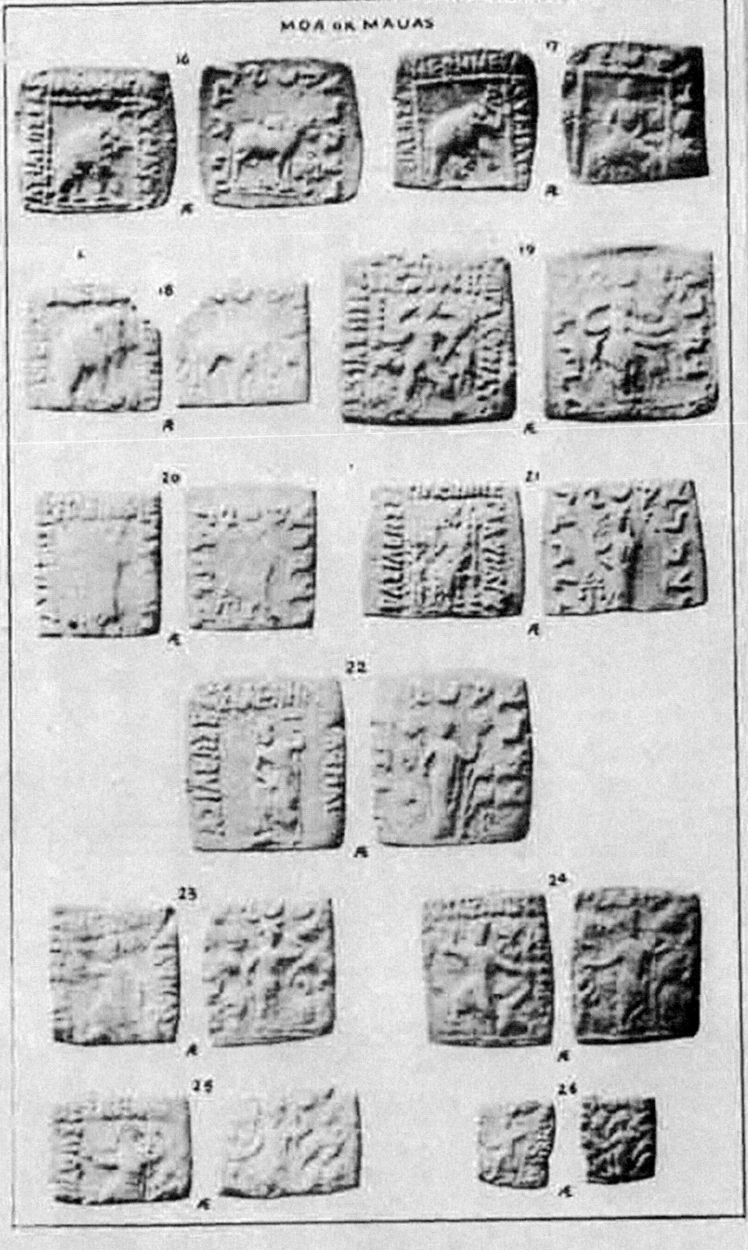

INDO-SCYTHIANS SAKAS. PLATE III.

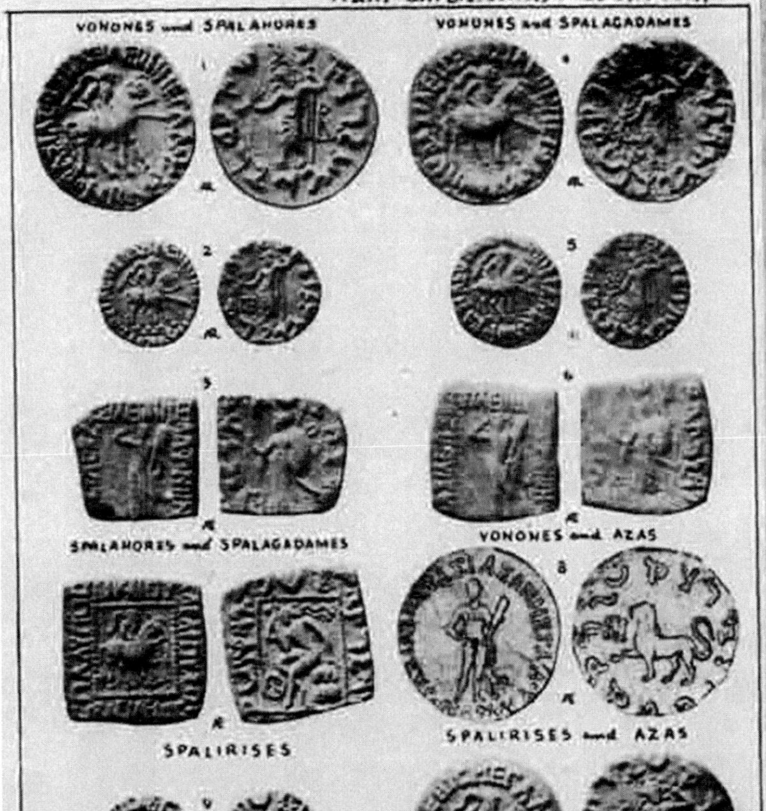

INDO-SCYTHIANS SAKAS. PLATE IV.

Num. Chron. Ser. III, Vol. X. Pl. VIII.

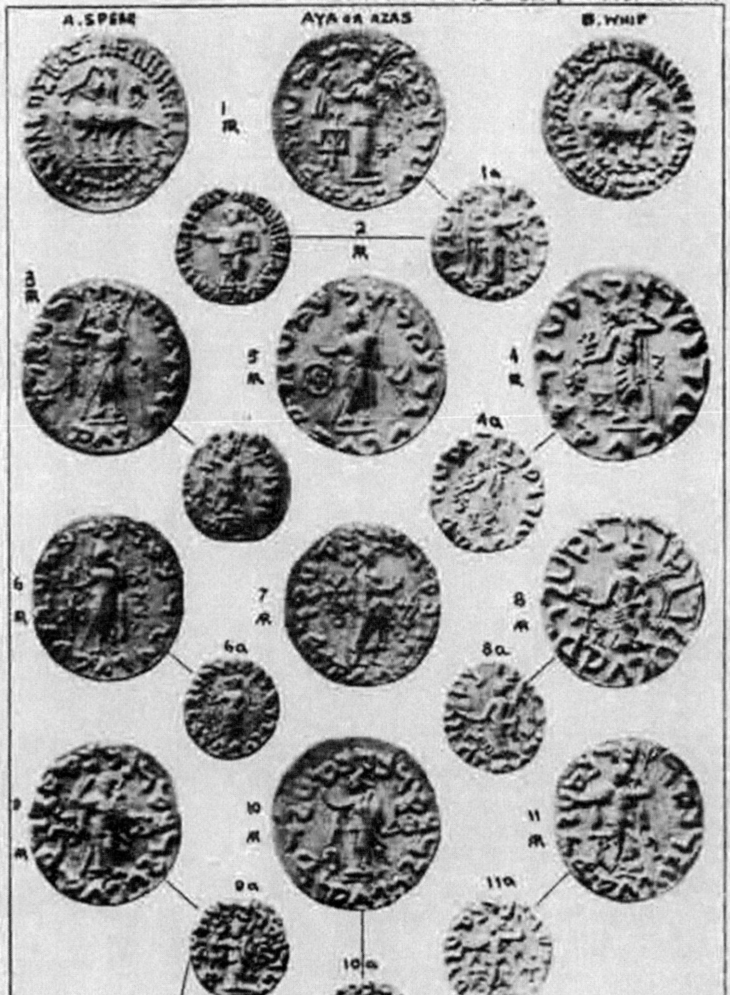

INDO-SOYTHIANS. SAKAS. PLATE V.

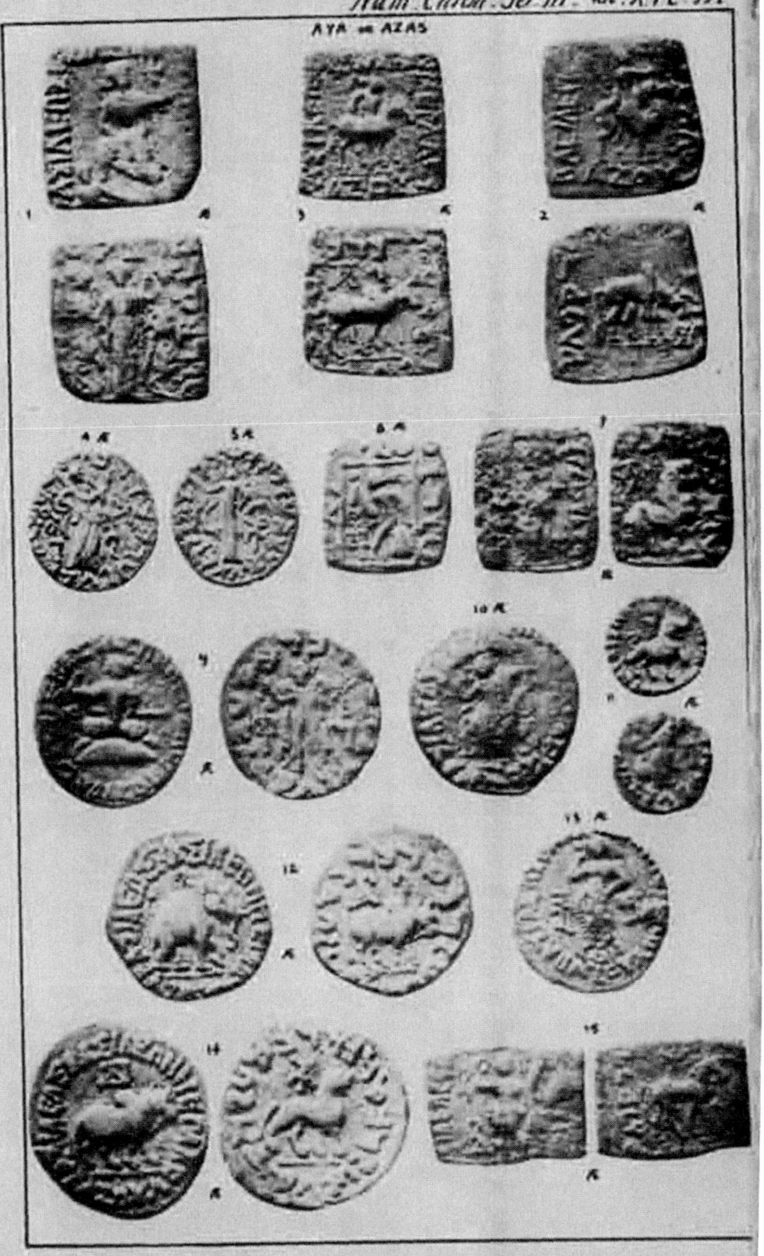

INDO-SCYTHIANS. SAKAS, PLATE VI.

Num. Chron. Ser. III. Vol. X Pl. X.

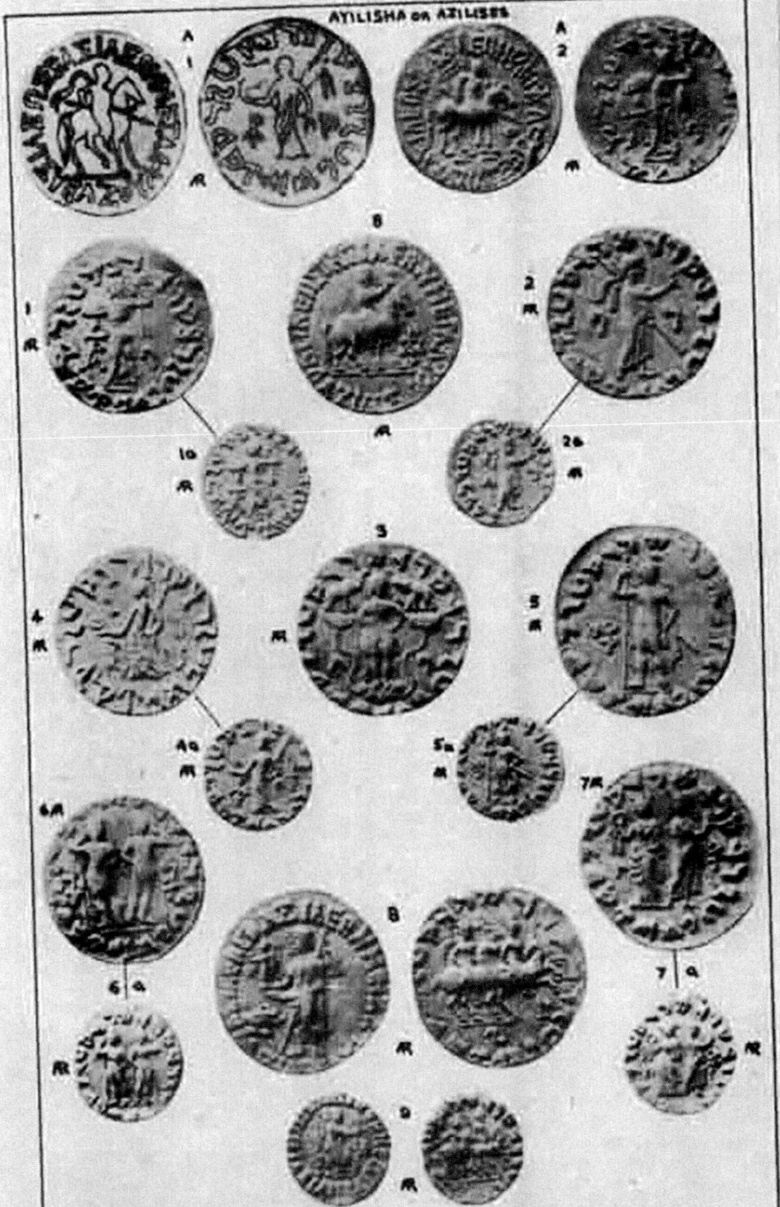

INDO - SCYTHIANS . SAKAS, PLATE VII

AYILISHA or AZILISES

INDO-SCYTHIANS. SAKAS, PLATE VIII.

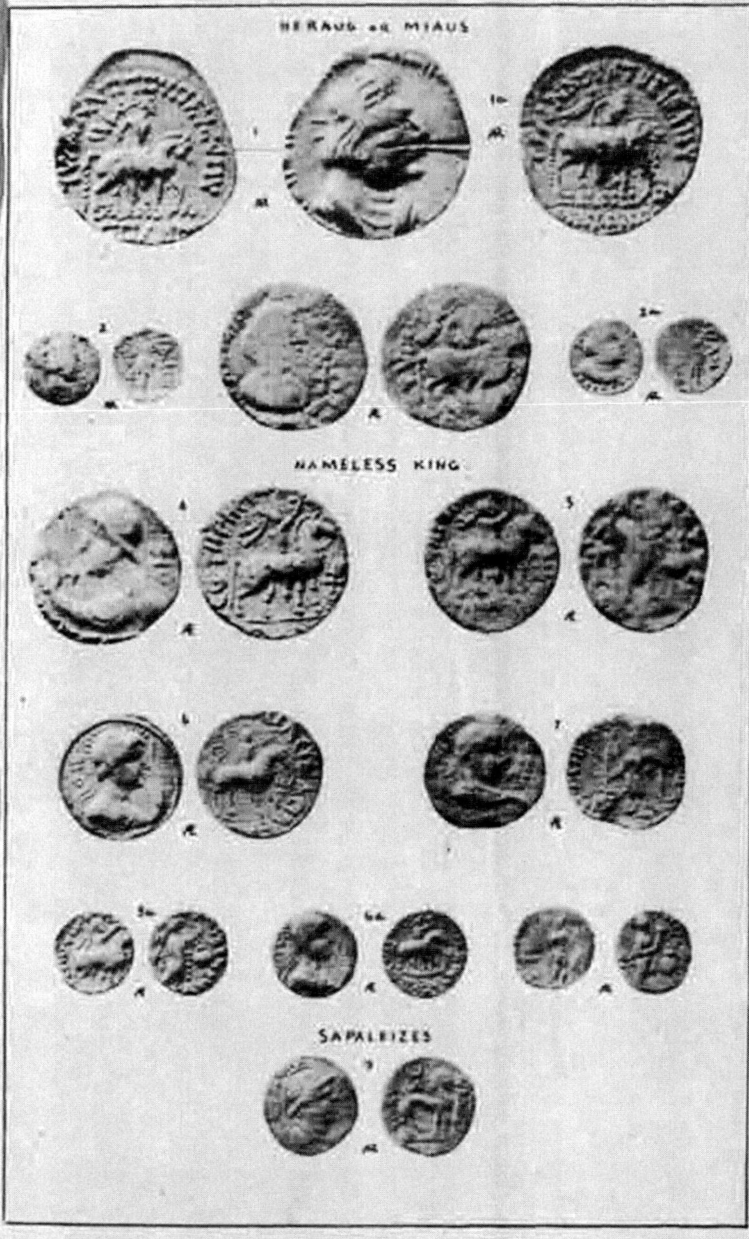

INDO-SCYTHIANS. SAKAS, PLATE IX

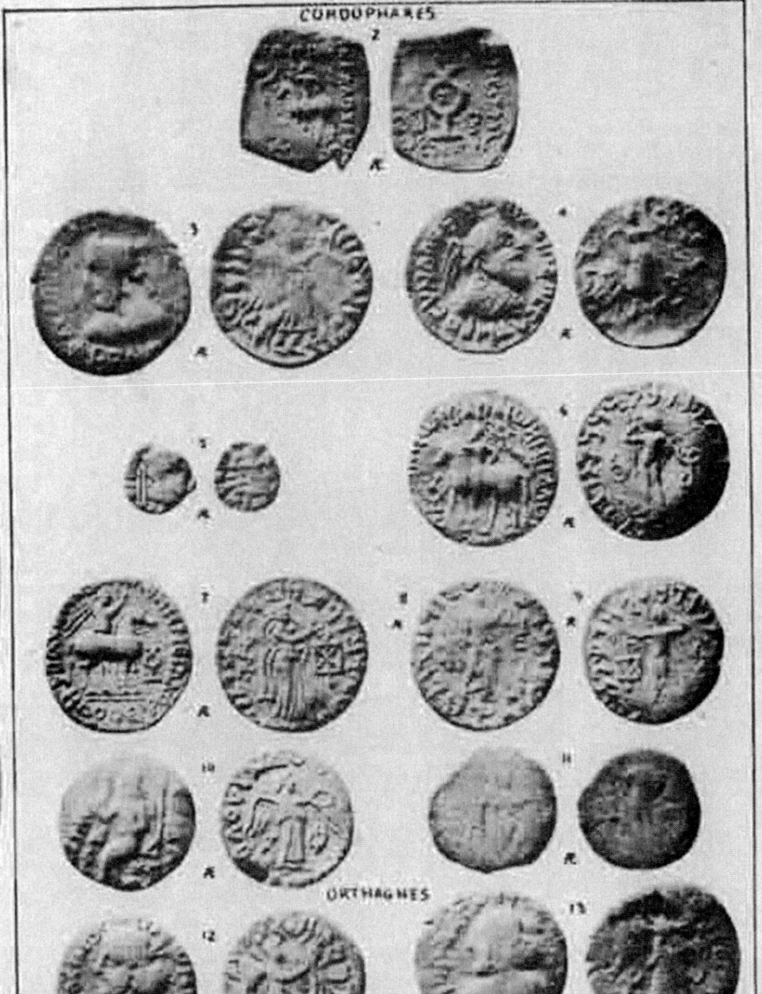

INDO-SCYTHIANS. SAKAS, PLATE X.

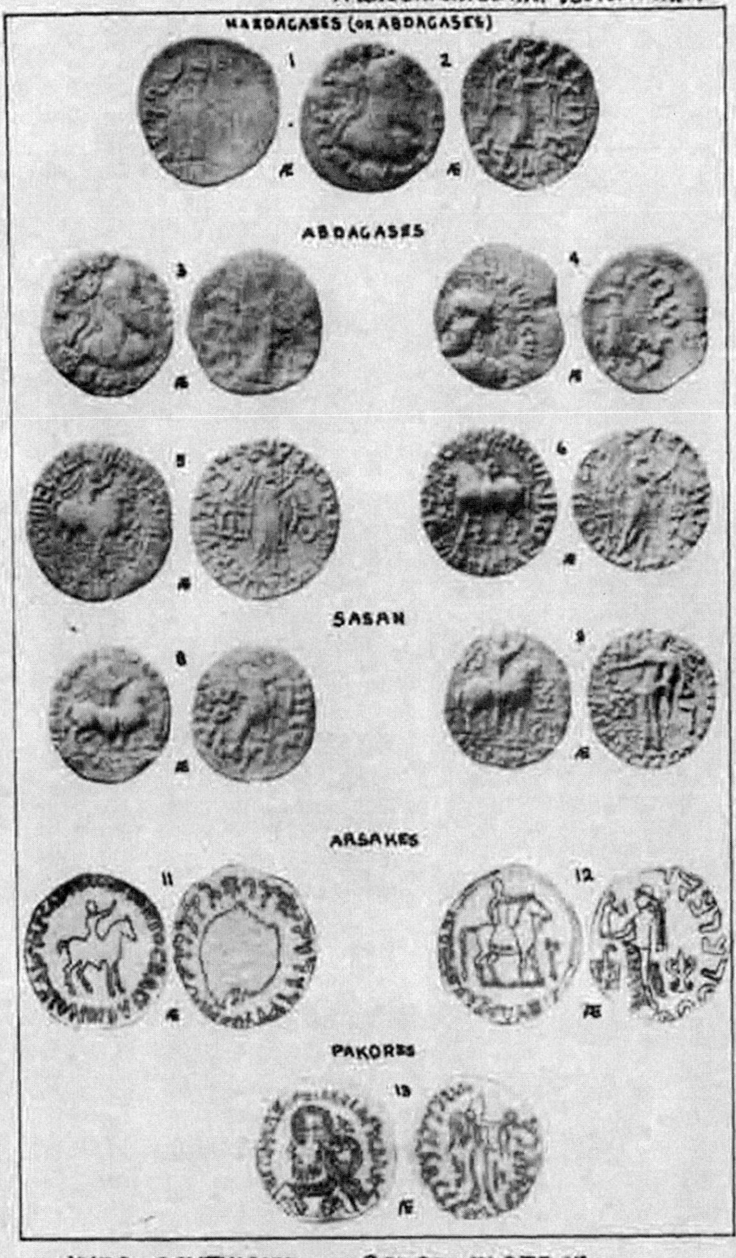

INDO-SCYTHIANS. SAKAS, PLATE XI

Num. Chron. Ser. III. Vol. X Pl. XV

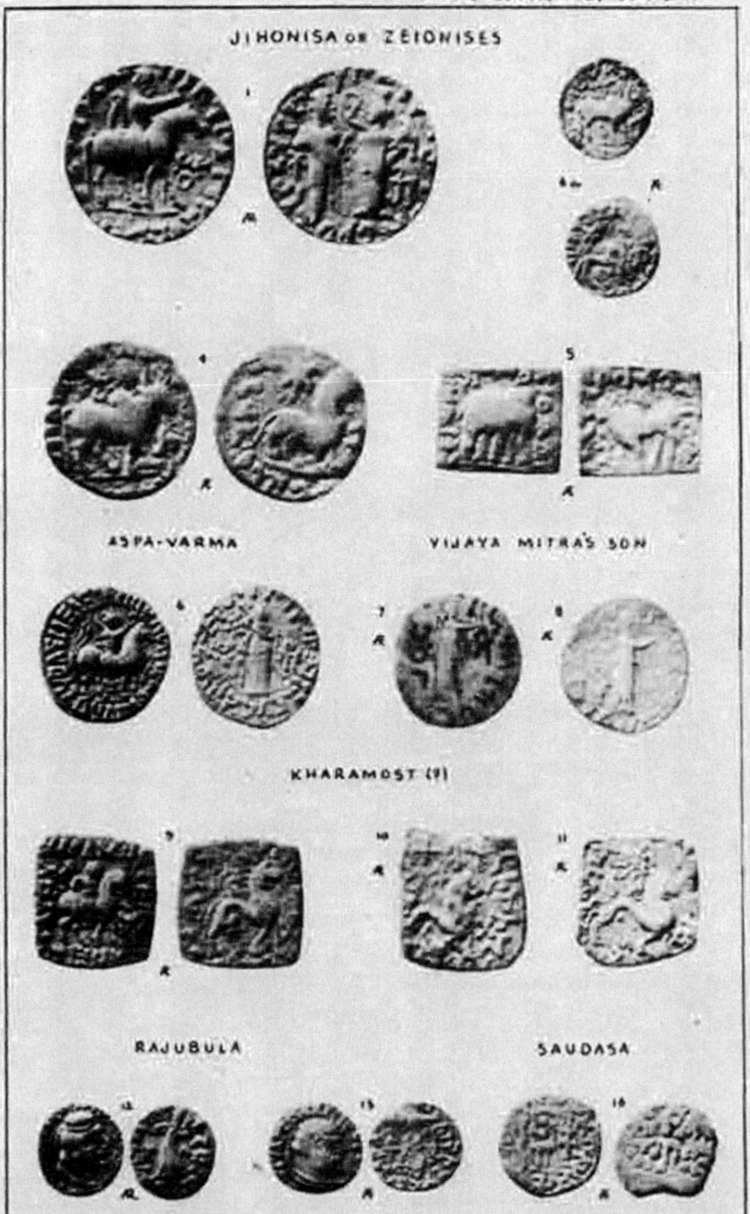

INDO-SCYTHIANS - SAKAS PLATE XII

Num Chron. Ser. III, Vol. X. PL.XVI.

INDO:SCYTHIANS. SAKAS. PLATE XIII.

Height of figure 2 ft.9in. (cf. Pl.V 9.)

COINS OF THE INDO-SCYTHIAN KING MIAÜS, OR HERAÜS.

PART II.

SUPPLEMENT.

BY

MAJOR-GENERAL SIR A. CUNNINGHAM,
R.E., K.C.I.E., C.S.I.

REPRINTED FROM THE NUMISMATIC CHRONICLE,
VOL. VIII., THIRD SERIES, PAGES 47—58.

LONDON:
1888.

COINS OF THE INDO-SCYTHIAN KING MIAÜS, OR HERAÜS.

In 1874 Mr. Percy Gardner published a tetradrachm similar to those represented in the accompanying Plate. He attributed the piece to Heraüs, King of the Sakas, by reading the legend [1]

ΤΥΙΑΝΝΟΥΝΤΟΣ ΜΙΑΟΥ ΣΑΚΑΒ ΚΟΙΙΑΝΟΥ,

as Τυραννοῦντος Ἡράου Σάκα Κοιράνου.

This assignment of the coin to a *Saka* king was eagerly adopted by Mr. Fergusson, who, by a bold conjecture, metamorphosed the *Turushka* king Kanishka, the sovereign of the *Kushâns,* into a king of the *Sakas*, and the founder of the *Sâka* era.[2]

But Mr. Fergusson was not the only rebel against "time-honoured" Sâlivâhana, whose name, as Professor Kern boldly suggested,[3] had been added to the Sâka era by the English. But this suggestion is utterly without foundation, as there are many inscriptions, both in Southern and in Northern India, dated in the *Sâlivâhana Sâka* era. I need only quote one of S. S. 1466, or A.D. 1544, from

---

[1] *Num. Chron.*, N.S., xii. p. 161.

[2] Royal Asiatic Society *Journal*, 1880, "On the Sâka, Samvat, and Gupta Eras."

[3] Dr. Max Müller, *India—What can it teach us?* p. 300.

Bâdâmi in Southern India, and another of S. S. 1583, or A.D. 1561, from Chamba, in the Punjab.[4] Does Professor Kern believe that the English ruled over India in those years?

In 1881 Dr. Oldenberg published a notice of the same coin,[5] in which he retained the reading of ΣΑΚΑ, and ignored the existence of the following letter B, while he objected to Κοιράνου, and proposed to read either *Koranou* or *Korranou*. He thus found "a decisive proof" that the *Korano* or *Gushân* princes, and more especially "Kanishka, must be regarded as *Sakas*." He then goes on to say that "we know from coins as well as from inscriptions of a mighty *Sâka* king Kanishka." With this statement I altogether disagree. I am well acquainted with all the inscriptions and coins of the Indo-Scythian princes, and I can state positively that neither coins nor inscriptions give the title of *Saka* to Kanishka. In the inscriptions he is always called by his own tribal title of *Kushân*, or *Gushân*, and on his coins he is invariably called *Korano*.

I presume, however, that Dr. Oldenberg refers to this coin of Heraüs as establishing his conclusion that Kanishka was a king of the Sakas, or *Saka-Kushâns*. But the reading of ΣΑΚΑ I dispute, as all my coins read ΣΑΝΑΒ and not ΣΑΚΑ. This word is, however, not always spelt in the same way. I find ΣΑΝΑΒ on six coins, the N being sometimes reversed, ΣΑΝΑΟΒ on one coin, and ΣΑΝΑΒΙΥ on one coin.

It is true that the N is sometimes reversed, but so it is sometimes both in ΤΥΡΑИИΟΥИΤΟΣ and in ΚΟΙΙΑ-

[4] *Indian Antiquary*, x. p. 67. *Archæol. Survey of India*, xxi. p. 136.

[5] *Indian Antiquary*, x. p. 215.

ИΟΥ. Of the latter form Mr. Gardner has given an instance in his footnote, page 47, quoting M. Tiesenhausen's coin.

Taking the various readings of *Sanab*, *Sanaob*, and *Sanabiu*, I think it probable that the term may be intended to represent the native title of *tsanyu*, or *chanyu*, "chief," or "king." As the last word on the small silver *oboli* is **ΚΟΡϹΑΝΟΥ**, there can be no doubt that the king belonged to the *Korsân*, or *Kushan* tribe. *Tsanyu* is a contraction of *Tsemli-Khuthu-tanju*, "Heaven's son great," or "Great Son of Heaven," = *Devaputra*. As the common pronunciation of the Greek **B** was **V**, the Greek form of **ΣΑΝΑΒ**, or **ΣΑΝΑΒΙΥ**, would approach very nearly to the native title.

With respect to the tribal name of *Kushân*, an examination of the earlier coins of Kujula Kadphizes shows that the first Greek forms of the name were *Korsna*, *Korsan*, and *Khoransu*, which agree with the title of **ΚΟΡϹΑΝΟΥ** on the *oboli* of Miaüs in the Plate. In common speech this name might become either *Korano* by the omission of *s*, or *Kushân* by the omission of *r*. But the Greek form I prefer to derive from the common practice of changing *s* to *h*, which would change *Korsano* into *Korhano*, or into *Korrhano*, or **ΚΟΡΡΑΝΟΥ**.

That the original form of the name was *Korsan*, or *Khorsan*, is, I think, supported by the name of the province of *Khorasân*, which was certainly occupied by this tribe. I suspect also that *Chorsari*, which Pliny says was the name given by the Scythians to the Persians, must refer to the Kushâns of Khorasân, who had come to be looked upon as Persians by the Scythians of the Jaxartes.

According to my view the legend of the tetradrachms is simply—

Τυραννοῦντος Μιάου Σανάβ Κορσάνου,

"Of the supreme king Miaüs, chief of the Kushâns."

On the oboli the legend is restricted to two lines, in which the name of the prince is spelt in two different ways, as ΜΙΑΟΥϹ and ΜΙΑΙΟΥ. With the tribal title of ΚΟΡϹΑΝΟΥ below, the whole legend is simply "Miaüs, the Kushân," or rather the *Korsan*.

The unique copper coin is unfortunately too much worn to give any assistance in reading either the name or the titles. But as it bears an Arian legend in addition to the Greek inscription it is invaluable as a proof that the territory over which the king ruled was not Bactria, but some country to the south of the Hindu Kush. On the Greek side I can read ΤΥΡΑΝ and ΚΟΡϹΑΝ; but of the Arian legend I can make nothing certain.

Of the find-spots of the tetradrachms I am unable to speak. But of the *oboli* I can say positively that my twelve specimens all came from Western Afghanistan, that is from Kabul and the country to the south of Kabul. A thirteenth obolus was actually found by Masson in No. 2 Tope at Kotpur, along with ten copper coins bearing the joint names of Hermæus and Kujula Kadphizes.[6] Masson describes the coin as "a small circular piece of silver, doubtful whether a coin from its smooth reverse, but on the obverse bearing the bust of a king, whose head was bound with the Greek diadem." I saw the piece in the Indian Museum in 1870 amongst Tope relics, and I at once recognised it as a coin of Miaüs, from the king's head being an exact representation of the head on the two tetradrachms which I then possessed. In the same Stûpa

---

[6] *Ariana Antiqua*, p. 66.

Masson obtained a clay seal (see *Ariana Antiqua,* Plate IV. Fig. 6 of Antiquities), with an armed figure standing with lance in hand. As my new coins of Kujula Kadphizes present the same armed figure we thus obtain a second connection with Kujula.

With respect to the date of Miaüs I think that the following facts all point to the latter half of the first century B.C.

1. One of his coins was found in company with ten copper coins bearing the joint names of Hermæus and Kujula.

2. The Greek Σ is used always in *Turannountos* and *Sanab,* but in Korsano it takes the round form, which is also found on some of the later coins of Hermæus.

3. The type of the king on horseback, with Victory flying behind to place a wreath on his head, is the prototype which was afterwards copied on the coins of Gondophares.

Taking these facts in conjunction with the find-spots of the coins, I infer that Miaüs must have ruled over the country to the south-west of Kabul, about Wardak and Ghazni, some time during the latter half of the first century B.C.

If my inference be correct we may, perhaps, gain some further information about this unknown king from the Chinese records. Turning, then, to their account of *Kipin,* that is of the country to the south-west of Kabul, I find the following facts recorded.

1. The first King of Kipin known to the Chinese is named *U-theu-lao* by Remusat[7] (or *Woo-tow-laou* by Wylie). He was reigning about the beginning of the

---

[7] Remusat, *Nouv. Mélanges Asiatiques,* i. p. 207.

first century B.C. He was succeeded by his son, who was defeated and killed by a rebel named *Yin-mo-fu*, son of the King of *Yung-Khiu*, assisted by the Chinese. *Yin-mo-fu* thus became King of Kipin. Having imprisoned the Chinese general Chao-te and killed some seventy of his officers, he sent an embassy to China to excuse his conduct. But the Emperor Hiao-yuan-ti had then stopped all communication with foreign countries, and the embassy was not received. As this emperor began to reign in 48 B.C., the conquest of Kipin by *Yin-mo-fu* may be placed about 50 B.C.[8]

2. The people of Kipin had gold and silver money which bore on one side the figure of a horseman, and on the reverse the head of a man. Wylie says a man on horseback and a man's face.[9] Now it is remarkable that the only coins which tally with this description are those of Miaüs and of the nameless king. But as there are neither gold nor silver coins of the latter the description can apply only to the former. This being the case, the coins with a horseman on one side and a king's head on the other should belong to *Yin-mo-fu*, the conqueror of Kipin, and Yin-mo-fu should therefore be *Miaüs*, or *Miaios*. There is a tempting resemblance between the two names, which, supported by both time and place, suggests the possibility of identifying *Yin-mo-fu*, King of Kipin, with *Miaüs*, or *Miaius*, whose coins belong to the same country as well as the same age.

With respect to the *name* of the king, I must confess that it is still uncertain. Twenty-five years ago, when I got my first two tetradrachms, I read the name as **HPAOY**,

---

[8] Remusat, *Nouv. Mélanges Asiatiques*, i. p. 206.
[9] *Num. Chon.*, N.S., ix. p. 79.

or Heraüs, as I noted at the time in the *Journal of the Bengal Asiatic Society.* In 1874, after Mr. Percy Gardner had published the British Museum coin, on which he also read the name as Heraüs, I was induced to examine the silver *oboli* of the same king which I had lately acquired. On some of them I found a *sloping* stroke in the first letter of the name, which seemed to agree with the first letter on the two tetradrachms, Nos. 3 and 4 of the accompanying Plate. I then read the names as ΝΙΑΟΥϹ, or ΜΙΑΟΥϹ, and also on some of the oboli as ΝΙΑΙΟΥ, or ΜΙΑΙΟΥϹ. On looking over the recorded names of Indo-Scythian kings, it struck me that the Greek name might *possibly* be a variant form of the Chinese name of *Yin-mo-fu.* Except for this possibility I cannot say that my present reading of Miaüs is preferable to my early reading of Heraüs. For the solution of the doubt we must await the discovery of a second specimen of the bilingual copper coinage, as the native rendering of the two names in Arian characters would be very different. *Heraüs* would most probably be 𐨱𐨅𐨪𐨩𐨯, *Herayasa,* while *Miaüs* would be 𐨨𐨁𐨀𐨩𐨯, *Miayasa.*

But whether the name of the king be Heraüs or Miaüs, it is certain that he belonged to the ΚΟΡϹΑΝΟ, or *Kushân* tribe, and consequently that he could not have been a *Saka.* I will now try to make this clear. For many centuries before the arrival of the Yuechi horde in Bactriana, the provinces on the Jaxartes and Oxus had been occupied by the Sakas, or Sacæ, where they successively opposed the armies of Cyrus, Darius, and Alexander. Their language, as shown by their names as well as by the Scythian version of the cuneiform inscriptions of Darius, has little in common with that of the Kushâns who formed one of the five tribes of the Yuechi—a great

Turkish horde. Darius records the suppression of the rebel Sarukha, a leader of the Sakas. Herodotus describes the Scythians in the army of Xerxes as Amurgian Scyths who carried the battle-axe called *Sagaris*. They were therefore the same people whom Darius calls *Saka-Humavarga*. There can be little doubt therefore that they were the same as the *Sagaraukæ*, who also carried the *Sagaris*, from which they must have derived their name. I have long ago identified the *Sagaraukæ* with the *Sarduchæ* of Trogus by reading A for Δ, and eliding the *g*. The words of Trogus are very important:[10] "Scythicæ res additæ, reges Thocarorum Asiani, interitusque Sarducharum." Now the *Thocari* are the Yuechi, who were called *Tushâras*, or *Tukharas*, by the Indians, and *Tu-ho-lo* by the Chinese; and the *Asiani* must be the *Kushâns*, or Gushâns, whose chief conquered the other four tribes, and took the title of "King of the Kushâns." The Sarduchæ are the *Sai*, or *Sakas*, who were driven out by the Kushâns. Now this title of "King of the Kushâns" is found on all the coins of Kujula Kadphizes, the Yuechi chief who conquered Hermæus, the last of the Greek kings of India.

That the Yuechi were a different race from the Sakas is shown by their history as related by the Chinese annalists. In the beginning of the second century B.C. they were driven by the Hiungnu from their home in the province of Shensi, near the Great Wall of China. They retired to the west, and, being again defeated and their king killed by the Hiungnu, they migrated still farther to the west, and settled in the country along the Jaxartes in B.C. 163. In a short time they spread over the whole of the provinces on both banks of the Oxus, from which,

[10] Justini, *Prol.*, chap. xlii.

about 130 to 126 B.C., they expelled the *Ta-Hia*, or Bactrian Greeks, and the *Sai*, or *Sakas*. One hundred years later the chief of the Kuei-shwang, or Kushân tribe, having subdued the other four tribes, united the whole horde of the Yuechi, and took the title of "King of the Kushâns," after which he conquered the Kabul Valley, where he came into contact with the Greek king Hermæus.

Now this title of "King of the Kushâns" is the same that was borne by Kanishka, who is styled in Court's Manikyâla inscription "*Samvardhaka Gushâna vansa*," or "the aggrandizer of the Kushân race." In the Sanskrit history of Kashmir he is called a *Turushka*, or Turk. Hwen Thsang calls him a *Tuholo*, or Tukhâra, while Biruni and other early Muhamedan writers call him a Tûrk, to which Biruni adds that his ancestor, the founder of the family, was Barhatigin. As Tigin is a Tûrki word, this statement furnishes another proof of the Tûrki origin of the Kushâns.

Hwen Thsang says that the language of *Folishisatangua*, or Kabul, was different from that of *Tsau-ku-ta*, or Kipin.[11] Again, in speaking of *Tsau-ku-ta*, or Kipin itself, he says that the writing and language were different from that of other countries.[12] But if the *Kushâns* were *Sakas*, the language of the Kushâns of Kâbul and of the Sakas of Kipin (Sakastene) would have been the same. The *Kushâns* are, in fact, separately distinguished from the *Sakas* in the Allahabad Pillar Inscription of Samudra Gupta under the well-known title of *Daivaputra Shâhi*, which was used by Kanishka and his successors in all their inscriptions.

---

[11] Beal, ii. p. 285; Julien, ii. p. 190.
[12] Beal, ii. p. 284; Julien, iii. p. 188.

In the face of all these facts I do not see how it is possible to maintain the identity of the *Sakas* and the Kushâns. Even if the word which I read as **ΣΑΝΑ** should hereafter be found to be actually **ΣΑΚΑ**, as read by Mr. Gardner and Dr. Oldenberg, I should object to these two distinct peoples being rolled into one tribe of *Saka-Kushâns*. My explanation would rather be that *Heraüs*, or *Miaüs*, was the king of both peoples—of the Kushâns by inheritance, and of the Sakas by conquest.

I will now describe the different coins of this king which I have given in Plate III.

Tetradrachms.

Obv.—Bare head of king, diademed, to right, with long hair and moustaches, surrounded by border of fillets.

Rev.—King on horseback, to right, left hand holding bridle, right hand resting on bow-case attached to saddle. Victory flying behind with wreath in outstretched hand to crown the king. Legend in corrupt Greek characters in one half-circle above, and two straight lines below.

No. 1.—ΤΥ/ΑΝΝΟΥΝΤΟΣ ΗΙΑΟΥ ΣΑИΑΒ
. . . ΙΑΝΟΥ.

2.—ΤΥ/ΑΝΝΟΥΝΤΟΣ ΗΙΑΟΥ ΣΑИΑΒ
ΚΟ((ΑΝΟΥ.

3.—ΤΥ/ΑΝΝΟΥΝΤΟΣ ΜΙΑΟΥ Σ . Ι . Ν . Ι . ΟΒ
ΗΝΥ⫛ΝΟΥ.

4.—ΤΥ/ΑΝΝΟΤΟΥΟΣ ΗΑΟΥ ΣΑИΑΒ
ᒣΠΑΗΟΥ.

5.—ΤV/ΑΝΝ ΟΥΟΥΝΣ ΟΑΟ'//, ΣΑΝΑΒΙV
ᒣИΑΗΟΥ.

6.—ΤV/ΑΝΝΟΥΝ ΕΟΑ ΒΥ
ΥΠΙ ΙΑΝΟΥ.

The British Museum specimen agrees very closely with Nos. 1 and 2, but the coin of M. Tiesenhausen, quoted by Mr. Gardner, appears to be more like No. 4. My No. 6

is an ancient forgery thickly plated. The other five coins average 226 grains, the heaviest, No. 4, being 240 grains.

OBOLI.

The small silver coins preserve very successfully the portrait of the king as shown on the tetradrachms. The weight varies from 8 to 9, 9½, 10½, and 11 grains. Mr. Thomas[13] notices one of these oboli in the possession of General Pearse, but he seems to have looked upon it as belonging to the barbarous imitations of the oboli of Eukratides, as he describes it as "an example of an exceptionally common class of silver coins," whereas General Pearse's and Masson's specimens are the only coins that I know of in addition to my own.

Obv.—Bare head of king to right, as on the tetradrachm, in a dotted circle.

Rev.—Male figure, standing to right, with both hands raised. Greek legend in two perpendicular lines.

No. 7.—	·IAIOY.	:KOPCANOY.
8.—	·IAIOY.	:KOPCANou.
9.—	·WIAIOY.	:KOΓCANOY.
10.—	·NIAOYC.	. OIIAyou.
11.—	MIAOY	KOΓCANOY.
12.—	WIAOYC.	. OPCA.

COPPER CHALKOUS.

13. *Obv.*—King's head to right, with Arian legend illegible.

Rev.—King on horseback to right, with Victory flying behind, as on the tetradrachms. Greek legend imperfect.

I can read **TYPAN** to left, and **KOIC** below, but I do not see any trace of letters between the horse's feet.

---

[13] *Bactrian Coins and Indian Dates.*

Some day, perhaps, a lucky find will give us the king's name in Arian characters. The legend on the right looks as if it was *Maharayasa.*

With respect to the letter B at the end of the word ΣΑΝΑΒ, Mr. Thomas has a curious note in which, by some legerdemain, he makes it an undeveloped form of a well-known monogram Ƨ. This he takes for *Drangia;* but unfortunately in the Greek spelling of the name ΔΡΑΓΓΙΑ there is no N, while there are two *gammas,* of which there is no trace in the monogram.

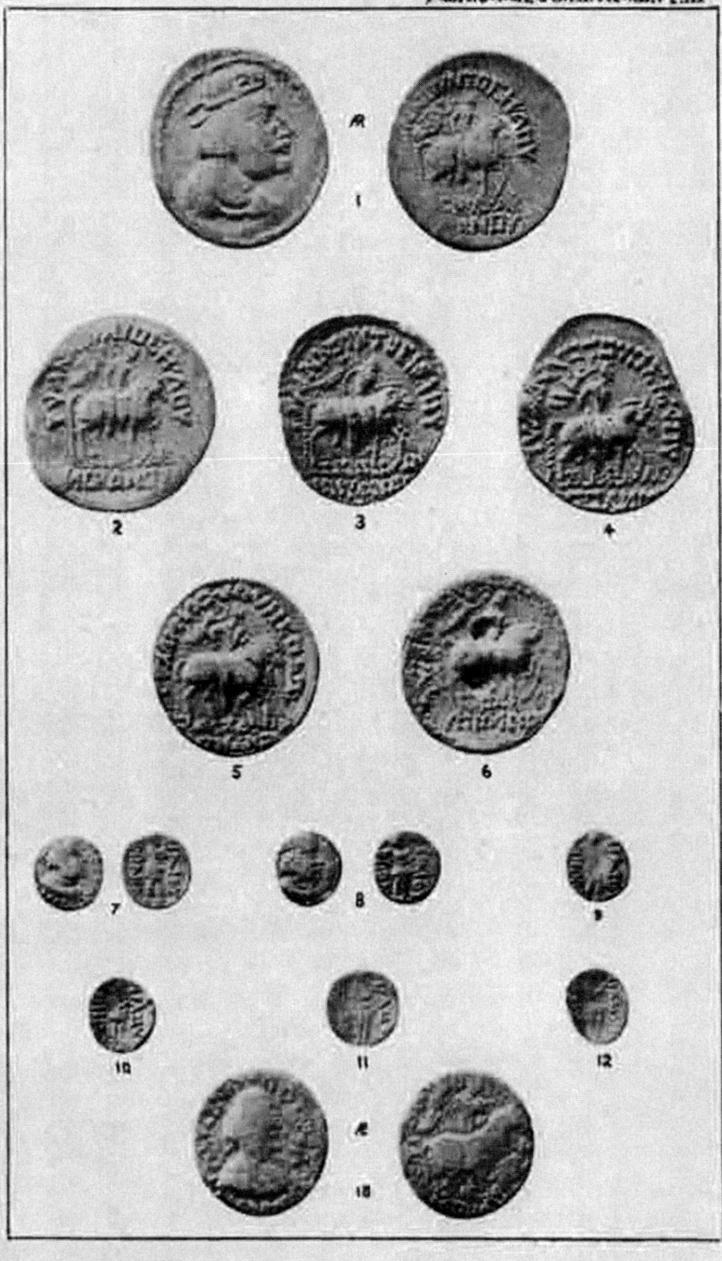

MIAÜS, OR HERAÜS CHIEF OF THE KUSHANS.

COINS OF THE KUSHÂNS,

OR

GREAT YUE-TI.

PART III.

BY

MAJOR-GENERAL SIR A. CUNNINGHAM,
R.E., K.C.I.E., C.S.I.

REPRINTED FROM THE NUMISMATIC CHRONICLE,
VOL. XII., THIRD SERIES, PAGES 40—82.

LONDON:
1892.

COINS OF THE KUSHÂNS, OR GREAT YUE-TI.

Class C.

(See Plates IV.—VIII.)

Before describing the coins of the *Kushâns*, it is necessary that I should state my reasons for considering them a separate race, quite distinct from the *Sakas*, or Sacæ Scythians. This is the more necessary as the *Turki* nationality of the famous King Kanishka has lately been denied by Mr. Fergusson, relying on the erroneous reading of the legend of a single coin. The coin was a tetradrachm of Heraüs, or Miaüs, on which the legend of **ΣΑΝΑΒ ΚΟΡϹΑΝΟΥ** was read as **ΣΑΚΑ ΚΟΙΡΑΝΟΥ**, or King of the Sakas. In my original paper on the coins of this chief,[1] I suggested that the word **ΣΑΝΑΒ** might be only the Greek form of the title of *Tsanyu* or *Tanju*, which is itself a contraction of the Chinese *Tsem-li—Khu-thu—Tan-ju*, or "Heaven's-son-Great," or "Great son of Heaven." My suggestion has since been confirmed by the acquisition of a duplicate copper coin, on which in Gandharian characters I read the Indian title of *Deva-putra*, which has exactly the same meaning. As this title is used by the three Kushân kings Kanishka, Hu-

[1] *Num. Chron.* 3rd Series, viii. 47, and x. Pl. IX. fig. 3.

vishka, and Vâsu Deva, its use by Miaüs would seem to prove that he also was a Kushân, as I had already pointed out by my reading of ΚΟΡϹΑΝΟΥ.

The earliest notices of the Kushâns we owe to the Chinese. In B.C. 165 the Great *Yue-ti*, being driven across the Jaxartes by the *Huing-nu*, succeeded in establishing themselves in Sogdiana. After some time they advanced to the Oxus, and about B.C. 126, they were found by the Chinese envoy Chang-kao in full possession of Bactriana, from which they had driven out the *Ta-hia*, or Greeks, and the *Sai*, or Sakas. The horde then consisted of five tribes. One hundred years later, or about 20 B.C., the chief of the Kushân tribe subjugated the other four tribes, and took the title of "King of the Kushâns." This king, named *Kieu-tsiukhio*, then crossed the Caucasus and occupied the Kabul valley. He has been identified by general consent with *Kujula Kadphizes* of the coins, who was the contemporary of the last Greek King Hermæus. His son, named *Yun-Kao-ching*, is said to have conquered India. As *Yun*, *Hun*, and *Wan* are only dialectical variants of the same term, I have identified the conqueror of India with the Hima or Wema Kadphises of the gold and copper coins, and also with *Wen*, the common ancestor of no less than ten of the reigning families of the *Yue-ti* in Bactriana and Sogdiana.[2] All of these chiefs bore the title of *Shao-wu*, which I long ago identified with the ΖΑΟΟΥ of the coins of Kozola Kadaphes.[3]

---

[2] Remusat, *Nouv. Mélanges Asiatiques*, i. 227.

[3] *Num. Chron.* 1872, p. 181. My reading of ΖΑΟΟΥ for ΖΑΘΟΥ is not alluded to by Prof. P. Gardner in the *Brit. Mus. Cat.*, published in 1886, p. 123, where he notes the correction.

As these Chinese accounts are generally corroborated by the few statements of classical authors which have come down to us, I will now compare them together.

1. Strabo (*Geogr.* xi. 8-2) states that "the best known tribes (of Scythians) are those who deprived the Greeks of Bactriana, the Asii, Pasiani, Tokhari, and Sakarauli, who came from the country beyond the Jaxartes." Here, then, *Sakarauli* are clearly the *Sakas*, and the *Tokhari* are the *Yue-ti*, who drove out the Sakas. The *Pasiani* I would identify with the *Kushâns*. Trogus also refers to the same events when, after noting the rebellion of Theodotus, he says [*Prolog.* xli.]: "Deinde qua re pugnantes Scythicæ gentes *Saraucæ* et *Asiani* Bactra occupavere et Sogdianos."

2. The death of the Parthian King, Phraates II., B.C. 126, in battle with the Scythians, as related by Justin [xlii. 1], I would refer to the retreat of the Sakas southward before the *Yue-ti*. The death of the next Parthian King, Artabanus II., in B.C. 123, in battle with the *Thogarii*, I would refer to the advance of the *Tokhari*, after the defeat of the Sakas.

3. The Chinese account of the subjugation of the four tribes of the *Yue-ti* by the chief of the Kushâns (the fifth tribe), is confirmed by the statement of Trogus (*Prolog.* xlii.), "Additæ res Scythicæ"; "reges *Thogarorum Asiani*, interitusque Saraucarum." This I take to be a succinct record of the fact that the Kushâns (*Asiani*) gave kings to the *Tokhâri*, and defeated the Sakas (Saraucæ).

4. Both Trogus and Justin spell the name of this people with *Th*, as if derived from a Greek source. I notice this spelling for the purpose of referring to a statement of Pliny, who says that the stone *Callaina*, of a pale

green colour, is found in the country of the *Phycari*.[4] As he locates the Phycari at the back of the Indian Caucasus, I would correct the name to *Thychari*, by changing the Greek Φ to Θ. This change is supported by the fact that the Callais or Callaina stone, the "Turquoise," is most plentifully found at Nishapur in Khorasân, in the Western extension of the Caucasus. We thus learn that the *Tokhari* had pushed their conquests westward as far as Nishapur, before the time of Pliny, or say as early as 50 A.D. By the Hindus these princes were named in Sanskrit *Tushâra*, or "men of the snowy land." But the Pali or spoken form of the name was *Tukhâra*, which was the original of the Τοχαροί of Strabo and Ptolemy, and of the *Tu-ho-lo* of the Chinese. The name is still preserved in *Tokhâristan*.

The successor of Yun-kao-ching (or Wema Kadphises) was *Kanishka*, of whom we possess several brief but independent notices, all of which give the most clear and satisfactory evidence that he was not a Saka.

According to the Raja Tarangini (i. 170), he was a *Turushka*, or Turk (*Turushkânwaya*).

In Court's Manikyâla inscription, he is called "the aggrandizer of the Gushân race" (*samvardhaka Gushâna vansa*).

According to Biruni (Sachau's translation, ii. 11), Raja Kanik was the descendant of the *Turki* chief, *Barhatagin*,[5] the founder of the *Shâhiya* rule in Kabul. He is further described as being dressed like a *Turk*, in a high hat and boots, which is a *very exact* description of the costume of

---

[4] *Nat. Hist.*, xxxvii. 33.

[5] I would identify him with *Burtechino*, or the "dun wolf," who was believed to be the progenitor of the whole race.

the Kushân kings, Wema Kadphises and Kanishka, as seen on their coins.

Having thus shown, as I believe conclusively, that Kanishka was a *Kushân Tukhâra*, it follows that he could not have been the founder of the Saka era. The era is, in fact, always ascribed to a *Saka King* in hundreds of inscriptions. In one of the most ancient inscriptions, indeed, the establishment of the era is referred to the *abhisheka*, or "installation" of the Saka king. I believe that the actual founder of the *Saka* era was the *Saka* king *Chashtana*, the *Tiastanes* of Ptolemy, whose descendants certainly made use of it in dating their coins and inscriptions.

But if Kanishka did not found the Saka era, it does not seem likely that he would have used it. What, then, is the era which is found in the inscriptions of the three Kushân kings, Kanishka, Huvishka, and Vâsu Deva, in both the Gandharian and Indian characters. This I believe to have been the Seleukidan era. My reason for this belief is the fact that the Kushâns make use of the Macedonian months. The names of *Artemisios*, *Panemos*, and *Apellaios* were first read by myself. *Daisios* followed soon after; and I am now able to add *Peritios*. It seems therefore a reasonable conclusion that the Kushâns must have adopted the Macedonian calendar of the Seleukidæ. If so, the date of these three Kushân kings might be explained by the omission of the hundreds of the Seleukidan era, which we know was a common practice in India in reckoning the *Sapt Rishi kâl*, or "Era of the Seven Rishis." This mode is used in fact throughout the Raja Tarangini. I find the same mode also on the coins of the Rajput Chief, *Malaya Varma Deva*, which bear the shortened date of S. 83, as well as the full date S. 1283.

This practice of expressing curtailed dates, by leaving out the hundreds, had already been adopted on some of the coins of the Greek kings, Eukratides and Heliokles. Mr. Thomas thus explained the letters ΠΓ = 83, on the coins of Heliokles, by pointing to the full date of ΡΠΓ = 183, on a tetradrachm of the same king in the British Museum. In the same way I would explain the letters ΝΑ = 51, and ΟΓ = 73, on the tetradrachms of Eukratides as being intended for 151 and 173 of the Seleukidan era.

The earliest and latest dates of Kanishka yet found are S. 7 and S. 28, which, if referred to the Saka era would be A.D. 85 and 106. But if read as 407 and 428 of the Seleukidan era, they would correspond with A.D. 95 and 116. The difference from the Saka era is only ten years; but I must confess that I feel a strong repugnance to the use of the Saka era by the Kushâns. I fully believe that the Saka era was *founded* by a Saka king; but as it is not *impossible* that the Kushâns *might have adopted* the same era, I am willing to make use of it as giving at any rate a very close approximation to the true dates of the Kushân kings. Their dates would, therefore, be as follows:—

B.C. 10. Kujula Kadphises.
A.D. 30. Wema Kadphises.
,, 70. Kujula Kara Kadphises.
,, 78. Kanishka.
,, 120. Huvishka.
,, 150. Vâsu Deva.
,, 176 = S. 98—latest date of Vâsu Deva.

Kujula-Kadphises.

The coins of the Scythian chief, Kujula Kadphises, King of the Kushâns, are very numerous both in the

Kabul valley and in the Western Panjâb. From his coins we learn that he was the overthrower of the last Greek king, as we find the name of the Greek Hermæus associated with that of the Scythian Kujula Kadphises on the same coins. On those with the joint names of Hermæus and Kujula, the Greek legend is invariably blundered, as ΒΑΣΙΛΕΩΣ ΣΤΗΡΟΣ ΣΥ ΕΡΜΑΙοΥ. But the same blundered legend is also found on the small coins with the figures of Victory and of Zeus seated, which bear the name of Hermæus alone, although the native legend is quite correct. Fifty years ago, I suggested that the letters ΣΥ might possibly be intended for Συγγενής, the "kinsman" of Hermæus, by the marriage of the Greek king's daughter with the Scythian conqueror. In this manner Seleukos and Chandra Gupta became allies; and at a later date the Sassanian Hormisdas II. married the daughter of the Kushân King of Kabul. Such an alliance would have secured for Kujula a favourable reception by the Greek subjects of Hermæus. I only offer this as a mere conjectural explanation of the puzzling ΣΥ.

The coins Nos. 5 and 6 of Plate XIV. are specimens of a new and rare type, on which the king is represented, with a helmet, on the obverse, and armed with a spear and shield on the reverse. A clay seal with the same figure is given in *Ariana Antiqua*, Pl. IV. 6, amongst the relics found by Masson in the Kotpur Stûpa.

Kozola-Kadaphes I take to be only a variant spelling of the same king's name, on the issue of a different mint. The head seems to be imitated from the coins of Augustus, his contemporary.

The coins with the two-humped camel were formerly assigned to Azas. Several years ago I read the name in the long native legend as *Kujula-Kara-Kadphises.* He must have been a king of the Kushâns, as he takes the well-known Kushân title of *Deva-putra.* I conjecture that he may have been the eldest son and immediate successor of Kujula Kadphises, and, therefore, the predecessor of Wema Kadphises. So far as I know, his coins are rarely found to the west of the Indus.

WEMA-KADPHISES.

The coins of *Wema Kadphises* offer little variety. The reverses, without a single exception, are confined to the worship of the Indian god, Siva. On some, the god is represented standing alone, holding a trident in his right hand, with the tiger's skin on his left arm, and a water vessel in the hand. On others he is accompanied by his bull, Nandi. On the small gold coins, *quarter dinârs,* the type is simply the trident of Mahadeva with the axe attached to the side.

On a single double dinâr the king is seen sitting on a throne with both feet resting on a footstool, and holding a flower in his right hand. On the other coins he is represented holding a club either in front of his face or resting on his right shoulder. On a single gold dinâr he is seen riding in a two-horse chariot with his club resting on his right shoulder and a small driver in front.

The Greek inscriptions are invariably in the nominative case, either BACIΛEVC BACIΛEωN CωTHP MEΓAC OOHMO KAΔΦICHC as on the *copper* coin, or simply BACIΛEVC OOHMO KAΔΦICHC as on the gold coins. The native inscription is always in the possessive case, *Maharajasa rajadhirajasa sarvaloga iṣvarasa mahiṣvarasa hima kathpiṣasa tradata.* I have long ago identified *Hima*, or OOHMO, with *Wen*, the common ancestor of all the Kushân kings. *Wen* is identical with the variant pronunciation of *Yen* and *Hen*. The Chinese give this name at full length as *Yen-kao-ching*, and attribute to him the conquest of India. His rule probably extended from 30 to 70 A.D.

KANISHKA.

The name of *Kanishka* has been preserved by the Chinese both in its full form as *Kia-ni-se-kia*, and also in its common spoken form as Ka-ni-kia, or *Kanikh*. It is found in the native history of Kashmir as Kanishka, a Buddhist prince of the Turushka race; and in its shortened form of Kanak it is preserved by Al Biruni as the Turki king of Kabul, who founded the great Stûpa at Parshâwar. In his inscriptions his name is invariably written Kanishka, both in Indian and Gandharian characters. On his coins the Greek spelling is KANHÞKOY and KANHÞKI, which may be rendered as *Kaneshka*, taking the abnormal Þ to be intended for *sh*.

On his coins we see the various changes of his religious belief. According to the Chinese pilgrim, Hwen Thsang, "he had no faith either in right or wrong, and he lightly esteemed the law of Buddha." His earliest coins show a preference for the pantheism of the Greeks in the worship of Helios, Salene, and Hephaistos. Then comes a mixture of Mazdean fire-worship and Indian nature-worship, followed by his conversion to Buddhism. The name of Kanishka is famous in Indian history as the great patron of Buddhism, who assembled a synod of five hundred monks in Kashmir, under Pârswika, for the compilation of an authoritative text of the Buddhist scriptures.

The inscriptions of Kanishka are dated in various years, from S. 7 to S. 28—which, if referred to the Saka era of 78 A.D., are equivalent to A.D. 85 and 106.

HUVISHKA.

Huvishka, the Hushka of Kashmirian history, was certainly the successor of Kanishka, as the dates of his inscriptions begin with S. 33, and continue at various intervals down to S. 51 of the Wardak record. The Buddha Gayâ Colossal Buddha, which is dated in S. 64, I would also attribute to his reign, as the impression of one of Huvishka's gold coins formed part of the Relic deposit under the throne of the Great Temple of Mahâbodhi at Buddha Gayâ. As the two extreme dates of S. 33 and S. 64 are equivalent to A.D. 111 and 142, I think that we may safely assign to him a long reign, from S. 32 to S. 72, or from 110 to 150 A.D. The Roman gold coins found in the Ahinposh Stûpa confirm this date, as the latest coin of Sabina, the wife of Hadrian, cannot be earlier than 136 A.D.

The coins of Huvishka present the same mixed cult of Mazdean and Indian origin as those of Kanishka, with a few additions such as the Mazdean *Ashavikhsho* and *Oaninda*, and the Indian *Mahasena, Skanda Kumāra*, and *Visâkha*. His gold coins, which are very numerous, present the king's bust, and on one rare variety the head only. A few very rare coins show the king seated or riding an elephant. The copper coins present the full-length figure, either riding on an elephant, or lounging on a couch, or sitting crossed-legged. On two very rare copper coins, now lost, the king was shown on his knees before the goddess NANA.

VASU-DEVA.

Vasu-Deva is connected with Kanishka and Huvishka by the similarity of his coinage in weight, make, and type, and in the peculiarity of using only Greek inscriptions. Three of his gold coins were found in a ruined Stûpa, below Ali Masjid, and there was a large number of them in the treasure trove of about 1,200 dinârs found at Peshâwar. They are common also all over the Punjâb and in North-west India. His inscriptions have hitherto been found only at Mathura and in the Indian character. But other inscriptions in Gandharian characters show that it was in use for some time after his reign. The dates of his Mathura inscriptions range from S. 74[6] to S. 98, or from A.D. 152 to 176. I think it probable, therefore, that his reign may have extended from 150 to 180 A.D.

The most notable peculiarity about his coins is the change in the symbol. His three predecessors, Wema Kadphises, Kanishka, and Huvishka, had all made use of the same symbol. But the symbol of Vasu-Deva must have had some marked significance, as it is used as the sole type of one of his copper coins (Pl. XXIV. fig. 1) with his name in Indian characters, written perpendicularly, *Vasu*. This particular symbol continued down to the time of the Guptas. The only innovation that I notice on the coins of Vasu-Deva is the representation of the god Siva, with three heads and four arms, in the orthodox Indian fashion.

---

[6] Originally I read this date as 44, but as the symbols for 40 and 70 are very similar I have no hesitation in correcting my reading to 74 (see *Archæol. Survey* iii., Pl. XV., No. 8), as we know certainly that Huvishka was reigning from S. 33 to S. 51.

TYPES OF THE COINS.

As many of the coin types of the great Kushân kings, Kanishka, Huvishka, and Vasu-Deva, appear to me to refer to the worship of the seven planets, and the various functions assigned to their regents, I have thought it most convenient to arrange them in the same order as the names of the seven week-days. I find about thirty different types, most of which appear to be susceptible of explanation. The chief difficulty lies in determining the source from which each name may have been derived, whether from India or Persia. At the first glance we can see that the figure labelled ΜΙΙΡΟ is the Persian *Mithra*, or the sun, while that labelled ΜΑΑCΗΝΟ must be the Indian god of war, *Mahasena*. The goddess ΝΑΝΑΙΑ, or ΝΑΝΑ, must also have been derived from Persia, while CΚΑΝΔΟ-ΚVΜΑΡΟ is clearly the son of the Indian god Siva. The termination of all the male names in Ο shows a decided Iranian influence. But the Kushâns themselves were a Turki tribe of Scythians, of whose worship we know absolutely nothing. On examining the coins of the first two kings I find that *Kujula Kadphises* adopted the type of the standing Herakles, while Wema Kadphises adopted the type of the Indian god Siva with his bull. But as the Greeks had already, as early as the time of Alexander, identified that Indian god with Herakles, I infer that the chief object of the early Kushân worship must have been the Scythian Herakles, or *Sapaleizes*, whom I would identify with the Scythian god Gebeleizes of Herodotus. A figure of Herakles was carried in front of the army of Porus. The people of the plains also are said to have worshipped Herakles,[7] while the people of the hill country worshipped Σοροάδειος, that is *Surya Deva*, or the "sun," and not *Dionysos*, the "god of wine," as Khares, of Mytilene, erroneously translated the name by *οἰνοποιός*, or the "wine-maker."

The objects of worship in ancient India and Persia sprang from a common source. The gods of India are well-known. Those of Persia have been described by Herodotus, Strabo, and Diodorus. They comprised the sun and moon, and the four elements of fire, wind, earth, and water, with the firmament of Heaven over all. Heródotus adds that "these were the only gods whose worship had come down to them from ancient times; but they afterwards adopted the worship of Urania from the Assyrians." This new goddess is *Anaïtis* (*Nanaia* or *Venus*), whose worship was introduced by Artaxerxes Mnemon.

In the time of Herodotus the Persians had no temples and no images; but both temples and statues of *Mithra* and *Anaïtis* were introduced during the reign of Artaxerxes I. (B.C. 485—435). About four centuries later statues of *Omanos*, *Anaïtis*, and *Anadatus* were seen by Strabo in a temple of Kappadokia. The statue of Omanos, which was of wood, was carried in procession. The temples were Pyrætheia in which a perpetual fire was kept. These are the Fire Temples of the Parsi books, called *Azer* or *Ader*. Each temple received a separate name from the planet or power to which it was dedicated. The

---

[7] Strabo, xv. 1-58.

following lists are taken from Hyde's *Relig. Vet. Pers.* 100, and from the Bundahist (West, p. 21):—

Temples.			Planets.
Azur i Mihr . .	☉	Sun	MITHRA
Azur i Nûsh . .	☾	Moon	MAH
Azur i Behrâm .	♂	Mars	BAHRÂM
Azur-âyin . . .	☿	Mercury	TÎR
Azur i Khurdâd .	♃	Jupiter	AHURMAZD
Azur i Barzin . .	♀	Venus	ANAHID
Azur Zardusht .	♄	Saturn	KEWAN

These names clearly represent the seven planets. But there is another set of seven names, consisting of Ahurmazd and the Ameshaspentas, or Amshaspands. They were originally mere abstractions which, being afterwards personified, were held to be the offspring of Ahuramazda. Their names are—

Haurvatât, genius of health, presided over water.
Ameratât, genius of immortality, presided over trees.
Kshathra-vairya, perfect sovereignty, presided over metals.
Asha Vahishta, holy order, genius of fire.
Armaiti, Vesu Aramati, goddess of earth.
Vohumano, good thought, god of living beings.

The names of the Amshaspands are taken from the *Gâthas*, or earliest portions of the Avesta, which are generally admitted to be as old as the time of Darius Hystaspes. It must be remembered, however, that *Ormazd* is mentioned in the inscriptions by Darius himself.

During the six centuries between Darius and Kanishka

several of the names preserved in the Gâthas of the Avesta became much modified. The later forms of the Indo-Scythian coins, as Dr. West observes, "bear a strong resemblance to Pahlavi, with a general leaning rather towards modern Persian than towards Avesta forms." All of these changes will be noticed hereafter.

A Zoroastrian origin for some of these Indo-Scythian deities has been claimed by Dr. A. Stein, based on a new reading of the variant form of the Greek *ro* in the names *Kanishka* and *Huvishka*, and of their tribal name of *Kushân*. So far back as November, 1860, when I read the name of Huvishka in the Mathura inscriptions as they were exhumed, I recognised that he was the OOHÞKI of the coins, and the Hushka of Kashmir history, as well as the Huvishka of the Gandharian inscription on the Wardak Vase.[8] This change I explained by the well-known usage of the Turki dialects, which substitute *r* for an initial *s* or *z*. The title of ÞAO I took for the simple title of *Rao* or *Raja*. I see that M. Ed. Drouin notes that *Rao* is a modern form; but I believe this to be a mistake, as the title of *Rao* is commonly used by the bard Chand before A.D. 1200, and is found in all the bardic chronicles at a still earlier date. In fact, the Raos of Jesalmer are said to have used no other title from the very foundation of their kingdom in the first century A.D. But as the title of ÞAONANO ÞAO shows a decided Persian form like *Shâhâna-Shâh*, instead of the Indian form of *Râjâ-Râjânâm*,

[8] The identification of Hoerki with the Hushka of Kashmir I had made as early as 1845. See *Journal Bengal Asiatic Society* for that year, p. 431.

I am willing to accept Dr. Stein's reading of this abnormal form of *ro* with the side stroke lengthened upwards as *sh*.[9] It is, perhaps, not impossible that the Kushâns themselves may have pronounced the title as *Rao*, whilst all other people said *Shao*. But the Chinese form of the title *Shao-wu* seems to confirm the native pronunciation of *Shao*. I may note also the fact that *r* and *sh* were interchangeable letters in ancient Persia, according to Dr. West,[10] who says that in dealing with Avesta names "we have to recollect that *art* and *ash* (*r* and *sh*) are merely dialectical variants of the same sound, as ancient *arta* = Avesta *asha*, Avesta *peretotam* = *peshotam*, and Pahlavi *arda-vahishta* = *Ashavahisht*." Following these examples the title of *Shao* might have been dialectically pronounced *Rao* by the Kushâns. The earliest Kushân coins of Miaüs and Kozola Kadaphes spell the name as *Korsan* with the common *rho*. I suspect that the adoption of a modified form of the Greek *rho* as Þ, *sh*, may have been purposely intended to show its intimate connection with the original P or *r*. The Indian pronunciation of the title, as declared by the Indian inscriptions of Kanishka and Vasu Deva, was certainly *shâhi*; and the same pronunciation was perpetuated by the later coins.

The general adoption of some portion of the Mazdean cult was certainly due to Kanishka, as his predecessor, Wema Kadphises, was a steady worshipper of the Indian Siva, whose trident, with battle-axe attached, is seen on all his coins, along with the figure of the moon-crested

---

9 *Babylonian and Oriental Record*, vol. i. 155.
10 *Babylonian and Oriental Record*, vol. ii. 237.

god himself, and his bull Nandi. On the copper coins this king is represented with his right hand pointing downwards near an altar, which is usually described as a fire altar. This type of the king sacrificing was adopted by all his successors.

I possess a curious copper coin (Pl. XV. fig. 14) which must almost certainly belong either to Wema Kadphises or to his successor Kanishka. On the obverse is the king sacrificing, but turned to the right. On the reverse is a double-faced bust, the right face being beardless and the left face bearded. Before the former is the well-known three-pronged symbol of the Nameless King, and before the latter is the symbol used by Wema Kadphises and Kanishka. There are traces of legends on both sides, but nothing is legible. In my account of the coins of the Nameless King I have noted that both he and Wema Kadphises have the same peculiarity of using the nominative case, while the forms of some of the Gandharian letters, which are common to both, are not used on other coins. These facts are, perhaps, sufficient to show that the two princes were contemporaries. But this new coin seems to offer a closer connection between them, if, as I suppose, the double-faced bust gives us the heads of the two kings united together. Perhaps it was due to a league between them that the Saka chiefs were driven out of Northern India in the first century A.D.

The names of the deities represented on the coins of Kanishka are certainly not Scythian. The goddess NANA was of Babylonian origin, but her worship had been adopted by Artaxerxes Mnemon, who set up her statues in several of the principal cities of the Persian empire. On the coins which bear Greek inscriptions she is called NANAIA. Her figure may, perhaps, be a copy of some Persian statue; but its pose and action agree so closely with those of the other deities that I feel satisfied the whole were the offspring of the same period during the reign of Kanishka. The designs I would attribute to the school of Indo-Greek art, which about the same time produced so many fine specimens of architecture as well as sculpture.

The finest coins are those which bear the Greek title of BACIΛЄVC BACIΛЄωN with the figures of HΛIOC, CAΛHNH, HΦAICTOC, and NANAIA. These figures were afterwards copied exactly on the coins which bear the native title of ÞAONANO ÞAO, with the corresponding native names of MIIPO, MAO, AΘPO, and NANA. The remaining names are partly Persian and partly Indian with the single exception of HPAKIΛO, or Herakles, with whom the Indo-Scythians identified the Indian god OKÞO. This figure of Herakles is undoubtedly Greek; and the standing figures of OKÞO with a club are direct copies of it. But the other figures of OKÞO, with the trident and the bull Nandi, are certainly of Indian origin. Some have three heads and four arms. That the Indians possessed statues long before the time of the Indo-Scythians we know from the sculptured remains of Asoka's period at Bodh Gayâ and Sânchi. But we have also the direct testimony of Q. Curtius, who says that a figure of Hercules (*Herculis Simulacrum*) was carried in front of the army of Porus.[11]

On a single gold coin of Kanishka we have a represen-

---

[11] Q. Curtius, viii. 14—11. Herculis simulacrum agmini peditum præferebatur.

tation of Buddha, under the name of **BOΔΔO**. The figure is standing with the right hand raised in the act of blessing. He is also represented in the same attitude on some rare copper coins with the title of **CAKA MANO BOYΔO**, or *Sakya-Muni Buddha.*[12] On a few copper coins Buddha is represented sitting in native fashion on the ground, with his right hand raised in the act of teaching.[13] I have referred to these coin figures because they are the earliest representations of Buddha that have yet been found. The sculptures at Bodh Gayâ (B.C. 250) and at Bharhut (B.C. 150) are remarkable for the absence of any figure of Buddha. His empty throne, his hair (*chudâ-mani*), his bowl, and his foot-prints, are frequently shown; but I have not seen any Indian sculptured figure of Buddha himself prior to the time of Kanishka. The earliest figures are those found in Gandhâra to the west of the Indus. This is the more remarkable as the Indian representations of Lakshmi at Bodh Gayâ and Bharhut are found very exactly copied on the coins of the Indo-Scythian Azilises. Even at Sânchi, so late as the middle of the first century A.D., there are no figures of Buddha. I think, therefore, that the well-known designs of Buddha, both sitting and standing, which were spread all over India from Mathura to Ceylon, must be ascribed to the Indo-Greek sculptors of the Indo-Scythian king Kanishka, about A.D. 100. I may add also that the designer, whoever he was, has clad

---

[12] See *Brit. Mus. Cat.*, Pl. XXVI. 8, and XXVII. 2; also *Ariana Antiqua*, Pl. XIII. 1, 2, 3. This reading is Mr. Rapson's.

[13] See my coin in *Bengal Asiatic Society Journal*, for 1845, and Von Sallet, Pl. VI. 1.

the figures appropriately in Indian garments, in the *sanghâti*, or kilt, fastened round the waist, and the *uttara sanghâti*, or robe, which sometimes enveloped the whole figure, and at other times was so arranged as to leave the right shoulder bare. As the artist had daily opportunities of seeing Buddhist monks, he may be credited with clothing the Teacher in his native costume, instead of in the foreign garments of Greece, the *khitôn* and *himation*, as described in *Brit. Mus. Cat.* p. 133.

Kujula Kadphises, the founder of the Kushân kingdom, would appear to have been content with the simple religion of his ancestors, who worshipped the god of Death, a deity carrying a club, whom the Greeks identified with *Herakles*, and the Indians with *Yama* or *Siva*. His successor, *Wema Kadphises*, or *Yen-Kao-Ching*, the conqueror of India, continued the same worship, and adopted the Indian figure of the god Siva and his bull Nandi on all his coins. But a complete change took place after the accession of Kanishka, whose wide domains probably extended from the Caspian on the west to the junction of the Ganges and Jumna on the east. In Court's Manikyâla inscription he is expressly named as the "aggrandizer of the Kushân race," *Gushana-vansa Samvardhaka*. His territories embraced large portions of both Persia and India, with the natural consequence that the barbarian conqueror adopted much of the religions of the two conquered races. This result is clearly displayed on the numerous coins of Kanishka and his successor Huvishka, which are described in the following pages. Altogether, their coins give the names of no less than 33 deities, of which several are unmistakably Greek, while the rest are partly Persian, and partly Indian. Several of the names are, of course, only different appellations of a single deity with different functions. Thus the regent of the planet Mars, who represented the element of *Fire*, was also the god of *Battle*, with whom was associated the goddess of *Victory*. These three figures are all described in the group of the planet Mars.

As before stated, I have divided all the names into seven classes, according to my view of their affinities with the seven planets, and in the order of the seven week-days. The coins bearing the name and figure of Buddha form an eighth class. In the following lists the names are arranged in their respective groups. The letters K and H stand for Kanishka and Huvishka, the kings on whose coins the different deities are found. With the single exception of one piece of *Nanaia*, the gold coins of Vasu Deva present only the single type of *Siva*. His copper coins give all the seven deities in very rude style.

Since writing the above I have received a gold coin of Huvishka, with the reverse of **ΑΡΟΟΑϹΠΟ**, which has led me to reconsider the probable meaning of the name. I now think that it may be rendered by *Arvva-Aspa*, taking *arvva* as "air" in gentle motion, as represented by the *walking horse*. The word *arvva* in fact seems to be identical with the Greek *ἄυρα* and the Latin *aura*. The name of **ΑΡΟΟΑϹΠΟ** must therefore be assigned to No. IV. group of Mercury, following **ΟΑΔΟ**. The quick running figure of **ΟΑΔΟ** represents the "*Wind*," or *air in quick motion, i.e. ἄνεμος*, or *ventus*, as distinct from the atmosphere which we breathe. The name may also be read as *Arha-aspo*—and as *Arha* and *Arvva* are both names of Indra, the full name would mean "*Indra's* *steed,*" that is the "Wind" which brings the rain. Another similar name of the Wind is *Prishadaswa*, or *Prexaspes*, or the "Rain Steed."

The discussion on the meanings of the different names will follow with the next paper on the coins of Huvishka.

No.	Legend	Name	Equivalent	K	H
		I.—Sun. ☉.			
1	ΗΛΙΟϹ	Helios		K	
2	ΜΙΙΡΟ	Miiro	P. *Mihir*	K	H
3	ΑÞΑ⋞ΙΧÞΟ	Ashavikhsho	P. *Asha-Vahishta*		H
4	ΑΙΝΟ - ?	Aino - ?			H
5	ΟΓΒΟΡ	Ombor ?			H
		II.—Moon. ☾.			
1	ϹΑΛΗΝΗ	Salene		K	
2	ΜΑΟ	Mao	P. *Mah*	K	H
3	ΜΑΝΑΟ · ΒΑΓΟ	Manao-bago	P. *Mana-baga*	K	H
		III.—Mars. ♂.			
1	ΗΦΑΙϹΤΟϹ	Hephaistos		K	
2	ΑΘÞΟ	Athsho	P. *Atar, Atash*	K	H
3	ΛΟΗ	Loë	Eng. *Lowe, Glow*		H
4	ΑΡΟΟΑϹΠΟ	Arvo-aspo		K	H
5	ΜΑΑϹΗΝΟ	Maaseno	S. *Mahâsena*		H
6	ϹΚΑΝΔΟ · ΚΟΜΑΡΟ	Skando-komaro	S. *Skanda-Kumâra*		H
7	ΒΙΖΑΓΟ	Bizago	S. *Visâkha*		H
8	ΟΡΛΑΓΝΟ	Orlagno	{ P. Verethragha / S. Vritraghan }	K	
9	ΟΑΝΙΝΔΑ	Oaninda	P. Vanainti		H
		IV.—Mercury. ☿.			
1	ΟΑΔΟ	Oado	P. Bâd. S. *Vâta*	K	H

No.	Greek legend	Reading	Original	K	H
		V.—Jupiter. ♃.			
1	ΜΑΖΔΟΟΑΝΟ	Mazdohano	P. *Mazdaonho*	K	
2	ΦΑΡΡΟ	Pharro	P. *Bâran* S. *Parjanya*	K	H
		VI.—Venus. ♀.			
1	ΑΡΔΟΧÞΟ	Ardokhsho	P. *Arta-dukhta* S. *Ard-dakshâ*	K	H
2	ÞΑΟΡΗΟΡΟ	Shaoreoro	P. *Sharewar* S. *Aira-vira* [14]		H
3	ΡΙΔΗ	Ride	S. *Riddhi*		H
4	ΝΑΝΑΙΑ · ΝΑΝΑ	Nanaia	P. Ânâhita	K	H
5	ΖΕΙΡΟ	Zeiro	P. Zahra		H
		VII.—Saturn. ♄.			
1	ΗΡΑΚΙΛΟ	Herakilo	. . . . .		H
2	ΟΚÞΟ	Oksho	S. *Ukshâ*	K	H
3	CΑΡΑΠΟ	Sarapo	*Sarapis = Yama*		H
4	ωΡΟΗ	Hôron	S. *Varun*		H
5	ΟΧÞΟ	Okhsho	. . . . .		H
6	ΟΑΧÞΟ	Oakhsho	. . . . .		H
		Buddha.			
1	ΒΟΔΔΟ	Boddo	S. Buddha	K	
2	CΑΚΑ . ΜΑΝΑ . ΒοΥΔΟ	Saka-mana Boudo	Sakya-muni Buddha	K	

N.B.—The letters K and H on the right hand stand for *Kanishka* and *Huvishka*.

[14] *Airavira*, Son of Earth (*Ira*), is *Kuvera*, the god of Riches. *Riddhi*, the wife of Kuvera, is the goddess of Fortune. As both presided over *metals*, they are represented in *armour*.

DESCRIPTION OF THE PLATES.

No.		Inches.	Grains.		Plate.
				N.B. Unless otherwise noted, all the obverse legends are in Greek letters, and all the reverse legends of the coins of Kujula Kadphises and Wema Kadphises are in native characters. These native characters I have hitherto called *Arian*. Lassen called them *Kabulian*, and Wilson named them *Arianian*. I now propose to style them *Gandharian*, because they were used throughout *Gandhâra*, to the east as well as the west of the Indus, from Kandahar to the Jumna. The name of Bactrian, or Indo-Bactrian, is certainly wrong, as no coins have yet been found to the north of the Indian Caucasus with any native characters, save those known as Chaldæo-Pahlavi. The coins of each king are numbered continuously on the left. The references to the Plates are given on the right.	
				HERMÆUS AND KUJULA KADPHISES.	
1	Æ	0·75	73 & 90	*Head of King* to r. ΒΑΣΙΛΕΩΣ ΣΤΗΡ□Σ ΣΥ ΕΡΜΑΙΟΥ. *Zeus enthroned*, with r. hand extended. *Mon.* No. 16, forming Χ□. *Maharajasa mahatasa Heramayasa.*	XIV. 1
2	Æ	0·6	42	*Head of King* to r., as on No. 1. Legend the same.	XIV. 2

DESCRIPTION OF THE PLATES—*continued.*

No.		Inches.	Grains.		Plate.
				Winged Victory, with palm and wreath to l. *Mon.* No. 16, with *pra.* *Maharayasa rayarayasa mahatasa Heramayasa.* N.B. Two reverses are given, so as to complete the native legend. The Greek legend on these two coins requires special notice. The *omega* is always omitted in ΣΩΤΗΡΟΣ, and the two letters ΣΥ are invariably inserted. I once thought that these letters might have been intended for Σύμμαχος, the "ally" of Hermæus. On No. 2 coin, with Victory, the high-sounding title of "King of Kings" (*rayaraya*) is curious. [*Brit. Mus. Cat.*, xxv. 1.]	
3	Æ	0·95	130	*Head of King* to r. ΒΑΣΙΛΕΩΣ ΣΤΗΡ□Σ ΣΥ ΕΡΜΑΙ□Υ. *Herakles* standing to front, with club in r. hand and lion's skin on l. arm. *Kujula Kasasa Kushana Yavugasa dhramathidasa.* [*Brit. Mus. Cat.*, xxv. 8.]	XIV. 8
4	Æ	0·9	151	*Head of King* to r. Κ□Ζ□ΥΛ□ ΚΑΔΦΙΖ□Υ Κ□ΡϹΝΑ. *Herakles* standing as on last, and Gandharian legend the same. [5 coins, author.]	XIV. 4
5 6	Æ	0·75	69 & 61	*Helmeted head of King* to r. ΚΟΖΟΥΛΟ ΚΑ . . . . . ΚΟΡϹΑΝ.	XIV. 5, 6

No.	Metal	Size	Weight	Description	Plate
				Soldier armed with spear and shield to r. *Kuyula Kasasa Kushana Yavuäsa.*	
				KOZOLA-KADAPHES.	
7	Æ	0·75	46	*Diademed head of King* to r. Like head of Augustus. ΚΟΖΟΛΑ ΚΑΔΑΦΕϹ ΧΟΡΑΝϹΥ ΖΑΟΟΥ. *King seated on chair.* Symbol to l. *Bra.* to r. *Kuyula Kapsasa dharma-thidasa Khushanasa Yaüasa.*	XIV. 7
8	Æ			A similar coin to No. 7, with *Victory* on the reverse, was lost by wreck of *Indus* steamer. On all these coins *Kujula* declares himself the King of the Kushâns. On the smaller coins, No. 7, which are more neatly executed, the tribal name, both in Greek and in the native character, is spelt with *Kh*, as *Khushân*. The title of ΖΑΟΟΥ is certainly the same as *Shaowu*, which the Chinese give to these *Yueti*. On the later coins of Kanishka it was shortened to *Shao*. The imitation of the head of Augustus Cæsar on No. 7 confirms the date of *Kujula*, which we derive from the Chinese, as lying between 20 B.C. and 80 A.D.	
				KUJULA-KARA-KADPHISES. [*Brit. Mus. Cat.*, xxiii. 7.]	
1	Æ	0·95	158	*Humped Indian Bull* to r. Buddhist symbol, No. 58, above. Greek legend corrupt. ΝΙΙΥΥΟΗΙΝΔΝΥΙΝ.	XIV. 9

DESCRIPTION OF THE PLATES—*continued.*

No.		Inches.	Grains.		Plate.
				Two-humped Bactrian Camel to r. Gandharian *mon.*, No. 57, to r. *Maharayasa Rayarayasa Devaputrasa Kuyula Kara Kaphsasa.* [2 specimens.]	
2	Æ	0·9	167	*Humped Bull* as on No. 1, with Buddhist symbol above. Corrupt Greek letters, ΠΜΤΗΥΙΥ. *Bu.* *Two-humped Bactrian Camel* to r, with *ka* and *chs.* *Kuyula Kara Kapasa Maharayasa rayatirayasa.* [Von Sallet, Pl. VI. 9, 10.]	XIV. 10
3	Æ	0·8	160	*Humped Indian Bull* to r. Greek letters illegible. *Two-humped Bactrian Camel* to r. Gandharian *mon.*, *Spasam.* *Maharajasa Mahatasa Kushana Kuya* (*la Kaphasa*). [5 specimens.]	XIV. 11
4	Æ	0·8	72	*Humped Bull* and Buddhist symbol above. ΒΥΠΝϾΙΒΥΠΝΕΙΝ [? for ΒΑϹΙΛΕΙ ΒΑϹΙΛΕΙ.] *Two-humped Bactrian Camel* to r. *Maharajasa raja* [*tirajasa Kuyula Kaphasa*]. [10 specimens.]	XIV. 12
5	Æ	0·6	67—26	Types and legends as on No. 4. When I first saw these coins, I read the name as *Kujulakasa* instead of *Kujula-kara*, as I remembered the name of *Liaka Kusalaka.* But as I find on 20 specimens that the last letter is certainly not *s*, but either *r* or *t*, I read	XIV. 13

				the name, with some confidence, as *Kujulakara*. I suppose that he may have been a son of the founder of the Kûshan dynasty.	
				Hema-Kadphises. [*Brit. Mus. Cat.*, xxv. 6.]	
1	*AV*	1·0	244·2	*King on throne* to front, with flower in r. hand; both feet on footstool. He wears a tall helmet, with front peak and fillet, and long tunic with sleeves, and large Tartar boots. Symbol, No. 58. ΒΑCΙΛΕΥC ΟΟΗΜΟ ΚΑΔΦΙCΗC. The *Indian god Siva*, standing in front of his bull Nandi, holding trident in r. hand; leopard's skin over left arm; Buddhist combined symbol over Bull. *Maharajasa Rajadirajasa Sarva-loga-iswarasa Mahiswarasa. Hima-Kathpisasa tradata.* The letter *pi* in the name has a St. Andrew's cross placed over its lower part, which I take to be the Gandharian letter *th*. This letter is properly a St. George's cross, +; but, as this upright form could not be added to *p* without absorption, I conclude that the sloping cross was adopted. The high-sounding title of *Sarvalokeswara*, "King of the	XV. 1

DESCRIPTION OF THE PLATES—*continued.*

No.		Inches.	Grains.		Plate.
				World," was probably assumed after the conquest of N. India, which is ascribed to *Yen-Kaoching*, the successor of *Kujula*. [*Brit. Mus. Cat.*, xxv. 7.]	
2	AV	1·0	245	*King squatted* in Eastern fashion, with crossed legs, wearing peaked helmet and diadem. Club in r. hand resting on shoulder; l. hand resting on knee. Symbol to l. The tunic is fastened at the neck by a couple of buttons or studs. Greek legend, as on No. 1.	XV. 2
				Siva standing in front of Bull, as on No. 1, and Gandharian legend the same.	
3	AV	1·1	245·5	*Bust of King* to r., with helmet peaked and filleted. Club on shoulder, held by right hand. Flames behind left shoulder, symbol above. Greek legend, as on No. 1.	XV. 3
				Siva standing in front of Bull; as before. Gandharian legend the same. [*Brit. Mus. Cat.*, xxv. 8.]	
4	AV	0·9	128·5	Types and legends as on No. 3, but without Bull. Symbol of Kadphises to l., Buddhist symbol to r.	
5	AV	1·0	243	*Bust of King* to l., helmeted, holding club upright in r. hand before face, and some small indistinct object in l. hand, perhaps an elephant-goad. Greek legend, as on No. 1, and symbol of Kadphises.	XV. 5

				Siva standing before Bull. Gandharian legend as before, and Buddhist symbol. [*Brit. Mus. Cat.*, xxv. 9.]	
6	AV	0·8	123·5	*Bust of King*, with Greek legend as No. 5, and symbol of Kadphises.	XV. 6
				Siva standing, without Bull. Gandharian legend as on No. 1. Symbol of Kadphises to l., and Buddhist symbol to r. [*Brit. Mus. Cat.*, xxxii. 18 ; *Ar. Ant.* x. 9.]	
7	AV	0·8	122·5	*King in Biga* to r., with club on r. shoulder. Small driver in front. Greek legend as before.	XV. 7
				Siva standing to front, with trident in r. hand, and leopard-skin over l. arm. Gandharian legend as before, and both symbols as on No. 4. [*Brit. Mus. Cat.*, xxv. 10.]	
8	AV	0·45	30·5	*Bearded head of King*, in picture-frame; fingers of hand appearing outside lower part of frame. Greek legend as on No. 1.	XV. 8
				Trident of Siva on stand, with battle-axe attached on l. ; club to r. Both symbols. Gandharian legend, *Maharaja Rajadiraja Hima Kathpisasa.* [*Brit. Mus. Cat.*, xxv. 11.]	
9	AR	0·7	56·5	*King standing* to l., with r. hand over small altar, and l. hand on hip. Trident to l., and club to r. ΒΑϹΙΛΕΥϹ ΒΑϹΙΛΕѠΝ ΜΕΓΑϹ ΟΟΗΜΟ ΚΑΔΦΙϹΗϹ.	XV. 9
				Siva standing, with Bull, as on No. 1. Buddhist symbol above.	

DESCRIPTION OF THE PLATES—*continued.*

No.		Inches.	Grains.		Plate.
				Maharajasa rajadirajasa Sarvaloga-iswarasa Mahiṣwarasa Hima-Kathpisasa tradata. N.B. The weight of this coin shows that it was intended for the equivalent of the Roman silver *denarius*, just as the gold coins of the Kushân kings had been assimilated to the Roman *denarius aureus*. But the name of the gold coin was also adopted as *Dinâr*, which is found in all the inscriptions of the Guptas. In fact, I look upon these Indo-Scythian *Dinârs* as a simple reissue of the Roman *Denarii Aurei* after recoinment. The two coins would, therefore, have been current at the same time, the recoined *Dinârs* in N. India, and the Roman *Aurei* throughout S. India. [2 coins, Author.]	
10	Æ	0·95	260	*King standing* to l., as on the silver coin. Trident and club. Kadphises symbol, and Greek legend as on No. 1. *Siva standing* before Bull, trident in r. hand, leopard's skin over l. arm, and water-pot in hand. Buddhist symbol over Bull. The whole surrounded by a circle of reels and pellets. No legend. [*Brit. Mus. Cat.* xxv. 13.]	XV. 10
11	Æ	1·05	263·2 Mean of 10 coins.	*King standing* to l., and Greek legend as on last. *Siva standing* before Bull, as on No. 10. Gandharian legend as No. 1.	XV. 11

12	Æ	0·85	128	Same as No. 11, but middle size. [*Brit. Mus. Cat.*, xxv. 13.]	XV. 12
13	Æ	0·7	59	Same as No. 11, but small size. [*Brit. Mus. Cat.*, xxv. 14.] [Author, *unique.*]	XV. 13
14	Æ	0·7	48	*Bust with two faces,* surmounted by an Indo-Scythian helmet. Left face, bearded, with Kadphises symbol in front. Right face, smooth, with symbol of Nameless King in front. *King standing* to r., sacrificing at small altar, like Wema Kadphises.	XV. 14

This coin is unfortunately in very bad preservation. There are traces of legends on both sides, but I cannot recognise any single letter with certainty. On the king's side the traces look like Greek.

In addition to the two symbols of Wema Kadphises and the Nameless King, I notice the following peculiarities, which are common to the coins of these two Princes.

1. Both use the same titles of ΒΑϹΙΛΕΥϹ ΒΑϹΙΛΕѠΝ ϹѠΤΗΡ ΜΕΓΑϹ in the nominative case.
2. Both make use of a circular margin composed of reels and pellets, in the place of the native legend.
3. Wema Kadphises holds a club upright before his face.
   The Nameless King holds a sceptre upright before his face.
4. Both use the same peculiar form of the Gandharian letter *j*, thus : 𐨗.

DESCRIPTION OF THE PLATES—*continued.*

No.		Inches.	Grains.		Plate.
				I may add that the coins of both kings are common in the Kabul Valley, throughout the Panjab, and in N.W. India, as far east as Benares and Ghazipur.	
				KANISHKA. THE SUN. ☉ HELIOS. MIIRO. [B.M. from Author.]	
1	*N*	0·9	123	*Standing figure of King, bearded,* with sword and spear; dressed in tunic, trousers, and boots, and holding r. hand over small altar. Cloak over shoulders, with ends flying out to front and rear. ΒΑϹΙΛΕΥϹ ΒΑϹΙΛΕѠΝ ΚΑΝΗϷΚΟΥ. *Radiate figure of Sun,* standing, dressed in long tunic; l. hand on hip, and r. hand extended, with forefinger pointing before him. Symbol like that of Wema Kadphises. ΗΛΙΟϹ.	XVI. 1
2	*N*	0·85	122	*King standing,* with spear in l. hand, and r. hand over altar, as on No. 1. ϷΑΟΝΑΝΟ ϷΑΟ ΚΑΝΗϷΚΙ ΚΟϷΑΝΟ. *Radiate figure of Sun,* as on No. 1, but with sword only. Kadphises symbol. ΜΙΙΡΟ.	XVI. 2

No.	Metal	Size	Weight	Description	Plate
				[*Dichalkon.*]	
3	Æ	0·8	128	*King* and Greek legend as on No. 1. *Radiate figure of Sun*, and symbol as No. 1. **ΗΛΙΟϹ.**	XVI. 3
				[*Hemiobolion.*]	
4	Æ	1·0	266	*King*, standing, as on No. 1. **ϷAO KANHϷKI.** *Radiate Sun-god*, as No. 1. **ΜΙΟΡΟ.** Kadphises symbol.	XVI. 4
				[*Dichalkon.*]	
5	Æ	0·8	126	Same types and legends as No. 4.	—
				[*Chalkous.*]	
6	Æ	·65	64	Same types and legends as No. 4. N.B. The copper coins of the Kushâns follow the weights of the drachma, didrachma, and tetradrachma. The first, of 66 grs., is the *chalkous*, the second is the *dichalkon*, and the third is the *hemiobol*. Taking the obolus at 11 grs., the rate of silver to copper was 1 to 48. This is the very same rate that I had already determined. (See *Num. Chron.*, 1873, p. 216.)	—
				THE MOON. MAO. ☾	
				[*Brit. Mus. Cat.*, xxvi. 1.]	
7	*AV*	0·85	123	*King standing*, with spear in l. hand, and r. hand over altar. **ΒΑϹΙΛΕΥϹ ΒΑϹΙΛΕѠΝ ΚΑΝΗϷΚΟΥ.** *Male figure of Moon standing*, with crescent behind shoulders; sceptre in l. hand, and r. hand extended, with fore-	XVI. 5

DESCRIPTION OF THE PLATES—*continued.*

No.		Inches	Grains.		Plate.
				finger pointing forward. **CAΛHNH**, and Kadphises symbol. [*Brit. Mus. Cat.*, xxvi. 9.]	
8	AV	0·85	122	*King standing*, as on No. 7, with crescent and sceptre. **ÞAONANO ÞAO KANHÞKI KOÞANO.** *Male figure of Moon*, as on No. 7. **MAO**, with Kadphises symbol. [*Unique.*]	XVI. 6
9	AV	0·8	120	*King standing*, as on No. 7. Same legend. *Four-armed Moon-god* enthroned to front; crescent behind shoulders; sceptre and callipers in two hands, and two indistinct objects in other hands; feet on footstool. Kadpbises symbol to r. **MANAO—BAΓO.**	XVI. 7
10	AV	0·55	30·5	*Bearded bust of King* to l.; sceptre in l. hand. Legend as on No. 8. *Figure of Moon* as on No. 7. Same symbol. **MAO.**	XVI. 8
11	AV	0·5	30·0	*King standing* as on No. 7. Same legend. *Figure of Moon* as on No. 7. Same symbol. **MAO.** [*Brit. Mus. Cat.*, xxvii. 8.]	XVI. 9
12	Æ	1·05	260	*Bearded figure of King*, standing, as on No. 7. **ÞAO KANHÞKI.** *Standing figure of Moon-god*, with crescent. Symbol. **MAO.**	XVI. 10
13	Æ	0·8	130	Same types and legends as No. 12.	—
14	Æ	0·6	65	Do. do. do.	—

				MARS. ATHSHO. [B.M. from Author.]	
15	AV	0·85	123	*Bearded figure of King*, standing, spear in l. hand, r. hand over altar. **BACIΛЄYC BACIΛЄωN KANHÞKOY.** *Standing bearded figure*, with sword; l. hand on hip; r. hand holding wreath. Symbol of Kadphises. **HΦAICTOC.** [*Brit. Mus. Cat.*, xxvi. 4.]	XVI. 11
16	AV	0·8	120	*Bearded figure of King*, as on No. 15, with spear, and r. hand over altar. **ÞAONANO ÞAO KANHÞKI KOÞANO.** *Male figure of god*, with sword and wreath. Symbol. **AΘÞO.** [*Brit. Mus. Cat.*, xxv. v.]	XVI. 12
17	AV	0·5	30	Same types and legends as last. [*Brit. Mus. Cat.*, xxvi. 16.]	—
18	AV	0·5	30	*Bearded bust of King*, with sceptre to l. Legend as No. 16. *Male figure of god*, with sceptre and wreath. Symbol. **AΘÞO.** [*Brit. Mus. Cat.*, xxv. 14.]	XVI. 13
19	AV	0·8	123	*Bearded figure of King*, with legend as No. 16. *Male figure*, with sword and sceptre; helmet surmounted by bird with expanded wings. Symbol. **OPΛAΓNO.** [*Brit. Mus. Cat.*, xxvi. 7.]	XVI. 14
20	AV	0·8	120	*Bearded figure of King*, with legend as No. 16.	XVI. 15

DESCRIPTION OF THE PLATES—*continued.*

No.		Inches.	Grains.		Plate.
				Bearded deity with wreath in r. hand, standing beside a bridled horse. Kadphises symbol. **ΑΡΟΟΑϹΠΟ.** [*Brit. Mus. Cat.*, xxvii. 1.]	
21	Æ	1·05	260	*Bearded figure of King.* Symbol. **ÞΑΟ ΚΑΝΗÞΚΙ.**	XVI. 16
22	Æ	0·8	128	Same types and legends as No. 21.	—
23	Æ	0·6	64	Do. do. do.	—
				MERCURY. OADO. ☿	
				[*Brit. Mus. Cat.*, xxvii. 6.]	
24	Æ	1·0	260	*Bearded figure of King*, standing, to l., as on 16. **ÞΑΟ ΚΑΝΗÞΚΙ.**	XVII. 1
				Male bearded figure, running, to l.; head rayed; holding up expanded dress with both hands. Kadphises symbol. **ΟΑΔΟ.**	
25	Æ	0·8	130	Same types and legends as No. 24.	XVII. 2
26	Æ	0·6	65	Same as No. 25, but god running to r.	XVII. 3
				JUPITER. PHARRO. ♃	
				[*Brit. Mus. Cat.*, xxvi. 15.]	
27	AV	0·8	124	*Bearded figure of King*, standing, as on No. 16. Legend the same.	XVII. 4

				Helmeted figure of deity, standing, to r.; spear in l. hand; indistinct object in r. hand. Kadphises symbol. **ΦΑΡΡΟ**.	
28	AV	0·5	30	Same types and legends as No. 27. [B.M., from Author.]	—
29	AV	0·75	122	*King, bearded*, standing, as on No. 16. Same legend. *Male figure* riding a horse, with two heads, to r. Kadphises symbol. **ΜΑΖΔΟΟΑΝΟ**.	XVII. 5
				VENUS Genetrix. ARDOKHSHO. Demeter. [*Brit. Mus. Cat.*, xxvi. 6.]	
30	AV	0·8	122·5	*Bearded King*, standing, as on No. 16. Legend the same. *Goddess*, standing, to r.; modius on head; holding cornucopiæ in r. hand. Kadphises symbol. **ΑΡΔΟΧÞΟ**. [*Brit. Mus. Cat.*, xxv. 13.]	XVII. 6
31	AV	0·6	30·0	Types and legends as on No. 30.	—
32	AV	0·85	120·5	*Bearded King*, and legend, as on No. 16. *Vira*, in Indian letters, in field. Gandharian letter, *pa*, to left. *Goddess*, with nimbus, seated on throne; holding wreath in r. hand, and cornucopiæ in l. hand. Kadphises symbol to l. Indian letter, *rû*, to r. above throne. **ΑΡΔΟΧÞΟ**. [Author, unique.]	XVII. 7
33	AV	0·8	125	*Bearded King*, as on No. 16. Greek legend, in stiff square characters, as on No. 16. Indian letter, *pa*, in field.	XVII. 8

DESCRIPTION OF THE PLATES—*continued.*

No.		Inches.	Grains.		Plate.
				Goddess, with nimbus, seated on throne without back; holding flower in r. hand, and wheat stem in l. hand. Kadphises symbol. ΑΡΔΟΧÞΟ.	
				VENUS. NANAIA. Artemis, Persephone.	
34	Ꝋ	0·95	125·5	*Bearded King*, and Greek legend as on No. 16. *Draped goddess*, standing, to r., with nimbus and lunar crescent; sword on her left side, and sceptre in r. hand, with half-animal top. Kadphises symbol to r. NANA to l. [*Brit. Mus. Cat.*, xxvi. 11.]	XVII. 9
35	Ꝋ	0·5	30·2	Types and legends as No. 34.	—
36	Ꝋ	0·85	120·5	*Bearded King*, and legend, as No. 34. *Draped goddess*, with rainbow and crescent; sword at her l. side, and sceptre in r. hand. Kadphises symbol. NANA ÞAO. [*Brit. Mus. Cat.*, xxvii. 11.]	XVII. 10
37	Ꝋ	0·5	30·2	Typos and legends as on No. 36.	XVII. 11
38	Ꝋ	0·55	31·0	*Bearded bust* of King with sceptre to l., as on No. 10. Same legend. Draped figure of Goddess, as on No. 34. Kadphises symbol. NANA.	XVII. 12

				[Author. Unique.]	
39	Æ	0·5	30·5	*Bearded bust* of King, with sceptre. **ÞAO KANHÞKI.** *Draped figure* of Goddess. Kadphises symbol. **NANA.** [*Brit. Mus. Cat.*, xxvi. 3.]	XVII. 13
40	Æ	0·9	130	*Full-length figure* of King to l., with r. hand extended over altar. Greek legend. **BACIΛEYC BACIΛEωN KANHÞKOY.** Draped figure of Goddess, with nimbus and crescent; sceptre in r. hand, and flat dish in l. hand. Kadphises symbol. **NANAIA.** [*Brit. Mus. Cat.*, xxvii. 5.]	XVII. 14
41	Æ	1·05	260	*Bearded King*, standing, as before. **ÞAO KANHÞKI.** Draped Goddess, as before. Kadphises symbol. **NANA.**	XVII. 15
42	Æ	0·85	130	Same types and legends as No. 41.	—
43	Æ	0·6	60	Do. do. do.	XVII. 16
				SATURN. OKSHO. Hades. [*Brit. Mus. Cat.*, xxvi. 12.]	
44	AV	0·8	123	*Bearded figure* of King, standing, to l., as usual, with light cloak over shoulders; spear in l. hand, and r. hand over altar. **ÞAONANO ÞAO KANHÞKI KOÞANO.** *Four-armed male deity* to front. In his two r. hands small hand-drum, and water-vessel with mouth downwards;	XVIII. 1

DESCRIPTION OF THE PLATES—*continued.*

No.		Inches.	Grains.		Plate.
				in l. hands, trident and antelope. Kadphises symbol to l. ΟΚÞΟ to right.	
45	AV	0·5	33	Same types and legends as No. 44. [*Brit. Mus. Cat.*, xxvi. 17]	XVIII. 2
46	AV	0·5	80	*Bearded bust of King*, with sceptre. Same legend as No. 44. *Figure of same god*, ΟΚÞΟ, as on Nos. 44 and 45.	XVIII. 3
47	Æ	1·05	260	*King, bearded*, and standing, as before. ÞΑΟ ΚΑΝΗÞΚΙ. *Four-armed deity* (the Indian *Siva*, as *Yama*). In two r. hands, small drum and wreath; in two l. hands, trident and antelope-skin. Kadphises symbol to l. ΟΠÞΟ to right.	XVIII. 4
48	Æ	0·8	130	The same as 47, in middle size.	XVIII. 5
49	Æ	0·7	70	The same as 47, in small size.	XVIII. 6
				BUDDHA.	
				[*Brit. Mus. Cat.*, xxvi. 8.]	
50	AV	0·8	109·2	*Bearded figure of King*, standing, to l., as before. Legend the same. *Buddha*, standing, to front, with nimbus; clad in long robes to mid-leg; carrying alms-bowl in l. hand; r. hand advanced to front, as if in act of blessing. Kadphises symbol. ΒΟΔΔΟ. N.B. This is one of the usual attitudes of the standing figures of Buddha.	XVIII. 7

				[*Ar. Ant.*, xiii. 2.]	
51	Æ	1·0	—	*Bearded figure* of King, and legend, as usual, on copper coins. *Figure of Buddha*, with nimbus, standing, to front; hands raised before breast. Legend beginning from upper left hand, and continuing round on r. hand, in boustrophedon fashion. **CAKA MA.** Kadphises symbol. **OΔYOBON** (to be read from right to left).	XVIII. 8
52	Æ	1·0	—	Similar. [Author.] [*Arian. Ant.*, xiii. 1. Middle size.]	XVIII. 9
53	Æ	0·8	—	*Figure of King*, and legend, as on No. 51. *Buddha*, standing. Greek legend, beginning from left of head downwards, and continuing from Buddha's left foot upwards. **CAKA MANO BOYΔO.** This reading I owe to Mr. Rapson.	XVIII. 10
54	Æ	—	—	Similar. [*Arian. Ant.*, xiii. 3. Small size.] [Author.]	—
55	Æ	0·95	—	*Bearded King*, standing. **ÞAO KANHÞKI.** *Buddha, seated*, with left hand in lap, and right hand raised in the attitude of blessing. **ΔYOBO**, to be read backwards, as, (**CAKO MAN**) **O BOYΔO.**	XVIII. 12
56	Æ	—	—	Similar. [Author, in *Bengal Asiatic Soc. Journal*, vol. 14, pt. 1, p. 430 (Plate 2).] Similar. [Author.]	
57	Æ	0·95	—	*King Kanishka, standing*, armed. **PAO KANHÞKI.** *Buddha, seated*, on pediment, with both hands raised in front	XVIII. 14

DESCRIPTION OF THE PLATES—*continued.*

No.		Inches.	Grains.		Plate.
				of breast. Greek legend incomplete. Reading on left, CAK; and on right, N BOYΔ.	
				HUVISHKA (?).	
58	Æ	0·95	—	Oblong thick coin, taken from a sketch made in 1842. Coin lost. *Obv.*—King riding on an elephant. Legend in very corrupt Greek letters, quite unreadable. *Rev.*—Buddha seated, with left hand on knee, and right hand raised in front of breast, in the attitude of blessing. Legend in large *Gandharian* characters: *Jayatasa* . . . *Hashtrashka—ṣa* . . . In 1842 I read the name as *Hystaspes*, tentatively. But, with a very slight correction, it reads quite clearly, *Huvishka*. As the elephant-rider on the obverse is the commonest type of Huvishka's copper coins, this reading of the name seems very probable. The use of the Gandharian letters in this legend is quite unique.	XVIII. 15

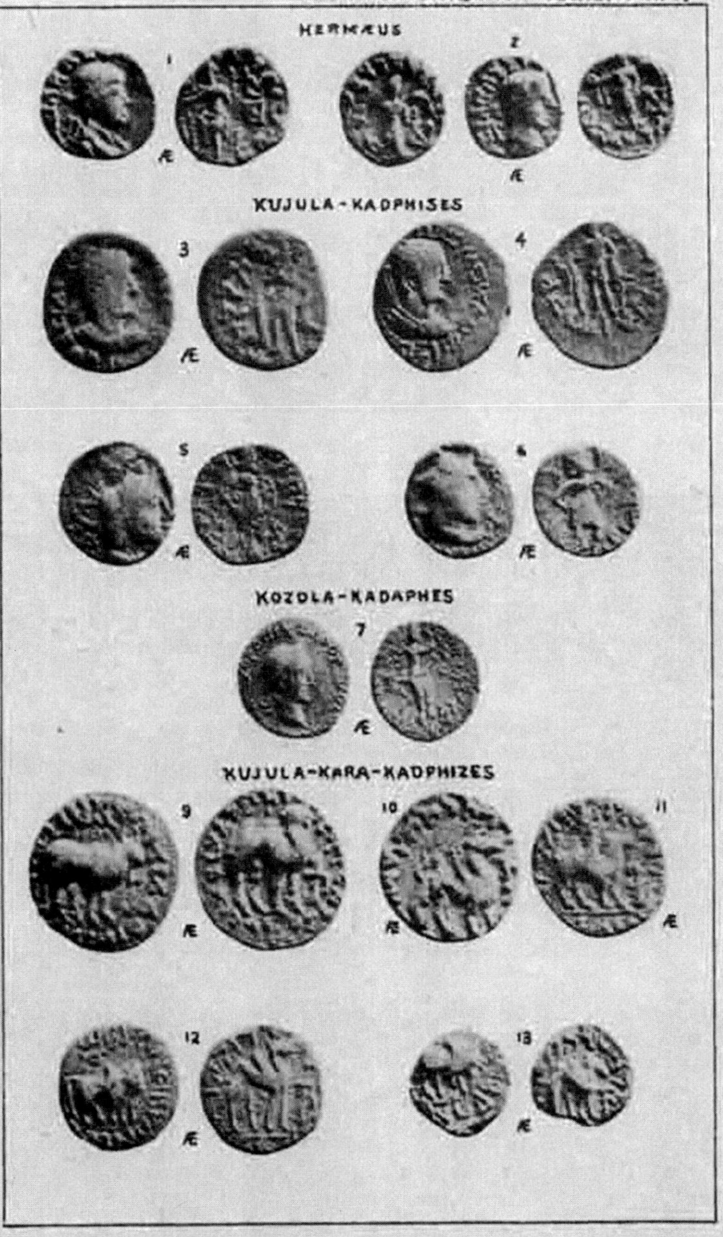

INDO-SCYTHIANS. KUSHANS. PLATE XIV.

Num. Chron. Ser. III. Vol. XII. Pl. V.

INDO-SCYTHIANS. KUSHANS PLATE XV

Num. Chron. Ser. III. Vol XII. Pl. VI.

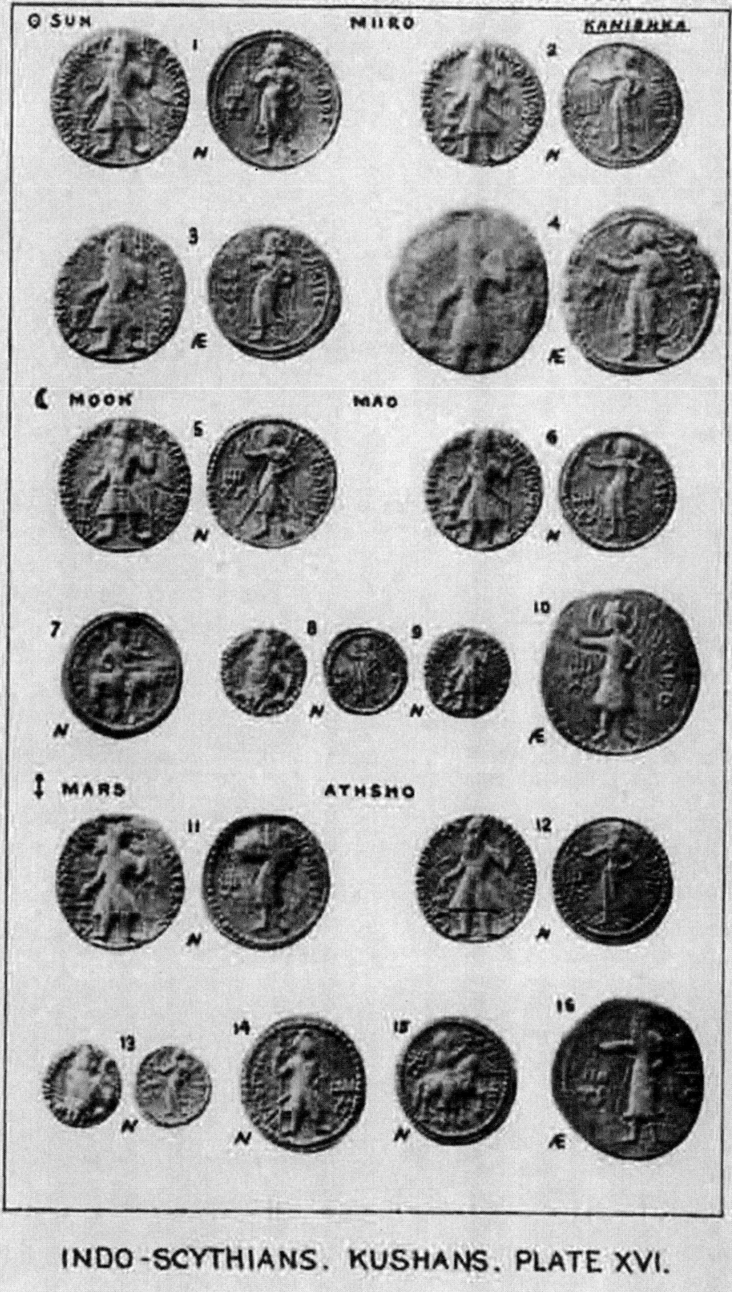

INDO-SCYTHIANS. KUSHANS. PLATE XVI.

Num. Chron. Ser. III. Vol. XII Pl. VII

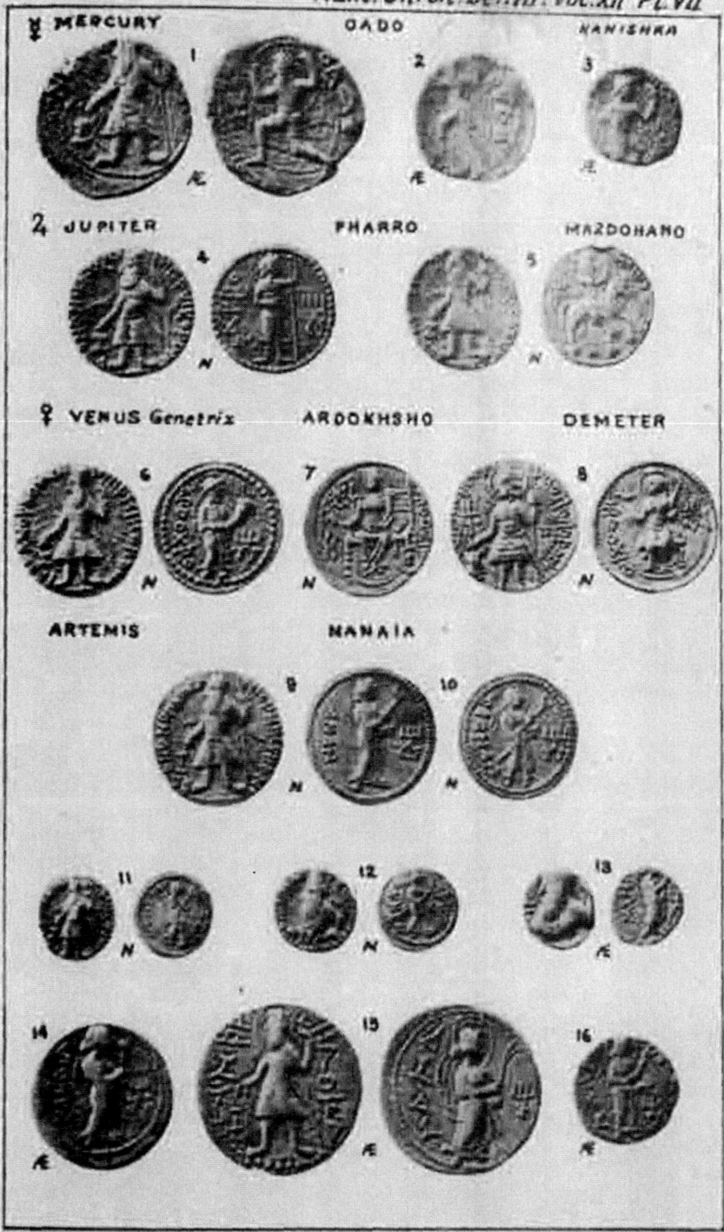

INDO-SCYTHIANS. KUSHANS. PLATE XVII.

Num. Chron. Ser. III. Vol. XII. Pl. VIII.

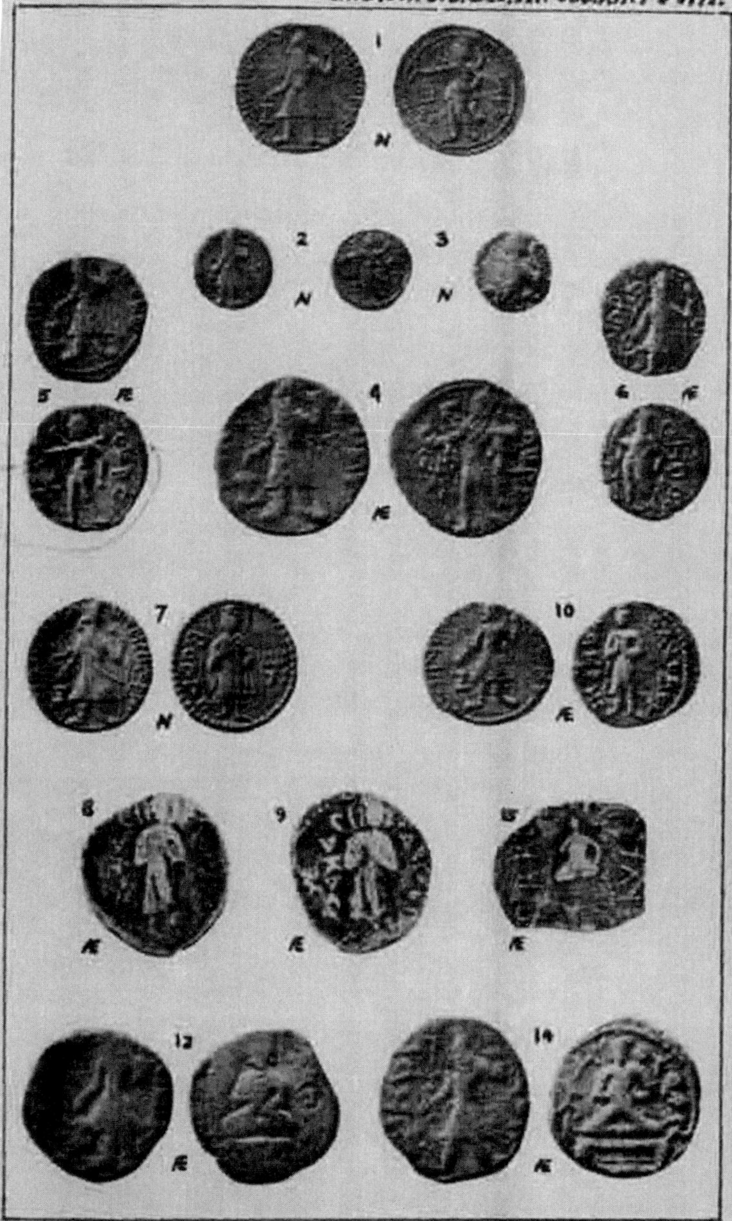

INDO-SCYTHIANS. KUSHANS PLATE XVIII

COINS OF THE KUSHÂNS,

OR

GREAT YUE-TI.

BY

MAJOR-GENERAL SIR A. CUNNINGHAM,

R.E., K.C.I.E., C.S.I.

REPRINTED FROM THE NUMISMATIC CHRONICLE,

VOL. XII., THIRD SERIES, PAGES 98—159.

LONDON:

1892.

COINS OF THE KUSHÂNS, OR GREAT YUE-TI.

(See Plates IX.—XIV.)

Huvishka.

The gold coins of Huvishka offer four different busts of the king, which, to save needless repetition, I will now describe. All four representations are given in Plate XIX., marked A, B, C, D, by which letters they will be quoted.

	Plate.
A—is a very rare large head of the King, covered with a round jewelled helmet with spreading crest, and the ends of the diadem hanging down behind. A large ornamental ear-ring is in the ear, and flames spring from the shoulders. The legend, in badly-formed Greek letters— **ÞAONANO ÞAO OOHÞKI KOÞANO.** *Shaonano Shao Hoveshki Koshano.* "The King of Kings HUVISHKA, the Kushân."	XIX. A.
B.—Half-length figure of the King to left, with *pointed helmet*, thickly jewelled, holding sceptre in left hand, and club in right hand before face. On some coins the sceptre is changed for the *ankus*, or "elephant-goad," which refers to the King as an elephant rider, as seen on his copper coins.	XIX. B.
C.—Half-length figure of the King, with *round jewelled helmet*, to *left*, club and *ankus* in hands.	XIX. C.
D.—The same half-length figure of King to the *right*.	XIX. D.
On some of the coins the King's name is **OͰOHÞKI**, *Huveshki*.	

DESCRIPTION OF THE PLATES.

No.		Inches.	Grains.		Plate.
				[*Brit. Mus. Cat.*, xxvii. 24.]	
1	*N*	0·80	121·1	*Half-length figure* of King, as C. *Sun-god*, **MIIPO**, radiated to right, and *Moon-god*, **MAO**, with crescent behind shoulders. Symbol of Huvishka, No. 58, between the figures. This symbol differs from that of Wema Kadphises and Kanishka by the simple addition of a short horizontal bar between the upper and lower members.	XIX. 1
				[*Brit. Mus. Cat.*, xxviii. 5.]	
2	*N*	0·75	122	*Half-length of King* to l., as C; also to r., as D. *Radiate figure of Sun-god*, **MIIPO**, to right, holding callipers in right hand, sword by his side Huvishka symbol to r.	XIX. 2
3	*N*	0·75	121	*Half-length of King*, as C; name, **OꟷOHÞKI**—*Huveshki.* *Sun-god* radiate to l., sceptre in r. hand, l. hand on hip. Huvishka symbol. **MIꟷPO**. *Brit. Mus. Cat.*, xxviii. 4, Sun-god faces to r.	XIX. 3
				[*Brit. Mus. Cat.*, xxviii. 2.]	
4	*N*	0·75	123·5	*Half-length of King*, as B, but round helmet. *Sun-god radiate* to r. Sceptre, sloping, in r. hand; l. hand resting on sword by side. Huvishka symbol.	XIX. 4

5	AV	0·80	122·5	*Half-length of King*, as B, but round helmet. Sun-god radiate to l., sceptre in l. hand, r. hand extended, sword by side. Huvishka symbol. **MIIPO**.	XIX. 5
6	AV	0·80	122·5	*Head of King*, as A. Legend as on A. *Sun-god radiate* to l., carrying sceptre and sword. Huvishka symbol. **MIIPO**.	XIX. 6
	AV	0·50	—	A quarter-Dinar, of same type.	
7	AV	0·75	123	*Half-length of King*, as B, and also as D. *Sun-god radiate* to l., right hand extended, l. hand on sword. Huvishka symbol. **MIOÞO** (*sic*).	XIX. 7
8	AV	0·85	122·5	*Half-length of King*, as B, with round helmet. *Sun-god radiate* to r., holding sceptre in r. hand, wreath in l. hand. Huvishka symbol. **MIOPO**.	XIX. 8
9	AV	0·70	120	*Half-length of King*, as B, with round helmet. *Sun-god radiate* to l., holding wreath in r. hand, l. hand on sword. Huvishka symbol. **MIOPO**.	XIX. 9
10	AV	0·75	—	Same as No. 9, but Sun-god has a very small wreath. **MIPO**. [*Brit. Mus. Cat.*, xxviii. 1.]	XIX. 10
11	AV	—	—	Same as No. 9, but Sun-god has both sword and sceptre.	—

DESCRIPTION OF THE PLATES—*continued.*

No.		Inches.	Grains.		Plate.
				ARDVIKHSHO.	
				[*Brit. Mus. Cat.*, xxvii. 9.]	
12	*N*	0·80	122·5	*Half-length of King*, as B. *Sun-god radiate* to l., with sword, l. hand on hip, r. hand extended. Huvishka symbol. **ΑΡΔ⋖ΙΧϷΟ** = *Ardvikhsho.*	XIX. 11
				[*Bengal Asiatic Soc. Jour.*, 1845, Pl. II. 8.]	
13	*N*	0·80	125	*Half-length of King* to l., as C. *Sun-god radiate* to l., with r. hand extended, and l. resting on sword. Huvishka symbol. **Ο[?]ΒΟΡ** = *Ombor?* N.B. The second letter is very corrupt.	XIX. 12
14	*N*	0·50	31	Half-length figure of King to l., as C. *Rev.*—**ΜΙΙΡΟ**, as on No. 6.	XIX. 13
				[*Brit. Mus. Cat.*, xxviii. 6.]	
15	*N*	0·55	30	Half-length figure of King to l., as B. Sun-god radiate to l., with r. hand extended, and l. resting on sword. Huvishka symbol. **ΟΝΙΑ**, or **ΑΙΚΙΟ**, read from r. to l.	XIX. 14

The copper coins of Huvishka present three different obverses, as represented in Plate XIX. under the letters E, F, and G.

E.—The Raja is represented riding an elephant, with sceptre in right hand, and an elephant goad (*ankus*) in l. hand. Legend, in corrupt Greek characters—
ÞAONANO ÞAO OOHÞKE KOÞANO. See *Brit. Mus. Cat.*, xxix. 2.

F.—King seated on throne with radiated back, r. leg raised up and resting on seat, l. leg hanging down. *Brit. Mus. Cat.*, xxix. 5, 6.

G.—King seated cross-legged on cushions in Indian fashion. *Brit. Mus. Cat.*, xxix. 4.

DESCRIPTION OF THE PLATES—*continued.*

No.		Inches.	Grains.		Plate.
16	Æ	—	260	*King riding an Elephant* to r., as E. Legend as E. Sun-god radiate, as on copper coins of Kanishka. Huvishka symbol. MIIPO.	—
17	Æ	—	260	*King seated on throne*, with right leg raised, as F. *Sun-god radiate*, as on Kanishka's copper coins. 58 symbol. MIIPO.	—
18	Æ	—	260	*King sitting cross-legged* in Indian fashion, as G. Sun-god radiate, as on Kanishka's copper coins. 58 symbol. MIIPO.	—
				THE MOON. ☾ MAO. [*Brit. Mus. Cat.*, xxvii. 17.]	
19	*N*	0·75	122	*Half-length of King*, as C. Legend as A. *Four-armed Moon-god* seated on throne, to front, with feet on footstool; crescent behind shoulders. In two left hands, sceptre and callipers; in two right hands, indistinct objects. No. 58 symbol. MANAOBA ΓO. [*Brit. Mus. Cat.* xxvii. 23.]	XX. 1
20	*N*	0·80	122	*Half-length of King*, as C. *Moon-god* to right, with crescent behind shoulders. In l. hand, sceptre; in r. hand callipers. No. 58 symbol. MAO to l.	XX. 2

21	AV	0·70	123	*Half-length of King*, as B. *Moon-god* to r., with crescent behind; sceptre in r. hand; sword at side. Huvishka symbol, No. 58 to r. **MAO** to l. [*Brit. Mus. Cat.*, xxvii. 21.]	XX. 3
22	AV	0·75	122	Similar to No. 21, but Moon-god to left, and King figure as C. [*Brit. Mus. Cat.*, xxvii. 19.]	XX. 4
23	AV	0·85	122·6	Half-length of King, as B. Moon-god to l., with crescent; sceptre in l. hand; r. hand extended. Huvishka symbol to l. **MAO** to right.	XX. 5
24	AV	0·80	122	Half-length of King, as B. Moon-god, with crescent, facing l.; r. hand extended; l. hand on hip. Symbol, and **MAO**. [*Brit. Mus. Cat.*, xxvii. 20.]	XX. 6
25	AV	0·50	30·2	Same types as No. 23. [*Brit. Mus. Cat.*, xxvii. 22.]	—
26	AV	0·70	124	*Half-length of King*, as C. *Moon-god with crescent*, sceptre in l. hand, sloping; sword by side. Huvishka symbol. **MAO**.	XX. 7
27	AV	0·80	122	*Half-length of King*, as B. *Moon-god* to l., with crescent; l. hand on sword; r. hand holding wreath. Huvishka symbol to l. **MAO** to r.	XX. 8
28	AV	0·80	122	*Half-length of King*, as B. *Moon-god* to l., with crescent; sceptre and sword; wreath in r. hand. **MAO**.	XX. 9
29	AV	0·50	30·2	A quarter-Dinar, of same type.	
30	Æ	0·80	260	[*Brit. Mus. Cat.*, xxix. 2, 4, 5. Three obverses, E, F, G.]	XX. 10

DESCRIPTION OF THE PLATES—*continued.*

No.		Inches.	Grains.		Plate.
31	Æ	—	—	*Moon-god* to l., with crescent, as on copper coins of Kanishka.	—
32	Æ	—	—	Left hand on sword, right hand extended. Symbol. **MAO**.	—
				MARS. ‡ ATHSHO.	
33	AV	0·80	123	*Half-length of King*, as B. *God of Fire* standing to r., with flames rising from shoulders, and carrying smith's hammer in right hand, and tongs in left hand. Huvishka symbol to right. **ΑΘÞΟ** = *Athsho.* [*Brit. Mus. Cat.*, xxvii. 8.]	XX. 11
34	AV	0·80	121·5	*Half-length of King*, as B. Type of Fire-god, as last. Huvishka symbol. **ΑΘΟÞΟ** = *Athosho.*	XX. 12
				VANINDA. [*Brit. Mus. Cat.*, xxviii. 18.]	
35	AV	0·80	121·5	Half-length of King, as C, with round helmet. Victory, winged, to left, holding out wreath in right hand, and carrying trophy or cornucopiæ in left. Symbol to l. **OANINΔAO**, sometimes **OANINΔA**.	XX. 13
36	AV	0·75	122	Half-length of King, as C.	XX. 14

				Victory, winged, to right, carrying wreath and trophy, or cornucopiæ. Symbol. **OANINΔO.**	
				MAHASENA.	
				[*Brit. Mus. Cat.*, xxvii. 16.]	
37	*N*	0·75	122	Half-length of King, as C. Male deity to front, with nimbus, holding in r. hand a standard surmounted by a bird; his l. hand resting on sword. Huvishka symbol. **MAACHNO.**	XX. 15
				SKANDA-KUMÂRA AND VISÂKHA.	
				[*Brit. Mus. Cat.*, xxviii. 22.]	
38	*N*	0·80	122·5	Half-length of King, as C. Two male figures, standing, to front, both nimbate, and carrying sword and sceptre. Symbol between them. **CKANΔO KOMAPO BIZAΓO.** [*Ariana Ant.*, Pl. xiv. 11. *Brit. Mus. Cat.*, xxviii. 23.]	XX. 16
39	*N*	0·50	—	Same types and legends as No. 38. [*Brit. Mus. Cat.*, xxviii. 24.]	
40	*N*	0·75	122	Half-length of King, as C. Three figures standing side by side in a temple, each nimbate. The middle figure is inscribed, **MAACHNO**; that on the left, **CKANΔO KOMAPO**; and that on the right, **BIZAΓO.**	XX. 17

DESCRIPTION OF THE PLATES—*continued.*

No.		Inches.	Grains.		Plate.
				All these three names belong to Kârttikeya, the Indian god of War. The last name, *Visâkha*, the "Divider," is given to him as *Shan-mukhi*, or the "Six-faced," because he divides the year into two portions of six months each. [*Brit. Mus. Cat.*, xxvii. 1.]	
41	Æ	1·00	—	*King riding Elephant* to r., with sceptre and *ankus.* *Fire-god*, **ΑΘÞΟ** = *Athsho*, as on copper coins of Kanishka. Huvishka symbol.	XX. 18
42	Æ	0·90	—	*King riding Elephant.* Figure of *Fire-god, Athsho*, with hammer and tongs; with mistaken legend of **ΜΑΟ**, the "Moon." N.B. I attribute this blundered inscription to the ignorance of the die-sinker, and not to accident, as I have met with several specimens of **ΑΡΔΟΧÞΟ** with the cornucopiæ duly labelled **ΜΑΟ**. The blundered legends of the obverses also point to the same conclusion of the die-sinker's ignorance of Greek. [See *Prinsep's Essays* i., Pl. XXXII. 13.]	XX. 19
43	Æ	1·00	—	*Rude figure of King* riding Elephant. Jumbled Greek legend, as made out by Prinsep from four specimens: **ΟΙΛΗΩΗ ΟΙΛΡΟΙΛΗΙΛΗΡΟΛΙΩΗ.** Figure of *Fire-god*, as usual, with l. hand on hip, and r. hand extended. Huvishka symbol to l.; to right, **ΟΛΗ**. The obverse legend does not seem to retain any trace of	XX. 20

				the usual ÞAONANO ÞAO, but is more suggestive of BACIΛEWC BAϹIΛEWN.	
				Mercury. Oado. ☿	
				[Very rare; only 2 specimens.]	
44	Æ	0·90	—	*King riding Elephant* to r. Legend obliterated. *Male figure*, running quickly, to l., carrying a light scarf, which forms a canopy overhead. **OAΔO.** [Author, unique.]	XXI. 1
45	AV	0·80	122	Half-length of King, with pointed head-dress, as B. Bearded male figure, standing, to front, beside an ambling horse. Huvishka symbol. **APOOACΠO.** N.B. On the similar type of Kanishka the horse has only one leg raised.	XXI. 2
				Jupiter. Pharro. ♃	
46	AV	0·85	121·5	*Half-length figure of King*, in highly ornamented dress, to l., nimbate and diademed; with sceptre in l. hand, and, in r. hand, standard with bird on top. Legend corrupt. **ÞAONANO ÞAO OOHPKI KOÞANO.** *Male figure*, nimbate, to left; sceptre in l. hand, and holding out in right hand a flat vessel containing "grain seeds." Huvishka symbol. **ΦAPPO.**	XXI. 3

DESCRIPTION OF THE PLATES—*continued.*

No.		Inches.	Grains.		Plate.
				[*Brit. Mus. Cat.*, xxviii. 28.]	
47	AV	0·75	123	*Half-length of King*, as B, with sceptre and club. *Same figure* as on last, but helmet winged. In l. hand, sceptre, and in r. hand a closed bag. Huvishka symbol. ΦΑΡΟ.	XXI. 4
48	AV	0·80	123	*Half-length of King*, with sceptre and bird standard, as on No. 43. *Same figure* as on last, with sceptre in l. hand, and closed bag in r. hand; the whole surrounded by foliage. Symbol. ΦΑΡΡΟ.	XXI. 5
49	AV	0·80	123	*Half-length of King*, as C. *Male figure*, nimbate and diademed, with winged head-dress. In l. hand, sceptre; in r. hand, wreath. Symbol. ΦΑΡΡΟ. [*Brit. Mus. Cat.*, xxviii. 29.]	XXI. 6
50	AV	0·80	123	*Half-length of King*, as B, with round helmet. *Male figure*, nimbate, with winged head-dress; sceptre in r. hand, left on hip, holding *ankus*. Symbol. ΦΑΡΡΟ.	XXI. 7
51	AV	0·75	121	*Half-length of King*, as C. *Male figure* as on last, but turned to left, and without *ankus*. Huvishka symbol. ΦΑΡΡΟ.	XXI. 8
52	AV	0·75	123	*Half-length of King* to l., as C. *Same figure* as No. 51, but facing to r. Winged head-dress.	XXI. 9

				Sceptre in left hand, and flat vessel in right hand. Huvishka symbol. ΦΑΡΡΟ.	
53	AV	0·50	30·5	*Same types* and legends as No. 52. (See *Brit. Mus. Cat.*, xxviii. 30.)	
				[*Brit. Mus. Cat.*, xxviii. 25.]	
54	AV	0·75	122	*Half-length of King*, as C. *Male figure*, with winged head-dress, facing l.; holding flat vessel of *shooting corn* in r. hand, and resting l. hand on hilt of sword. Symbol of Huvishka. ΦΑΡΡΟ. [*Brit. Mus. Cat.*, xxviii. 26.]	XXI. 10
55	AV	0·80	122	*Same types* as No. 54, but the god holds sceptre in l. hand. Winged head-dress strongly marked. Flames or ornaments on shoulders. Symbol. ΦΑΡΡΟ. [*Brit. Mus. Cat.*, xxviii. 27.]	XXI. 11
56	AV	0·80	123·3	*Same types* as Nos. 54 and 55, but deity facing to right, and holding in left hand a flat dish filled high with fruits. Huvishka symbol. ΦΑΡΡΟ. N.B. Mr. P. Gardner describes the *patera* on these coins as containing *fire*, but the same vessel filled with fruits is seen on the coins of ΑΡΔΟΧÞΟ. [*Brit. Mus. Cat.*, xxviii. 31.]	XXI. 12
57	AV	0·80	122·4	*Half-length of King*, as C. *Male deity*, with winged head-dress and nimbus, standing on a small circular frame, his r. hand extended, and l. hand holding some indistinct object. Huvishka symbol. ΦΑΡΡΟ.	XXI. 13

DESCRIPTION OF THE PLATES—*continued.*

No.		Inches.	Grains.		Plate.
				[Rare.]	
58	Æ	0·85	—	King riding Elephant, as Plate XIX., fig. E. Male figure, standing, to left, with sceptre in left hand, and a bag in extended right hand. Huvishka symbol. **OIOAPO.**	XXI. 14
59	Æ	0·85	—	Same types as last. Huvishka symbol. **ΦAPPO.**	
60	—	—	—	*Sardonyx*—Seal. Author. Two figures, male and female, standing facing each other. The *Male* figure, with winged head-dress, holding sceptre in right hand, and flat vessel, with sprouting corn, in left hand—exactly like *Pharro* of the coins. The Female figure, with modius on head, and cornucopiæ in left hand—exactly like the *Ardokhsho* of the coins. A lunar crescent above, and a child behind the male figure. Inscription, in corrupt Greek letters: **XAÞOBAΛANO** = *Khasho Balano.* As the same legend is found on a seal of different type, it must be the owner's name (General Pearse).	XXI. 15
61	—	—	—	*Agate*—Seal. Author. Female figure, standing, with modius on head, and cornucopiæ in left hand. Right hand extended towards a child. Greek legend, in late letters, **ÞOOΓAO** = *Shao Gao*, the "Queen of Earth." *Gao* is one of the Old Avesta names for the Earth, as *Go* is one of the Sanskrit names.	XXI. 16

62	—	—	—	*Chalcedony*—Seal. *King's Antique Gems*, Plate IV., fig. 12. "Sassanian Queen and infant Prince, inscribed '*Armindochti*,'" vol. ii., p. 45. Female, standing to left before child, holding cornucopiæ in right hand. Legend, in Chaldæo-Pahlavi letters, *Armandukhta*, or "Queen Arman," that is, "Queen Earth." The old Avesta name for the Earth-goddess is *Armaiti*, which is the same as the Vedic *Aramati*. *Dukhta*, "Princess or Queen," was the common Sassanian royal title, as in *Arta-dukhta*, the Queen of Artaxerxes I., and also *Puran-dukht* and *Azermi-dukhta*, two of the late reigning Queens. *Zarman-dukht* was one of the Armenian Queens.	XXI. 17
				EARTH. ARDOKHSHO. DEMETER. [*Brit. Mus. Cat.*, xxvii. 12.]	
63	*N*	0·80	120·9	King riding Elephant to right, sceptre in right hand, *ankus* in left hand. ÞAONANO ÞAO OOHÞKO KOÞANO ÞAO. Draped female to right, holding cornucopiæ in both hands. Huvishka symbol. APΔOXÞO. [*Brit. Mus. Cat.*, xxvii. 10.]	XXII. 1
64	*N*	0·80	124·5	Half-length of King, as B. Usual legend. Draped female, standing, to r., holding cornucopiæ with both hands. Huvishka symbol. APΔOXÞO, in straight line.	XXII. 2

DESCRIPTION OF THE PLATES—*continued.*

No.		Inches.	Grains.		Plate.
65	AV	0·80	123	Half-length of King. Draped female, standing, to left, holding cornucopiæ before her. Huvishka symbol. ΑΡΔΟΧÞΟ.	XXII. 8
66	AV	0·80	122·5	Half-length of King. Draped figure of ΑΡΔΟΧÞΟ to left, holding cornucopiæ in l. hand, and wreath in r. hand. Huvishka symbol. [*Brit. Mus. Cat.*, xxvii. 13.]	XXII. 4
67	AV	0·80	122·5	Half-length of King, as C. Draped female to l., holding cornucopiæ in l. hand, and wreath in r. hand. Huvishka symbol. Legend, ΔΟΧÞΟ—perhaps corrupt. [*Brit. Mus. Cat.*, xxvii. 11.]	XXII. 5
68	AV	0·50	30·6	Half-length of King, as C. Figure of ΑΡΔΟΧÞΟ, as on No. 63. [*Prinsep's Essays* ii., Pl. XXXII. 13.]	
69	Æ	0·90	—	King riding Elephant, nimbate, with sceptre and *ankus.* Goddess standing to front, with cornucopiæ in l. hand, and r. hand on hip. Huvishka symbol. ΑΡΔΟΧÞΟ. [*Bengal Asiatic Soc. Jour.*, 1845, Pl. II. 10.]	XXII. 6
70	Æ	0·90	—	King riding Elephant, as on No. 66. Goddess, nimbate, to left, with cornucopiæ in l. hand, and wreath in r. hand.	XXII. 7

No.	Metal	Size	Weight	Description	Plate
				SHAHREWAR, OR AIRAVIRA. *God of Wealth.*	
				[*Brit. Mus. Cat.*, xxviii. 17.]	
71	*N*	0·80	122·5	Half-length figure of King, as B. Male figure to right, fully armed, with helmet, spear, and shield. Huvishka symbol. ÞAO PHOPO, in straight line.	XXII. 8
				[*Brit. Mus. Cat.*, xxviii. 19.]	
72	*N*	0·80	123	Half-length figure of King, as B. Male figure, fully armed, to r., with helmet, spear, and shield. Huvishka symbol. ÞAϷPHOPO, in curved line.	XXII. 9
				[*Brit. Mus. Cat.*, xxviii. 18.]	
73	*N*	0·80	123	Half-length figure of King, as B. Male figure with spear to left, shield on right arm. Huvishka symbol. ÞAOPHOPO.	XXII. 10
				RIDÊ, OR RIDDHI. *Goddess of Fortune.*	
				[*Brit. Mus. Cat.*, xxviii. 20.]	
74	*N*	0·80	122	Half-length figure of King, as B. Armed female, standing, to right, with helmet, spear, and shield. Huvishka symbol. PIΔH. N.B. *Riddhi*, the goddess of Fortune, was the wife of the Indian *Kuvera*, the god of Wealth, who was also named *Airavira.*	XXII. 11

DESCRIPTION OF THE PLATES—*continued.*

No.		Inches.	Grains.	Venus or Artemis. Nanaia. Persephone. [*Brit. Mus. Cat.*, xxviii. 10.]	Plate.
75	AV	0·85	122·6	King sitting cross-legged, helmeted and diademed, holding in left hand standard surmounted by bird; right hand on front of breast. ÞAONANO ÞAO OOHÞKO KOÞANO ÞAO. Draped figure of the goddess NANA to right, with crescent on head, and deer-headed sceptre in right hand, with sword on left side. Huvishka symbol to right. NANA to left.	XXII. 12
76	—	—	—	*Agate*—Seal. Author. The goddess Nanaia, standing, with crescent overhead, and her peculiar symbol in left hand. Legend not read.	XXII. 13
77	AV	0·75	120	Half-length figure of King to left, as B, with usual legend: ÞAONANO ÞAO OONÞKE KOÞANO. Draped figure of the goddess NANO to left, with crescent and nimbus; with deer-headed sceptre in right hand, and left hand on hip. Huvishka symbol. [*Brit. Mus. Cat.*, xxviii. 11.]	XXII. 14
78	AV	0·80	120	Half-length figure of King, with round helmet. The goddess NANO, standing, to the front, with her symbol in right hand, and vessel of shooting corn in left hand.	XXII. 15

				[Author, only 2 coins.]	
79	AV	0·80	121	Half-length of King to left, with sceptre and club, as B. The goddess **NANO**, with nimbus and crescent, to right, as Artemis, holding bow in left hand, and drawing an arrow with right hand from quiver at her back. Huvishka symbol. [*Brit. Mus. Cat.*, xxviii. 7.]	XXII. 16
80	AV	0·75	122·3	Types as No. 79, but legend **ϸ PO**, perhaps **ZHPO** = *Zahra*, the Persian name for Venus. According to Hesychius, *Zarētis* was the Persian *Artemis*.	XXII. 17
81	—	—	—	*Jacinth*--Seal. Author. The goddess *Nanaia*, sitting to front on a recumbent Lion; crescent on her head, and symbol in right hand. General Pearse has a duplicate in red carnelian, with the same inscription. The letters are, apparently, corrupt Greek —**ΦΡΕΙΧΟΔΑΝΟ**. N.B. As the same legend is found on another seal of quite a different subject, it is probably only the name of the owner. [*Author, now in Brit. Mus.*]	XXII. 18
82	AV	0·80	122	Half-length of King, nimbate, to left, as B, holding sceptre in left hand, and club in right hand. The goddess **NANO**, with nimbus, crescent, and sceptre, seated on a Lion, as on the gem No. 78. The Lion's feet are apparently fettered. Huvishka symbol to left.	XXII. 19

DESCRIPTION OF THE PLATES—*continued.*

No.		Inches.	Grains.		Plate.
83	AV	0·75	—	Half-length of King, with nimbus, diadem, and pointed helmet, as B. Goddess, with nimbus and crescent, standing to right, holding patera with shooting corn in left hand, and her peculiar sceptre in right hand. Symbol. ÞAO NANA. On some specimens the legend is NANA ÞAO. [Author.]	XXII. 20
84	AV	0·55	80	Half-length of King to left, as B. The goddess NANA, nimbate, to right, carrying her peculiar symbol with half-deer on top. Huvishka symbol. [*Author, lost by wreck.*]	—
85	Æ	1·10	260	*King, nimbate,* to left, sitting cross-legged on a pile of cushions, his head covered with a round helmet, holding in right hand a club before his face, and resting his left hand on his hip. Legend imperfect. *King Huvishka, kneeling,* with hands joined before the goddess *Nanaia,* who is standing, fully draped and nimbate, with her peculiar symbol in her right hand, and looking towards the King. Behind her is Huvishka's symbol, and her name, NANA. Over the King's head is inscribed, PAΓ PAΓAN, "King of Kings," and round the top of the coin an imperfect legend, beginning with OHOIAΓOΓɯ.	XXII. 21

No.	Metal	Size	Weight	Description	Plate
				[*Lady Sale, lost in Mutiny.*]	
86	Æ	0·15	260	*King*, nimbate and diademed, *riding Elephant*, to r. Legend illegible.	XXII. 22
				King Huvishka kneeling before the goddess *Nana*, as on No. 85. Legends the same, as far as readable.	
				N.B. By a strange fatality both of these important and interesting coins have been lost. Of No. 86, Lady Sale's coin, nothing now remains but a slight tracing of my original drawing. But of No. 85 I still possess a leaden impression, which was recovered uninjured after six months' submersion in the wreck of the steamer *Indus*.	
				The attribution of both coins to Huvishka is rendered quite certain by the types of the King riding and sitting cross-legged, as well as by the peculiar symbol, which is found only upon the coins of this Prince.	
	Æ	—	—	There are copper coins, with the reverse of NANA, of all three types, E, F, G, of obverse, but they are rare, and generally in poor condition. Specimens may be seen in *Ar. Ant.* xiii. 7, and in Author's collection.	
				SATURN. OKSHO. SIVA, or YAMA.	
				[*Brit. Mus., from Author.*]	
87	*N*	0·75	123	*Half-length figure of King* to left, as C. Legend as usual.	XXIII. 1
				Two standing figures, male and female, facing each other. On right, the Indian god Siva, nimbate and four-armed, holding a deer and trident with two left hands, and a	

DESCRIPTION OF THE PLATES—*continued.*

No.		Inches.	Grains.		Plate.
				small drum and water-vessel, with water dropping, in two right hands. On left the goddess Nanaia, diademed and holding her peculiar symbol. Huvishka symbol between them. To right, **OKÞO**; to left, **NANO**. [Brit. Mus., from Author.]	
88	*AV*	0·50	30	Same types and legends as the last. [*Brit. Mus. Cat.*, xxviii. 14.]	XXIII. 2
89	*AV*	0·85	125	*Half-length of King* to left, as C. The Indian god *Siva* to left, nimbate, with four arms and crescent on head, holding in two right hands a small drum and water-vessel with mouth downwards, from which water is dropping, and in two left hands a trident and a Deer or Antelope. Symbol. **OKÞO.** [*Brit. Mus. Cat.*, xxviii. 15.]	XXIII. 3
90	*AV*	0·80	123	Half-length of King to left, with club and bird-sceptre. Three-headed and four-armed figure of *Siva* to front, holding in two right hands drum and water-vessel, and in two left hands trident and club. Crescent surmounting heads. Symbol. **OKÞA.** [*Brit. Mus. Cat.*, xxviii. 16.]	XXIII. 4
91	*AV*	0·75	123	Half-length of King, as B. Four-armed figure of *Siva*, nimbate and naked, except waist-	XXIII. 5

				cloth, with wheel and Deer in two right hands, and drum and trident in two left hands. Huvishka symbol. **OKÞO.** [Unique, with Deer.]	
92	Æ	—	—	King riding Elephant to right. Four-armed figure of *Siva*, holding trident and Deer in two left hands, and small drum and noose in two right hands. Huvishka symbol. **OKÞO.** [Seal. *Mr. Franks.*]	XXIII. 6
93	—	—	—	Standing figure of Siva, with two arms, holding trident and water-vessel. Legend to l., in Gandharian letters, *Sanghavasasa*. Legend to r., in Indian letters, *Si* . . . . —not read.	XXIII. 7
				SARAPO. [*Brit. Mus. Cat.*, xxviii. 21.]	
94	*N*	0·75	123	Half-length of King to left, as C. Usual legend, but name **OΗOHÞKI**, for *Huveshki*. Deity, standing, to left, with short sceptre in left hand, right extended. Huvishka symbol. **CAPAΠO.** [Author.]	XXIII. 8
95	*N*	0·50	80	Half-length figure of King, as on No. 94. The god Sarapis, seated on throne, with modius on head, sceptre in left hand, and noose (?) in right hand. Huvishka symbol. **CAPAΠO.**	XXIII. 9

DESCRIPTION OF THE PLATES—*continued.*

No.		Inches.	Grains.		Plate.
				ÔRON. *Varuna* (?). [*Brit. Mus. Cat.*, xxviii. 32.]	
96	AV	0·80	122	Half-length figure of King to left, as C. Male figure to left, bearded and nimbate, with modius on head, sceptre in left hand, and right hand extended. Huvishka symbol. ꞶPOH. N.B. This figure is almost the same as that of the next, No. 97.	XXIII.10
				OKHSHO. [*Unique*, Author.]	
97	AV	0·80	121·5	Half-length of King, as on the last. Male figure to left, same as No. 96. Huvishka symbol. OXÞO = *okhsho.*	XXIII. 11
				OAKHSHO. [*Unique*, Author.]	
98	AV	0·75	121·5	Half-length of King. Male figure, nimbate, standing, to left, holding upright spear in right hand, and some unknown object in left hand. Huvishka symbol. OAXÞO = *Oakhsho.*	XXIII. 12

No.	Metal	Size	Weight	Description	Plate
				N.B. This figure is quite different from those of **OKÞO** and **OXÞO**, which forbids the possibility of the legend being only a blundered version of the former.	
				HERAKILO. HERAKLES. [*Brit. Mus. Cat.*, xxvii. 15.]	
99	AV	0·80	123	Half-length figure of King, as B. Bearded male figure, standing, naked, to front; in right hand, a club; in left hand, an apple, with lion's skin hanging over arm. Huvishka symbol. **HPAKIΛO**. [Author, rare.]	XXIII. 13
100	Æ	1·00	189	King riding Elephant to right. Figure of Herakles, with club in right hand, as on 99. Legend, **HPAKIΛO**, imperfect. [Author, rare.]	XXIII. 14
101	Æ	1·00	182	Both types same as 100, but legend, **OKÞO**, corrupt.	XXIII. 15
102	Æ	1·00	250	King riding Elephant, as on 100. Herakles, standing, to front, with club in r. hand resting on shoulder. Huvishka symbol. **HPAKIΛO**.	XXIII. 16
103	Æ	1·00	170	King riding Elephant. Herakles to front, crowning himself with r. hand, and club in l. hand resting on shoulder. Lion's skin over arm. **HPAKIΛO**.	XXIII. 17

DESCRIPTION OF THE PLATES—*continued.*

No.		Inches.	Grains.		Plate.
				VASU-DEVA. [Author, unique.]	
1	Æ	0·60	54·5	King's name, written perpendicularly, VASU, in Indian letters, as seen also on the gold coin No. 12. The peculiar monograph, or symbol of *Vasu Deva*, which is found on all his coins.	XXIV. 1
				[*Brit. Mus. Cat.*, xxix. 8.]	
2	*N*	0·85	122·5	King, standing, to left, diademed and nimbate, dressed in long tunic, trousers, and Tartar boots, conical helmet; sword girt on left side, sceptre (or *hasta pura*) in left hand, and his right hand pointed downwards towards a low altar. Legend, in Greek letters, ÞAONANO ÞAO BAZO ΔHO KOÞANO. Fully draped figure of the goddess *Nanaia*, with nimbus and crescent; holding her peculiar sceptre in right hand, and a flat dish in left hand. Symbol of Vasu Deva, No. 59, to right, and NANA to left.	XXIV. 2

				[Author.]	
3	AV	0·80	123	King, standing, to left, as on No. 2. Legend, incomplete from want of room, ÞAONANO ÞAO BAZOΔHO K. The Brit. Mus. specimen has the legend complete. The Indian god *Siva*, as *Yama*, with three faces, standing, to front, with trident in left hand, and noose in right hand. The Vasu Deva symbol to left, and legend, OÞHO, to right, perhaps only a blunder for OKÞO, which is the legend on a fine specimen belonging to Mr. Theobald. Two Brit. Mus. specimens read *oshko* and *oksho*. A fifth specimen appears to read OԿ3O = *okzo*. N.B. As holder of the noose, *pasa*, Siva as Yama is called *Pâşi* and *Pâşapati*. He is thus represented in the Temple of *Dharma Raja* (or *Yama*) in the fort of Kangra. [*Brit. Mus. Cat.*, xxix. 11.]	XXIV. 3
4	AV	0·50	31	Same types and legends as on No. 3. A quarter-Dinar. [Author. Quarter-Dinar.]	XXIV. 4
5	AV	0·55	26·5	King, standing, to left, as on Nos. 2 and 3, with trident in field to left over the altar. Greek legend as on No. 2. The God *Siva*, with one head and two arms, holding trident in left hand, and noose in right hand. Behind is the Bull *Nandi*. Vasu Deva symbol, No. 59, to left, and legend to right, OKÞO.	XXIV. 5

Before describing the different figures of *Siva* on the reverses of Vasu Deva's money, it will be convenient to give a short account of the variant obverses, which for the sake of brevity may be afterwards referred to as A, B, C, D, E, and F.

	Plate.
Fig. A.—represents the Raja, nimbate, standing to the left, holding an erect sceptre (or *hasta pura*) in his left hand, and pointing downwards with his right hand towards a small altar. His dress is a long tunic, with trousers, and Tartar boots. He wears a conical helmet, and a sword at his left side. Behind his head there is a small flower on an upright stalk. Legend, in corrupt Greek letters, **ÞAONANO ÞAO BAZO ΔHO KOÞANO.**	XXIV. A
Fig. B.—The Raja, as on A, with the addition of a trident over the altar. Legend as on A.	XXIV. B
Fig. C.—The Raja as on A. Legend corrupt, reading simply, **ÞAONANO ÞAO BAZ ΔHO**, with the shortened name of *Baz-Deo*, and omitting the tribal name of *Koshano*.	XXIV. C
Fig. D.—The Raja as on A. The legend very corrupt, the name being spelt **AAZO AHO**, and the tribal name omitted.	XXIV. D
Fig. E.—The Raja as on A, with the addition of a trident to the left, and a symbol like the united Buddhist *Tri-ratna* and *Dharma-Chakra* on the right. Legend as on A.	XXIV. E
Fig. F.—The Raja as on A, but the execution rough and rude. Trident to left, and Buddhist symbol to right. Three dots overhead, three dots between feet, and six dots to right. Legend very corrupt, all the vowels being simply **O**.	XXIV. F

There are other varieties of these obverses. Some have a *Swastika* between the feet, and one has a small circle under the left arm. The groups of dots also differ—some having five, six, seven, or eight pellets.

DESCRIPTION OF THE PLATES—*continued.*

No.		Inches.	Grains.		Plate.
				[Very common.]	
6	AV	0·80	124·5	King, standing, as on A, B, C, D, E, F, with various legends, as just described. The Indian god *Siva*, as *Yama*, with one head and two arms, standing to left, with trident in left hand and noose in right hand. The god wears only the Indian *dhoti*. Behind is the bull *Nandi*, to the left the Vasu Deva symbol, and to the right **OKÞO**. [Author.]	XXIV. 6
7	AV	0·75	123	King, standing to left, as on A. Same legend. The Indian god *Siva*, standing to front, with three heads and two arms, holding trident and noose. The bull *Nandi* behind. Vasu Deva symbol to right, and legend **OKÞO** to lower left hand. [Author.]	XXIV. 7
8	AV	0·80	122	King, standing to left, as Fig. A. Legend the same. The Indian god *Siva*, standing to front, with three heads and two arms, as on No. 7. The bull *Nandi* behind, with head turned round. Vasu Deva symbol. Legend, **OKÞO**. [Author.]	XXIV. 8
9	AV	0·80	123·5	King, standing to front, as Fig. A. Legend the same.	XXIV. 9

DESCRIPTION OF THE PLATES—*continued.*

No.		Inches.	Grains.		Plate.
				The Indian god Siva, with three heads and four arms, standing to front. In two right hands, noose and water-vessel; in two left hands, trident and tiger's skin. The bull *Nandi* behind, with bell. Symbol No. 59. Legend, **OKÞO**. [*Ar. Ant.*, xiv. 22.]	
10	Æ	0·95	130	King, standing, as on the gold coins. Same legend. The god **OKÞO**, standing in front of the bull *Nandi*. [Author.]	XXIV. 10
11	Æ	0·70	—	Same types as No. 10, but Greek legend **ÞAO BAZO ΔHO**. [*Ar. Ant.*, xiv. 21.]	XXIV. 11
12	AV	0·75	—	King, standing, as on the gold coins. Same legend. The name of *Vasu* in field to right in Indian letters; the letter *g* under l. arm, and *bh* under r. hand. The goddess **APΔOXÞO** (Lakshmi), seated, with cornucopiæ. Symbol of Vasu Deva in field. [*Ar. Ant.*, xiv. 21.]	XXIV. 12
13	Æ	0·80	120	Same types as the gold coin No. 12. Obverse legend generally corrupt. Reverse legend, **APΔOXÞO**.	XXIV. 13

NOTES ON THE NAMES OF THE DEITIES.

I have reserved my explanations of the names of the Kushân deities to the last. I am particularly anxious that they may be accepted simply as attempts, more or less plausible, to ascertain the nature and functions of the numerous gods and goddesses whose names are found upon the coins of the two great Kushân kings, Kanishka and Huvishka.

The founder of the dynasty, *Kujula Kadphizes*, presents only the figure of the Scythian god of Death, who was identified with the Greek Herakles with his club. But as Kujula calls himself *Sacha-dharma-ṭhida*, or the "upholder of the true Dharma," it would seem that he had studied, and perhaps partially adopted, Buddhism.

His son, *Hima Kadphises*, presents only the figure of the Indian *Siva* or *Yama* with his "noose," who, as I conclude, was identified with *Gebeleizes* or *Sapaleizes*, the Scythian Herakles, or god of Death.

With his successors, Kanishka and Huvishka, we get an extensive Pantheon of Persian and Indian deities, which includes the sun and moon, and the five planets, besides the elements and numerous attributes. Thus the planet Mars is the element of fire, and also the god of War, with his attribute the goddess of Victory. So also the Earth, with her mines of metals, became the mother of the god of Wealth and of the goddess of Fortune. Likewise the deity of the lower world became the Regent of Water, and the god as well as the judge of the dead.

Some of my identifications seem to offer some hitherto unsuspected affinities with the Western Mythologies. Thus *Vaisravana*, or *Wessawana*, the father of *Kuvera*, may be *Iasiôn*, the father of *Ploutos*. Kuvera, the god of Wealth, was also called *Paulastya*, after his grandfather. *Verethraghna*, the god of War, may be Jupiter *Feretrius*. I suspect also that the name of the Indian *Maruts*, the twin brothers, is preserved in *Birutis* in the Troad, and in *Bruttium* in S. Italy, as both present the Dioskuri on their coins. *Birut* is only a slightly different form of *Marut*.

I.—The Sun. ⊙

1. Helios.—2. Miiro.—3. Asha-vikhsho.—4. Aino.
5. Ombor ?

1. Helios. This Greek name of the Sun is found only on the coins of Kanishka, both in gold and copper, which give the king's titles in the Greek form of ΒΑCΙΛΕΥC ΒΑCΙΛΕωΝ. The figure, with a rayed halo round the head, faces the left, with the right hand extended as if pointing to some object, and the left hand resting on the hip.

2. Miiro. This figure is an exact copy of *Helios*. On the coins of Huvishka the name is often spelt Mioro, and on a single specimen I find Miuro; but I have not seen any coin with *Mithra*. On these coins the titles are given in the native form of *Shaonan-shao*, with the tribal name of *Koshano* added. On a few specimens of Huvishka the figure holds out a wreath, and on one coin a pair of callipers, which I take to represent the Sun as a "measurer of time" by *years*. The same type occurs with the moon-god *Mao*, who was also a "measurer of time" by *months*.

The Greeks generally used the form of *Mithra*, as in the names of *Mithridates*, *Mithro-barzanes*, *Mithraustes*, *Mithræus*, *Aspa-mithres*, and *Mithrakenes*. But the true Persian form of *Mihr* is also found in *Meranes* and *Merdasas*, and better still in *Meherdates*.

3. ASHA-VIKHSHO is the usual figure of *Miiro* with the rayed halo. The name has been compared by Dr. Stein with that of the Mazdean Amshaspand, *Asha-vahishta,* which means literally "best goodness," and is supposed to refer to the brilliant light of the sun, as he is invoked to keep up the "splendour of light." I look upon him as simply an impersonation of "*Sunlight.*" Preferentially I read the fourth letter of the name as a digamma, thus making *Asha-vikhsho,* which I would refer to as *vîksha* = "sight" or "seeing."

4. AINO. The reading of this name is not certain, as the first letter is corrupt. But as it is so read by all, the name may perhaps be referred to *Ahan,* the "Day," as the sun is popularly known as the "Day-lord," *Aharpati,* and as *Divâkara,* the "Day-maker."

5. OMBOR (?) In this name the second letter is corrupt. The coin is very rare, as I have seen only one specimen of the type, of which I possess a cast.

II.—THE MOON. ☾

1. SALENE.—2. MAO.—3. MANAO-BAGO.

1. *Salênê.* The figure of *Salene* is exactly repeated in the representation of *Mao;* but the former coin gives the titles of the king in Greek, as **BACIΛЄYC BACIΛEωN,** while the latter gives them in the native language as *Shaonano Shao.* The figure is represented exactly in the same attitude as that of the sun-god, but instead of a rayed halo, it has a lunar crescent behind the shoulders.

2. *Mao.* In ancient Persia, as well as in India, the "Moon" was a male deity. *Mao* is the Zend form of the

ancient Persian *mâh*. In addition to a sword the moon-god nearly always carries a sceptre.

Another figure of the moon-god, with the same name of *Mao*, seems to be simply a repetition of the sun-god as a "measurer of time," with a pair of callipers in the extended right hand. The moon has been the recognised measure for months from time immemorial, and hence the word *mâh* signifies both moon and month in Persian. In Sanskrit the term is *mâs* for both. The Roman poet Catullus also calls Diana, "Goddess measuring the months" (xxxiv. *in Dianam*)—

> "Tu, cursu, Dea, menstruo
> Metiens iter annuum."

3. *Manao-bago* is a third representation of the moon-god, who is here undoubtedly the "god of measure," as declared by his name, *mâna* being "measure," and *baga* being "God," in ancient Persia. The figure, which is four-armed, is represented sitting on a throne with a lunar crescent behind his shoulders. One hand holds out a pair of callipers, a second grasps a sceptre, a third rests on the hip, while a fourth hand holds an indistinct object in the shape of a circle, surrounded by twelve dots which, by their number, may be supposed to typify the twelve months of the year, as well as the twelve signs of the zodiac. As the Indian moon-god, Soma, is usually represented with four arms, and a lunar crescent behind the shoulders, I infer that the figure of *Manao-bago* must be of Indian origin.

The copper coins offer only the common standing figure with the lunar crescent behind the shoulders, and a sceptre in the left hand. The right hand is simply extended to the front.

There are several varieties of the standing figure of *Mao* on the gold coins. On some he carries a sword only, on some a sceptre only, whilst on others he carries both sceptre and sword. On a fourth variety the right hand holds out a wreath.

The personal names connected with the moon are not very numerous. From the shorter form *Mao* (Persian *Mah*) were formed *Madates* and *Masistes*, besides *Ha-Ma-datha*, the father of Haman. From the longer name of *Manao* were probably formed *Monobatus* and *Monœses*.

III.—Mars. ♂

1. Hephaistos.—2. Athsho.—3. Loë.—4. Maaseno.
5. Skando-Komaro.—6. Bizago.—7. Orlagno.—8. Oaninda.

Mars is represented under a greater variety of names than any other of the planetary deities.

1. Hephaistos. As the god of "Fire" his figure was probably borrowed from a Greek source. He is represented with a hammer and a pair of tongs, with flames springing from his shoulders. The same figure is repeated with the name of **AΘÞO**, or *Athsho*, for the old Iranian *Ader* or *Azer*="Fire"—or in modern Persian *âtash*. A few coins give **AΘOÞO**, or *Athasha*, which is clearly intended for *Atash*.

2. Athsho, or Athro, is a bearded figure, holding out a wreath in the right hand, and resting the left hand on the hip or on the hilt of his sword, in the same pose as the figures of *Miiro* and *Mao*. I take this figure to represent the Element of *Fire* (*Brit. Mus. Cat.* xxvi. 4). There are many personal names formed with the old Iranian *Atur* or *Ader* = *Fire*—as *Atradates*, *Atropates*, *Atrines*, *Artabazus*, *Artabanus*, *Artaphernes*, *Artabandes*, *Artagerses*, *Artabaris*,

Artembares, *Artazostra*, &c. But I cannot find a single name formed with the modern Persian *Atash*.

3. Loë. A similar figure on a copper coin is labelled ΛΟΗ. Only four coins with this legend have yet been discovered. From the obverse type of the king riding an elephant the coin might be assigned to Huvishka; but the corrupt Greek legend is quite unintelligible. I possess one of the four specimens; the coins were originally published by Prinsep (see E. Thomas's *Prinsep*, vol. i., Pl. XXII., Fig. 12). The short legend was the same on all. I think the word must certainly refer to *fire* or *heat*. In India the extreme heat of the summer air is called *luh*; and in England we have *glow* and *glow-worm*, as well as *luke-warm*; besides *lew* and *lowe* in *lowe-bell*, a bell with a light placed inside, which was used for fishing at night. I suspect that the word may be connected with the Scythian *Roï* or *Rhoi*, which appears in the name of *Rhoisakes*, the "friend of *Rhoï*." *Rheo-mithres* would have the same meaning; but of *Rhoi-metalkes* and *Rhoi-skuporis*, I cannot even guess the meaning. I find *Rhôsakis* mentioned as a noble Persian under Ochus, who was descended from one of the seven conspirators. There was also a Persian *Rhoisakus* at the battle of the Granicus. The word *Loë* must also be connected with the old Greek Λύκη and the Sanskrit *Luk*, both signifying "light," and also with the Latin *lux* and *luces*. *Lohita* and *Rohita* are also used to denote the *red* colour of fire. Hence *Agra*, or "fire," is called *Rohitâswa* and *Lohitâswa*, or the "red steed" of Mars. The name was common in Persia as *Rhodaspes*. Iron, the metal now dedicated to Mars, is called *Loha*; but as iron is not red, I conclude that *bronze* was the original metal which was considered emblematic of fire, its green and red tints resembling those of the

planet. *Ayas* also is another name for *iron*, but as may be inferred from the Latin *æs*, it must have been originally given to bronze. The full name of iron would appear to have been *Kâlâyas*, or "black bronze," to distinguish it from the well-known *ayas* or *æs*.

4. MAASENO.

5. SKANDO-KUMARO.

6. BIZAGO.

All these three names are genuine titles of the Indian god of War, who is also known as *Kârtikeya*.

Mahâsena simply means a "general," or "commander of an army."

Skanda-Kumâra is the "Prince Skanda." Skanda is also used alone.

Visâkha is the name of one of the two nymphs, or personified asterisms, by whom the infant Skanda-Kumâra was suckled.

In all these representations the god of War carries a sword and a spear. From the latter weapon he derives his Indian names of *Sakti-dhara* and *Sakti-pâni*, or "spear-holder," and "spear in hand," just as the Roman Mars was called *Quirinus* from carrying a *quiris*, or "spear." All of the three figures are standing to the front, as if on show. The Quirinal hill must have been named after the god *Quirinus* who carried the *quiris*, and not the god after the hill, as usually stated.

7. ORLAGNO, or ORTHAGNES. This name has been compared by Benfey with *Verethragna*, the Zoroastrian War-god. The Indian form of the name is *Vritrahan*, an abbreviation of *Vritraghan*, which was a personification of Indra as the "cloud-striker," or "foe-killer." The form of *ghan* is preserved in *Amitra-ghâta*, the Greek *Amitrochades*, and it is still used in the well-known name of the

Kachwâha Rajputs as *Kachhapa-ghâta*, or "tortoise-killers." When Indra gave place to Ormazd, the warrior *Vritraghan* was made into a War-god, as *Verethragna*, which has been gradually contracted to *Varahrân* and *Bahrâm*. It is possible that the name is preserved in the Roman Jupiter *Feretrius*.

The name of *Orlagno* on the Kushân coins I would correct to *Ordagno*, on authority of the Saka names of *Orthagnes* and *Orthanes*, as well as on that of its well-ascertained identification with Verethraghna.

On the gold coins of Kanishka the god is represented armed with sword and spear, and wearing a helmet crowned by a bird with expanded wings, which Dr. Stein has identified with the bird *Vâraghna*. In the Bahrâm-Yasht the god Verethraghna is represented as "flying with great flapping wings, the swiftest of the flying."[1] The flapping wings of the bird are seen on the helmet of *Ordagno* on the coins.

As noticed above, I think it probable that the god of Victory, Verethraghna, may be identified with the Roman Jupiter Feretrius, in whose temple all *spolia opima* were dedicated. This dedication alone would seem to indicate that Feretrius was a "War-god." If this identification be correct, then the Roman name must be earlier than the separation of the Eastern and Western Aryas, and the consequent degradation of Indra. Could the Sabine word *quiris*, "a spear," have any connexion with the common Indian word *chărri*, a "stick or lance"? The Sabine words *hirpus*, a "wolf," and *teba*, a "hill," would seem to countenance an Eastern connexion.

8. *Oaninda*, or *Vaninda*, is a winged female figure

---

[1] Spiegel, 103.

carrying a trophy-stand in her left hand, and holding out a wreath in her right hand. As the figure of *Vaninda* is a very close copy of the Greek Nikê, Dr. Stein has identified her with the female genius *Vananiti uparatât*, or "victorious superiority," who is always joined with *Verethraghna* in the invocations of the Avesta. According to Haug, p. 217, the *Vanant Yasht* is "a very short prayer addressed to the star *Vanant*, by which the Dasturs understand the Milky Way."

IV.—Mercury. ☿

1. Oado or Vado.—2. Arvoaspo.

Oado, or *Vado*. The old Persian name for the "wind" was *bâd*, Sanskrit *vât*, or as rendered on the coins in Greek ΟΑΔΟ = *Vado*. The element is appropriately represented as a running figure with distended robes. The term *bâd* is often used in the composition of Persian names, as *Badizes* and *Badres*; and, perhaps, also in *Vasakes* and *Vagises*, with the shorter form of *Wâh*, the "wind."

By the ancient Persians the planet Mercury was called *Tigra* or *Tîr*, the "arrow," on account of the rapidity of its motion. The river *Tigris* was so called for the same reason. *Tigranes* preserves the full name of the planet, and so also does *Tigra-mitra*, which is found in the Wardak Inscription. The shorter form of *Tir* is found in *Tiridates* and *Tiribazus*; the former meaning "given by Mercury," and the latter the "worshipper of Mercury." It occurs also in *Teri-teukhmes*, or *Tiri-takhma*, "strong as Mercury."

One of the commonest old names for the planet, both in India and in Persia, was *Vayu*, and this, I believe, is found in 'Οιόβαζος, or *Vayu-Bazu*, the worshipper of *Vayu*, a Persian mentioned by Herodotus, ix. 115, as having been sacrificed by the Apsinthians to their god Pleistôrus.

2. *Arvoaspo*, or *Arhoaspo.* This name is found only on a single specimen of Huvishka, although it is not uncommon on the coins of Kanishka. In both cases it is corruptly spelt as ΔΡΟΟΑCΠΟ, as the initial should clearly be Α, making ΑΡΟΟΑCΠΟ. I have already noticed a similar misspelling in ΟΡΛΑΓΝΟ, for ΟΡΔΑΓΝΟ, the ΟΡΘΑΓΝΗC of the Saka series of kings. Dr. Stein is willing to accept the name as it stands for *Loharâsp;* but I prefer to consider it as a simple mistake.

The type shows a bearded male figure standing beside a bridled horse, with two legs on the same side raised as if ambling. There are only two bearded figures in the whole series of these Kushân coins, namely, ΑΘÞΟ, *Athsho*, the God of *Fire*, and ΟΑΔΟ, *Vado* or *Bâd*, the God of *Air* or Wind. Both *Arvva* and *Arha* are Sanskrit names of Indra, and joined to *Aspa* would mean "Indra's steed," that is the wind which brings the rain. A different form of the name, known in Persia, was *Prexaspes*, or *Prishadaswa*, the "Rain Steed"; but the commonest descriptive name for the wind was *Gandha-vâha*, or the "Scent-wafter," which is found on the coins in the form of *Ganda-phara*, or *Gondophares*, or *Undopharres.* The symbol of Mercury, ☿, is placed on many of the coins of this king.

The general of Khusru II, who made his master a prisoner, is named *Gurdanaspes* by the Emperor Heraclius, and *Gundabunas* by Theophanes. The first name may perhaps be corrected to *Gundanaspes*=*Gandhanaswa*, the "Scent Steed," and the latter to *Gundabares*, the "Scent-bearer."

V.—JUPITER. ♃

1. MAZDOHANO.—2. PHARRO.

In ancient India, as well as in ancient Persia, *Heaven* and *Earth* were the acknowledged parents of all creation. The *Rain* showers of the sky fertilised the earth, hence Heaven was called *Parjanya*, or the "Rain-god," or simply *Parjan*, the "Impregnator." Strabo (vv. 1—69) specially mentions that the Indians worshipped *Zeus Ombrios*, that is, *Indra*, the Rain-giver. Similarly, in Persia, Ormazd himself was the creator,[2] who, as *Bârân*, the giver of Rain, fertilised the earth. But as the old Iranians had dethroned Indra, and adopted *Ahuramazda* or *Ormazd* as the author of creation, we ought to find the name of *Ormazd* himself on the Zoroastrian coinage, and that of *Parjanya* on the Indian coinage of the Indo-Scythians. We do in fact find the names of **MAZΔOOANO** and of **ΦAPPO** on the coins of Kanishka, and of **ΦAPPO** on the coins of Huvishka.

1. MAZDOHANO. I take this name to be the same as the Avesta *Mazdaonho*, the plural of *Mazdao*. Ormazd himself is simply the Ahura, who is called *Mazdao*, the author of the Mazdean religion. The two primeval principles of good and evil were united in *Ahuramazda* himself, the beneficent spirit being called *Spenta-Mainyus*, and the hurtful spirit *Angro-Mainyus*.[3] In the Yasna (West, 189) these two spirits are called the "two creators," but they were not separate beings (p. 304), but spirits "inherent in his own nature." Hence I infer that the two-

---

[2] His nineteenth name was the "Creator."—Darmesteter, ii. 25.

[3] West's *Haug*, p. 301.

headed horse, which is ridden by *Mazdaonho*, may be intended to typify the two spirits of good and evil, which were inherent in the one supreme creator, Ormazd.[4] As the lord of all, the Armenians called the planet Jupiter by his name. He is also said to be the father of the *Amesha-Spentas*, and of the powerful goddess *Ashi-Vanguhi*, whose mother was *Spenta-Armaiti*, or the "Earth."

The name of the great *Ahura* is found in *Orobazus*, *Orophernes*, *Orodes*, and *Hurodes*. The name of Ormazd is found in *Ormisdates*, *Oromasdes*, and *Hormisdas*. *Baga*, or "the god," is also used for Ormazd, as in *Bagophanes*, *Bagopates*, *Bagasakes*, &c.

2. PHARRO. Throughout the ancient world there appears to have been a general belief that the great god of the firmament of Heaven was the author of all being, and that the Earth was the mother. In India we have this belief very clearly announced in the Vedas, with reference to *Parjanya*. Three hymns are addressed to him. In *Rig Veda*, vii. 101—6, it is said, "He (Parjanya) rules as god over the whole world, he is the life of all that moves and rests." Again in *Rig Veda*, v. 83, it is said, "Praise *Parjanya*, worship him with veneration, for he, the roaring Bull, *scattering drops*, gives seed fruit to plants." In the *Atharva Veda*, xii. 1—12, its full belief is announced, "The Earth is the *mother*, and I am the son of the Earth; *Parjanya* is the Father."[5]

From Herodotus, iv. 59, we learn that the Scythians made the *Earth* the wife of *Zeus*. So also at the present day the Russian Slâvs worship *Parûn*, the great god, the husband of mother Earth.

---

[4] Dr. West suggests *Mazdovano* = "Mazda-uniting," *i.e.*—the two powers.

[5] Max Müller, 180, 183, 185.

In Greece the feeling was universal. In Athens newly married couples sacrificed to "Heaven and Earth," whose junction was called γάμος, or "wedding." In the Eleusinian mysteries the Heaven and Earth were called by mystic names, he as Ὕης, or the "Rain-god," and she as Τοκυῖα, or the mother "who brings forth." The same belief is frequently alluded to by the poets, as by Æschylus (quoted by Athenæus, xiii. 73):

> "Then, too, the *Earth* feels lone, and longs for wedlock,
> And *Rain*, descending from the amorous air,
> Impregnates his de iring mate ; and she
> Brings forth delicious food for mortal men—
> Herds of fat sheep, and corn."

So also Euripides speaks of Γαῖα μεγίστη, καὶ Διὸς Ἀιθὴρ,

> "O heavenly *Aether*, mighty *Earth*,
> *He*, that to gods and men gave birth,
> *She*, teeming mother, on whose breast
> Heaven's fertile rain-showers fall,
> From whence all living things spring forth,
> Both flower and fruit, both man and beast,
> Thee do mankind justly call
> Mother of all."

The same feeling about *Father Heaven* and *Mother Earth* was also common to the Roman poets, as in Lucretius, *de Rerum Nat.* i. 151:

> "Postremo peremit imbres ubi eos *Pater Aether*
> In gremium *Matris Terrai* præcipitavit."

And also in Virgil, *Georgic*, ii. 325:

> "Tum *pater* omnipotens fæcundis imbribus *Aether*
> Conjugis in gremium lætæ descendit, et omnes
> Magnus alit."

> "In fruitful showers Almighty Father Heaven
> Falls on the bosom of his happy spouse."

Having shown the wide extent of this belief in the ancient world, it now remains to prove that the god *Pharro* of the coins is identical with the "Rain-god" *Parjanya* of the Aryan peoples. I find no trace of the *name* in the Zoroastrian books. But though Indra was supplanted by Ahuramazda amongst the Iranians, yet the functions of the god of the firmament still remained, and Ormazd, the creator of the material world, possessed all the powers of Indra. As the bestower of all good things, he was the giver of the Rain that fertilised the Earth. It was by the agency of his son *Tishtrya* (the bright star Sirius) that he bestowed the Rains.[6] The Tir-yasht is dedicated to the propitiation of *Tishtrya,* the giver of Rain. At the present day the Heaven is called *Bârân,* the "fertiliser," from *bârish*=rain.

Practically the name of *Parjanya* would have been shortened to *Parjan,* just as *Aranya* and *Hiranya* became *Aran* and *Hïran.* In this slightly altered form of *Parjan* I think that I can recognise the god of Rain in the name of *Parshan-datha,* the son of Haman, the *Pharsannes* of the Septuagint, and the Varaz-tad or *Pharas-dates* of the Armenians. Here we see that the *j* of Sanskrit becomes *sh* in Hebrew, *s* in Persian, and *z* in Armenian. In Pharas-menes the *s* is still preserved. But just as *cursus* became *currus,* so I infer that *Pharsa* became *Pharra,* with the final *n* of *parjan* retained as in *Pharan-dates, Pharna-bazus, Pharna-zathres, Pherendostas,* &c.

There are several myths connected with the union of Heaven and Earth. Thus in India Parjanya, or Parjan, with his rain drops blesses the earth with his seed (*Rig Veda,* v. 83). In Greece, Zeus in a golden shower visits

[6] Darmesteter, p. lxi., ii. 97, *Tir-yasht.*

Danaë (dry earth), who gives birth to Perseus, *i.e.* as in Persian to *barz*=*σπόρος*=" seed," who thus becomes the conqueror of Medusa; in Sanskrit, *mrityus*, or " death."

The god *Pharro* is represented on the coins as a male figure, with sword, or sceptre, or sometimes with both; and always with a winged head-dress. In his right hand he generally holds a flat, shallow vessel, with some sprouts of corn rising upwards. Mr. P. Gardner calls this a vessel of *fire*. In my opinion the vessel contains *shoots of growing corn*, of which *Pharro*, the Rain-god, is the begetter. On some coins the god holds a small bag, which Mr. Gardner calls a purse. I take it for a bag of seed-corn, as one of my coins shows the small seeds inside the bag. On a single specimen I find the coin with the bag entirely surrounded by branches of foliage, which I take to denote a vegetable creation.

As an illustration of the significance of the vessel with corn-shoots I can quote the fact that at the New Year's Festival still held at *Yazd-i-Khast*, one of the last strongholds of Zoroastrianism, every house " *has a dish of green corn ready for the feast of No-roz*. The seeds are sown some weeks before, so that they might grow up green ready for the New Year's Festival." [7]

The same shallow dish of springing corn is also represented on some of the coins of the Earth-goddess *Ardokhsho*, and notably on some silver coins of the Saka kings Azas and Azilises. On these last the goddess carries the dish in her extended right hand, and a palm-branch resting on her left shoulder. Mr. P. Gardner hesitates to identify this figure, and suggests a city (?). But the *date-palm* is surely intended for a symbol of *abundance*.

[7] *English Illustrated Magazine*, January, 1890, p. 326. " Travels," by Mr. Theodore Bent.

As a last illustration of the connection of *Pharro* with the *Earth-goddess*, I can quote the engraved gem in my own possession on which the figures of Pharro and Ardokhsho are standing together with a child beside them. He has the winged head-dress and the dish of sprouting corn, while she carries the cornucopiæ [Pl. XXI. 15]. Similar representations of the Earth-goddess will be referred to presently. The junction of the two figures on the same seal with the child, and the cornucopiæ and the dish of growing corn, I take to be a clear declaration that the figures represent the Heaven and the Earth as the creators of all things living.

On the Indo-Scythian coins the Creator is known only as *Pharro*; but he was also commonly known as *Baga*, or "the God," which the Greeks frequently changed to *Mega* for euphony. Thus we have Pharnabazus, Bakabazus, and Megabyzas; Pherendostes, Megadostes, and Bagosakes; Pharnapates, Bagupates, and Megabates.

VI.—Venus Genetrix, Wife of the Lord of Heaven, ♀; The Earth = Demeter.

1. Ardoksho.—2. Shaoreoro.—3. Ridê.

4. Nanaia, Nana. { Venus of Babylon = Ishtar = Persephone. Nanaia, wife of the Lord of Hades.

1. In treating of *Pharro*, the Rain-god of the Firmament whose showers fertilised the earth, I have somewhat anticipated the functions of the Earth-goddess. In the Vedas she is named *Aramati*, and in the Avesta *Armaiti*. But neither of these names is found upon the coins, which give only Ardokhsho, or ΑΡΔΟΧÞΟ. I have described the figure of the Earth as represented on my seal, which gives the figures of *Pharro* and the *Earth* and their child

and their symbols. On another seal in my possession a similar female figure, with a child, is labelled in corrupt Greek ÞOOΓAO, or *Shao Gao,* or "Queen Earth" (Pl. XXI. 16). *Gao* is one of the Avesta names for the Earth. On a second seal which has been published by Mr. King (Pl. IV. fig. 12, *Antique Gems*), in my Pl. XXI. fig. 17, I find a similar female figure with child, labelled in Chaldeo-Pahlavi characters, *Arman-dukhta,* or "Queen *Arman,*" that is, the "Earth." Here, then, we have a direct proof that the female figure on the coins, which is labelled *Ardokhsho,* is actually an impersonation of the Earth-goddess.

The female figure named *Ardokhsho* is represented in two positions, either sitting or standing. When standing she usually carries a large cornucopiæ, which she appears to grasp with both hands. On a single specimen she carries the cornucopiæ in her left hand, and holds out a wreath in her right hand. This last type is also that of the coin with the shorter legend of *Dokhsho.* On a few rare specimens a flat dish filled with fruits, or young shoots of corn, is placed in the field near the feet of the goddess.[8] As a sitting figure she is seated on a high-backed throne, holding a cornucopiæ in her left hand, and a wreath in her extended right hand. This seated figure is almost an exact copy of the goddess Demeter on the copper coins of Azas.

The derivation of the name of *Ardokhsho* has not yet been ascertained; but as the shorter form of *Doksho* is found upon a few coins, and as *Dakshâ* is one of the Sanskrit names of the earth, I think that the name may

[8] Both Amos viii. 1, and Jeremiah xlviii. 32, speak of a "basket of summer fruits."

stand for *Arta-daksha* or *Ard daksha*, which thus became *Ardâksha* by the coalescing of the two *d's*. One of the Queens of Armenia, the wife of *Pâp*, was named *Zarman-dukht*, and *Artadukhta* was the Queen of Ardashir I. the Sassanian. That *Ardokhsho* represents the Goddess of the Earth, the Prithivî of the Indians and the *Spenta Armaiti* of the ancient Persians is certain. According to Haug p. 150, *Armaiti* created the material world, but Ormazd was the soul of it. As the mother of all she was the *Magna Dea* of the Mazdeans, and might thus have been called *Arto-dukhta*.

It is to this Venus, the bride of Heaven, and the mother of all things living, that Lucretius makes his noble address in the opening of his poem :—

"Aeneadûm genitrix, hominum divômque voluptas,
Alma Venus cœli subter labentia signa
Quæ mare navigerum, quæ terras frugiferenteis
Concelebras ; per te quoniam genus omne animantum
Concipitur, visitque exortum lumina Solis :
Te, Dea, te fugiunt ventei, te nubila cœli,
Adventumque tuum ; tibi suaveis dædala tellus
Summittit flores ; tibi rident æquora ponti,
Placatumque nitet diffuso lumine cœlum."

"O genial Venus, joy of gods and men,
Mother of Rome, who, as the seasons roll,
Fillest the ship-starred sea and corn-clad earth,
Through thee all living beings have their birth,
Spring into life, and hail the glorious Sun.
At thy approach the winds and clouds disperse,
The dædal Earth puts forth her sweetest flowers,
Rough ocean laughs, and well-pleased Heaven beams
Without a speck to dim his smiling face."

The planet Venus was called *Anâhid* or *Nanaia*. She is the *Venus Urania* who was added to the Zoroastrian creed by Artaxerxes Mnemon. The Earth-goddess was the *Zir-Banit*, or Zir-genetrix, the wife of *Bel Merodach*, just as Demeter, the wife of Zeus, was the mother of Persephone.

2. SHAHREWAR, or ÞAOPHOPO of the coins, whose full Avesta name of *Kshathra-vairya*, Prof. Darmesteter (I. lx.) translates as "perfect sovereignty," while Haug calls it (p. 306) "possession, wealth." But both agree that he was the "God of Wealth," and the "Lord of Metals." In this capacity he agrees exactly with the Indian *Kuvera*, the King of the Yakshas, and the God of Riches. In modern times *Kuvera* is represented as deformed, from a perverse derivation of his name from *Ku* = "bad" and *vera* = "body." But in early times the Yaksha Kuvera was noted for the comeliness of his person, as we learn from the story of Sakya Sinha's first appearance as an ascetic at Rajagriha, when the people wondered who he could be. "Some took him for Siva, some for Brahma, and some for *Vaisravana*" (or Kuvera, whose patronymic was Vaisravana).[9] The comeliness of his personal appearance is further vouched for by one of the sculptures of the Bharhut Stûpa (see my Stupa of Bharhut, Pl. XXII. fig. 1, p. 21). His statue is duly labelled *Kupiro Yakho*.[10] In the Vishnu Purana he is called "King of Kings," and the same title is given to him by the poet Kâlidâs in his Meghaduta, slok. 3.

As metals and wealth are dug out of the earth, Kuvera

[9] Hardy, *Manual of Buddhism*, p. 29. Mr. Beal also notes how 500 Rishis, flying through the air, mistook Buddha for Vaisravana, the god of Riches.—*Babyl. and Oriental Record*, v. 87.

[10] The change in the meaning of name of *Kuvera* I would attribute to the period of Greek ascendancy in N. India, when some attempt may have been made to identify the Indian *Kuvera*, the worker in metals, with the lame Hophaistos, the Greek god of Metal-Working; hence *ku* = "earth" was altered to *ku* = "bad."

was appropriately made the son of *Ira-vira*, or the "Earth" by Visravana (or Wessawan). He was therefore called *Airavira*, or the Earth's son, and as he was the grandson of Pulastya, he was also called *Paulastya*, or in the spoken form *Paulast* or *Paulat*. As all these names recall those of the Greek god *Ploutos*, who was the son of *Iasiôn* by *Demeter* (the Earth), it seems to me highly probable that the Indian myth of the god of Wealth had been known in Greece as early as the time of Hesiod.

From this account it appears that *Shahrewar* or *Kshatra-vairya*, the "genius of metals and the giver of wealth," is identical with the Indian *Airavira* or *Kuvera*.

3. Ridê, **PIΔH**, is a female figure, armed with helmet, spear, and shield, like the Greek Athene, and the exact counterpart of the male *Shahrewar*.[11] The similarity of the equipment suggests some connexion between the two figures, and as the male figure is the god of *Wealth*, I take the female figure to be the Goddess of *Fortune*, under the Indian name of *Riddhi*, ऋद्धि. The Zoroastrian representative of Fortune is the goddess *Ashi-vanguhi*, whom Haug [12] calls the "Spirit of Fortune." This name is now corrupted to *Ashi-shang*, and the goddess is identified with *Lakshmi* by the Parsi priests. The connexion between *Wealth* and Fortune is shown by the Indian names of *Srid* for Kuvera, and of *Sri* for Lakshmi.

Having read the Greek name as Ridê, **PIΔH**, my attention was struck by a remark of Prof. Darmesteter [13] that, "*ashi* is not the feminine adjective of *asha*, but is *ar+ti*, and means *bhakti*, or piety." I saw at once that the Sanskrit *Riddhi* might become *Arddhi* or *Arti*, the

---

[11] *Brit. Mus. Cat.*, xxviii. 20.
[12] West's *Haug*, p. 184. [13] ii. 270, note.

original of *Ashi*. Now *Riddhi* was the wife of Kuvera, and *Ashi-vanguhi* only means the "good *Ashi*," or *Arti* or *Riddhi*. She was the daughter of *Ahura-mazda* and *Armaiti* (the Earth), and the ancient Persians prayed to her for wealth, for victory, and for children. She is described as riding in a chariot, and there is a doubtful allusion to "*her shining wheel*." At least Spiegel thus translates the passage in the *Ashi Yasht* (ii. 118), which Prof. Darmesteter refers to her loud sounding chariot (ii. 119). Perhaps the round object which I have described above as a shield may be the wheel of fortune. The symbol had already appeared on one of the coins of King Moas, as a real wheel with radiating spokes, while on the coin of Huvishka the round object seems to be solid like a shield.

As *Ridê*, or *Riddhi*, is an undoubted Indian name, it seems to me highly probable that the names of her mother *Ardokhsho* and her brother *Shaorcoro* must also be of Indian origin, as I have already suggested, by deriving the former from Sanskrit *Dakshâ*, the "Earth," and the latter from *Airavira*, the earth's son.

4. Nana, or Nanaia, the Babylonian Venus, was one of the most ancient deities of the East. Her statue had been carried off from Erech by Kudur-Nahundi, king of Elam, 2300 years B.C.[14] In Assyria she was worshipped as *Ishtar*, in Phœnicia as *Astarte*, and the planet Venus is still called *Ashtar* by the Mendeans, and *Nâni* by the Syrians. Her worship was foreign to the original Mazdeism of Zoroaster; but during the reign of Artaxerxes Mnemon, B.C. 404—361, her statues were set up in Babylon, Susa, and Ekbatana, when her worship was also

---

[14] Geo. Smith, *Assyrian Discoveries*, p. 223.

introduced among the Persians and Bactrians on the east, and to Damascus and Sardis on the west. In Persia her cult was taught in the Abân Yasht, where she is described under the name of *Ardvi-Sura-Anâhita.* She is the Anaitis of the Greeks, and the Nana or Nanaia of Persian history and of the Indo-Scythian coins. As the Persian name for the planet Venus is *Zarah,* the adoption of the name of Anâhid shows that her worship was a foreign addition to the original cult.

In the Avesta *Ardvi-Sura-Anâhita* is " the high, powerful, undefiled spring of *water* " which flows down from heaven upon the earth. Her statue is described as carried forth in a standing position, and some details of her dress are given. In her hand she carried a *baresma* or barsom. On the coins Nanaia carries a peculiar symbol or sceptre, which may perhaps be intended for her barsom. Her golden crown is mentioned, but in the coins there is only a lunar crescent. This crescent, however, connects her with the moon, which agrees with the general opinion of antiquity. A bilingual inscription at Athens translates *Abd Tanat* by Artemidorus, and she is called *Tanata* in the cuneiform inscription of Artaxerxes. Plutarch says: " Artemis quam vocant Anaitida,"[15] and Hesychios says Ζαρῆτις was the Persian name of Artemis, *i.e. Zarah.* In the *Abân Yasht* it is said that she presided over the birth of children, and that women in labour prayed to her for a happy delivery. Here, then, she appears as Juno Lucina. By the Assyrians she was accounted the daughter of the moon-god. All connexion with the moon appears to be dropped in the Abân Yasht; and yet we have the lunar crescent preserved on all the Indo-

---

[15] Hyde, 94.

Scythian coins of Nanaia. Perhaps the crescent is meant in the description of her "well-made crown in the shape of a *ratha* with fillets streaming down." [16] But I should prefer to identify the *ratha* with her sceptre, which is sometimes represented with pendent fillets.

On some rare coins of Huvishka *Nano* is connected with *Oksho*, the two deities standing side by side and facing each other. As *Oksho* is certainly the god of Death, this connexion would seem to point to the identification of *Nano* with *Persephone*, the Queen of Hades. It is perhaps not impossible that the Assyrian myth of the "Descent of Astarte into Hades" may have been the original of the famous Rape of Persephone from the field of Henna.

On other coins *Nano* is represented as *Artemis*, holding a bow in the left hand, and with her right hand drawing an arrow from the quiver at her back. One coin of this type has a corrupt legend, which may be read doubtfully as **ZEIPO** or **ZEPO** for *Zahra*, the Persian name of Venus.

On a single coin and on two gems she is represented sitting on a lion. The legend on the coin is simply **NANO**, but both of the gems have an unread legend, **ΦPEIXꟷAΔH**, *Phreikhoadé*, which seems to offer some sort of approximation to the name of Persephone. As Homer calls her ἐπαινή, the "terrible," Persephone might be compared with the fierce goddess Durgâ, who is well known as *Sinha-rathi*, because she is represented "riding on a lion." As Durgâ was called *Kumâri*, or the "maiden," so also Persephone was generally known as the κόρη, or virgin goddess. In fact κόρη or κούρη is the same word as the Sanskrit *Kumâri*, which in its

---

[16] Abân Yasht, 128.

spoken form becomes *Kuäri*. I would suggest also that the title of *Despoina*, which was applied to Persephone as "mistress of the lower world," may have been originally *Dis-potnia*, or "wife of Dis," as *poina* would appear to be only a contraction of *πότνια*, or Sanskrit *patni*, a "wife."

On two very curious copper coins the Kushân king Huvishka is represented kneeling before the goddess Nana, who is standing as usual. Behind her is inscribed her name ΝΑΝΑ, and round the king's hand is inscribed his title of ΡΑΓ ΡΑΓ(ΑΝ)—or King of kings. Above is an incomplete legend beginning ΟΜΟΙΑΓΟΓϢ . . . . . Here there is no doubt of the Indian origin of the title, which is clearly *Raja Rajânâm*, and not the Persian *Shâhânu Shâh*.

As the brightest star in the heavens the planet Venus was called *barez* or *barzin*, the "*brilliant*," Sanskrit *bhrâj*, and her name was very common among Persian ladies.

The goddess *Nana* or *Nanaia* was closely connected with the god *Oksho*, as she is represented standing beside him on several gold coins, both large and small. From their positions facing each other they must certainly be husband and wife. In this case Nanaia will represent Persephone as Queen of the Lower World, or Hades. Except on one coin she is always represented standing, and fully clad, with a crescent on her head. In one hand she carries a peculiar short sceptre, which appears to be surmounted with the forepart of a deer. In the other hand she carries a small vessel holding some uncertain objects. The union of the goddess *Nana* with the god of the lower world is confirmed by Strabo, who saw the statues of *Anaïtis* and *Omanos* placed together in the same temple. *Omanos* is the Greek form of the Avesta *Vohumano*, in Sanskrit *Bahu+manas* or *Su+manas*, who was the Indian *Yama*, or Judge of Hades. His title of

Dharma Raja has the same meaning as the Avesta name. He must also be identified with the Roman Summanus. The name of *Omanos* is not found on the coins; but as *Oksho* is represented with a *club* and *noose*, we know that *Yama* is indicated. Summanus is directly identified with Pluto and Dispiter, by Martial and Arnobius.

The usual legend on the gold coins is either NANAIA or NANA or NANO; but it is extended to NANA ÞAO or ÞAO NANA. With this royal title of "Queen Nana" she generally carries a sword in addition to the sceptre.

A new type shows the goddess fully clad, holding a bow in her left hand, and drawing an arrow from a quiver at her back. This representation fully confirms her identification with Artemis. The same figure is found on an unique coin of Azas.

Another type shows the goddess sitting on a lion, with the crescent on her head, and her peculiar sceptre in her hand. This is one of the common representations of the Indian goddess *Devi*, the wife of Siva, who is therefore called *Sinha-vâhini*, or the "lion-rider." Siva in the form of *Yama* is the god of the Lower Regions, like *Oksho*. Homer calls Persephone ἐπαινή, "the terrible," and the Indian *Devi* is also called *Bhawâni*, "the terrible."

The Babylonian account of the "Descent of Ishtar into Hades" may be compared with the Greek account of the Rape of Persephone, and her consequent descent into Hades.

The planet was generally known as *malkat shawaïna*, or the "Queen of Heaven." Amongst others we have *Barsine*, the widow of Memnon and mistress of Alexander, and Stateira, the eldest daughter of Darius, who was also called *Barsine*, a name derived from *berez*, "brilliant," a title of the planet Venus. It seems, therefore, not improbable that the Greek *Persephone*, or *Phersephone*, may be only the Persian *Barsaphanes*. I find no personal names connected with *Nanaia*—perhaps because it was of foreign origin. But *Bidukht* was another Persian name according to Hyde (p. 90), which was probably in common use, as it is found in the same way as other female names, as *Arta-dukhta*, *Azermidukht*, *Purandukht*, and *Armandukht*. Perhaps the female names of *Parysatis* and *Pharsicis* may be made up from the title of *Berez*, or Venus, "the bright." *Orsabaris*, the daughter of Mithridates Eupator, may also be referred to *berez*.

5. Zeiro, or Zero, is found only on one coin, which is in the British Museum. As the same figure on other coins is named *Nano*, the corrupt legend is most probably intended for *Zahra*, the Persian name of Venus, or rather of Artemis, as the goddess is armed with bow and quiver. The wife of Haman was named *Zahra*, which in the Septuagint is rendered by *Sósara*, Σωσάρα. Omitting the initial syllable, this is the same name.

VII.—Saturn. ♄

1. Herakilo.—2. Oksho.—3. Sarapo.—4. Horôn.—
5. Okhsho.—6. Oaksho.—7. Omanos.—8. Sapal or Sabel.

1. Herakilo, or Herakles. On a single gold coin, and on several rare copper coins, there is a naked standing figure, armed with a lion's skin and club, and inscribed ΗΡΑΚΙΛΟ. The figure on the gold coin is clearly a rude copy of some one of the many known statues of Herakles. On the copper coins the attitude and the position of the club are varied.

2. Oksho, ΟΚÞΟ, is a standing figure, evidently sug-

gested by that of Herakles. But the figure has now become an Indian god with three heads and four arms. With one hand he grasps a club, which rests on the ground; the second hand holds a trident; the third a thunderbolt; and the fourth a water-vessel. (Huvishka.)

A second representation of *Oksho*, also with three heads and four arms, shows him as a naked mendicant with trident, *damara* or drum, *chakra* or wheel, and deer. This is the Phallic Siva. (Huvishka.)

A third representation of *Oksho*, with one head and four arms, shows him carrying trident, drum, and water-vessel, and holding a deer. This is the common form on the coins of Kanishka.

A fourth representation of *Oksho* shows the god with one head and two arms, carrying the trident, and the *pâsa* or noose on coins of Vasu Deva.

A fifth representation of *Oksho* shows the god with one head and two arms, armed with trident and noose, standing in front of the humped bull Nandi. (Vasu Deva.)

A sixth is similar to the last, but the head of the bull is turned round, boustrophedon. (Vasu Deva.)

A seventh shows the god with three heads and four arms, standing in front of the bull Nandi. Some two-headed figures also have four arms.

3. *Sarapo* is represented both sitting and standing. The former type occurs only on the small gold coins, but the figure corresponds so closely with that of the Greek Plutôn that there can be no doubt it is intended for the king of the Lower World. He is represented with a *modius* on his head, as described by Suidas, seated on a throne, with a sceptre in his left hand and a "noose" in his right hand. It is not a *wreath*, but is the regular Indian *pâsa*, or

"noose," from which *Yama* gets his titles of *pási* and *pâsi-pâna*, or "noose-in-hand."

On the larger coins Sarapo is represented as a standing figure with a simple head-dress, and a short sceptre or rod in his left hand. His right hand is extended with fore-finger pointing, as shown in the figures of *Miiro* and *Mao*, but it is empty.

Both Porphyry and Suidas say that Sarapis presided over the "invisible world." [17] Suidas adds that the statue of Sarapis bore on its head a measuring vessel, and in the hand a cubit, or measuring rod for fathoming the depth [of the Nile].[18] Diodorus calls him the Egyptian Pluto. Porphyry couples Serapis with Hekatè. No derivation has yet been found for the name, but it seems not impossible that the name may be identical with शरव *Sarava*, one of the titles of the Indian Siva (? *Sarvva-pa* = Lord of all).) Perhaps *Sarapis* may represent "Time," and would thus symbolize the annual rise and fall of the Nile, as well as the gradual growth and decay of heat, and its renewal every year. *Sarpa*, the serpent which renews its skin, is known to the languages of India, Greece, and Rome. I would identify *Sarapis* with the Greek *Minos*, the Indian *Yama* or *Dharma Raja*, and the Zoroastrian *Bahman* or *Vohumano*, all of whom sat to judge the dead. *Vohumano* in fact is described as "rising from a golden throne to welcome the souls of the dead into Paradise."

4. *Hôron*, ωPOH, and 5, *Okhsho*, OKÞO, are found only on two very rare coins; the latter, in fact, I believe to be unique. I couple them together because the two figures are exactly alike. Both are bearded; each has a *modius*

---

[17] Prichard, *Egyptian Mythology*, 98. [18] Prichard, 91.
[19] Haug, 255.

on his head, each holds a sceptre in his left hand, and each points downward with his right hand. Perhaps both may refer to the god of water, of which the *modius*, or water vessel, would be a symbol. In this view the name of *Hôron* might be compared with *Varuna*, the Indian god of water, while that of *Okhsho* might be referred to *Akshara*, or *Akhra*, a name of Siva, which in the Vedas is also used to designate "water."

These are mere guesses, but of the next I cannot even make a guess.

6. *Oakhsho* or *Vakhsho*, ΟΑΧÞΟ. This figure differs entirely from ΟΧÞΟ as well as from ΟΚÞΟ, so that there is no possibility of the legend being blundered. The figure is that of an old man holding a long sceptre in his right hand, and carrying what looks like a dolphin or fish in his left hand. If I could be sure as to the fish or dolphin, I should be inclined to accept the figure as the god of the "Ocean."

7. OMANOS, ΩΜΑΝΟΣ, is coupled by Strabo [xv. 3. 15] as being placed with *Anaïtis* in a common shrine. He must therefore be Hades, the lord of the Under World. The name of *Omanos* has already been identified by Haug (p. 255) with *Vohumano* or *Bahman*, who is described as rising from his throne to welcome the souls of the dead. As the name means the "right-minded," in Sanskrit *Su-+manas* or *Sumati*, in Greek Eumenes, this form of the god is clearly the same as the Indian *Yama*, or Judge of the Lower World, and the Roman Summanus, or Pluto.[20] His name is not found on the coins, but as the god is represented with *club* and *noose* under the name of *Oksho* we

---

[20] *Summanus* is directly identified with Pluto and Dispiter by Martial and Arnobius. The Indian *Yama* is also named *Saman*, or the "Killer," from *sam*, to kill.

know that *Dharma Raja* is intended, which is one of Yama's titles.

8. *Sapal* or *Sabal.* The name of *Sapal* does not occur on any of the *Kushân* coins, although it appears on most of the *Saka* coins. It is found in the name of *Sapaleizes,* whom I believe to be the same as *Zamol-xis* or *Gebel-eizes,* to whose realm the dead were supposed to go (Herod. iv. 94). *Zamol* and *Gebel* appear to be only variant forms of *Sapal.* The word is, no doubt, connected with the Sanskrit *Ṣava,* a "corpse," from which Ṣiva received his title of *Ṣavara,* or "receiver of the dead." It is also connected with the Latin *sepelio* and *sepulcrum,* and with the Hebrew *Sheol,* or *Shaul,* as Gesenius writes it. The country occupied by the Saka Scythians received the general name of *Zabulistan,* and their capital was called *Sigal.* But the name was very widely spread over all the countries between the Indus and the Euphrates. Thus we learn from Tacitus (*Annal.* xii. 18) that when the Parthian king, Gotarzes, arrived at Mount *Sambulas* he sacrificed to Hercules, the principal god, whose shrine was on the mountain. Pliny also (*Nat. Hist.* vi. 27) calls the same hill Mount *Kambalidus.* Omitting the epenthetic Greek *m* before *b,* we get *Sabula* and *Kabala* as the actual name of the hill, in which I recognise the two forms given by Herodotus of *Zamol-xis* and *Gebel-eizes.* On some rare Indo-Scythian coins I find the name of *Sapal-eizes.* I think, therefore, that this god, who was worshipped on the mountain of Sambulos, was actually Hercules himself, whose name is not otherwise mentioned by Herodotus.

In the curious legend of the "Descent of Ishtar into Hades," the god or king of Hades is called *Iskalla,* a name which is clearly identical with *Sakal,* and, therefore, with *Sapal.* As I have already shown that Herakles, as Nergal, was the god of the dead, it follows that he must be the same god as *Iskalla* or *Sapal*. Hence we see how easy it was for Herakles, the god of Death, to be the victor in all encounters.

The name of *Sapal* or *Sapar* is found in every country occupied by people of Scythian race, from the Saparnian *Hyrkani* on the Caspian, to the Sabellian *Hirpini* on the Tiber, who worshipped Sancus, the Samnite Hercules. In Ariana we have the names of Sapaleizes, Spalahora, and Spalirises, and the Spartani of Zapaortene. In the West we have Sparamizes and Parmizes, Sparadokus, Spartokus, and Spartacus. In another form we have Skolopitus, king of the Skoloti, and the more contracted forms of Saulius and Sauloë. In both countries the wolf was called *hirkus* and *hurk*, and a bull *teba* and *tiba*.

Buddha.

The coins with the figure of Buddha are extremely rare. He is represented both standing and sitting, but only on the coins of Kanishka. The gold coin, which is unique, was found in the Stûpa at Ahin-posh, near Jelalabad, and two copper pieces were found in Ventura's Manikyala Stûpa. These three are all of the standing type. I have obtained only three specimens of the sitting type during my long career.

On the gold coin the legend is simply BOΔΔO = Buddha.

On the copper coins the legend is longer, and is rather difficult to read, as the latter part is reversed in boustrophedon order. Beginning at the upper left hand I read CAKAMA, continued from the lower right in reverse order, ·NOBOYΔO. For this reading I am indebted to Mr. Rapson.

On left CAKAMA.
On right OΔYOBON.

The copper coins are in three sizes, like those of Kanishka's money generally (see *Ariana Antiqua*, xiii. 1, 2, 3; see also Thomas's *Prinsep's Antiquities*, Pl. VII. fig. 21, and *Journal Bengal Asiatic Society*, 1845, Plate II., fig. 7).

In the same Plate, fig. 6, I have given a specimen of the seated Buddha.

These figures are of some interest as they are the earliest known representations of Buddha. They would also seem to have been the original representations, as all the Indian figures follow the same types.

Num. Chron. Ser. III. Vol. XII. Pl. IX.

INDO-SCYTHIANS. KUSHANS. PLATE XIX.

Num. Chron. Ser. III. Vol. XII. Pl. X.

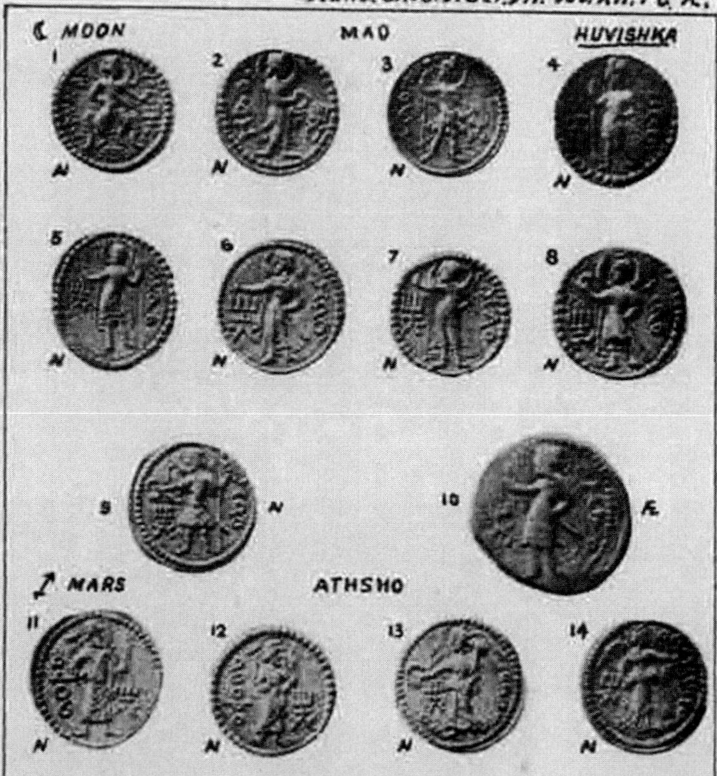

INDO-SCYTHIANS. KUSHANS. PLATE XX.

Num. Chron. Ser. III. Vol. XII. Pl. XI.

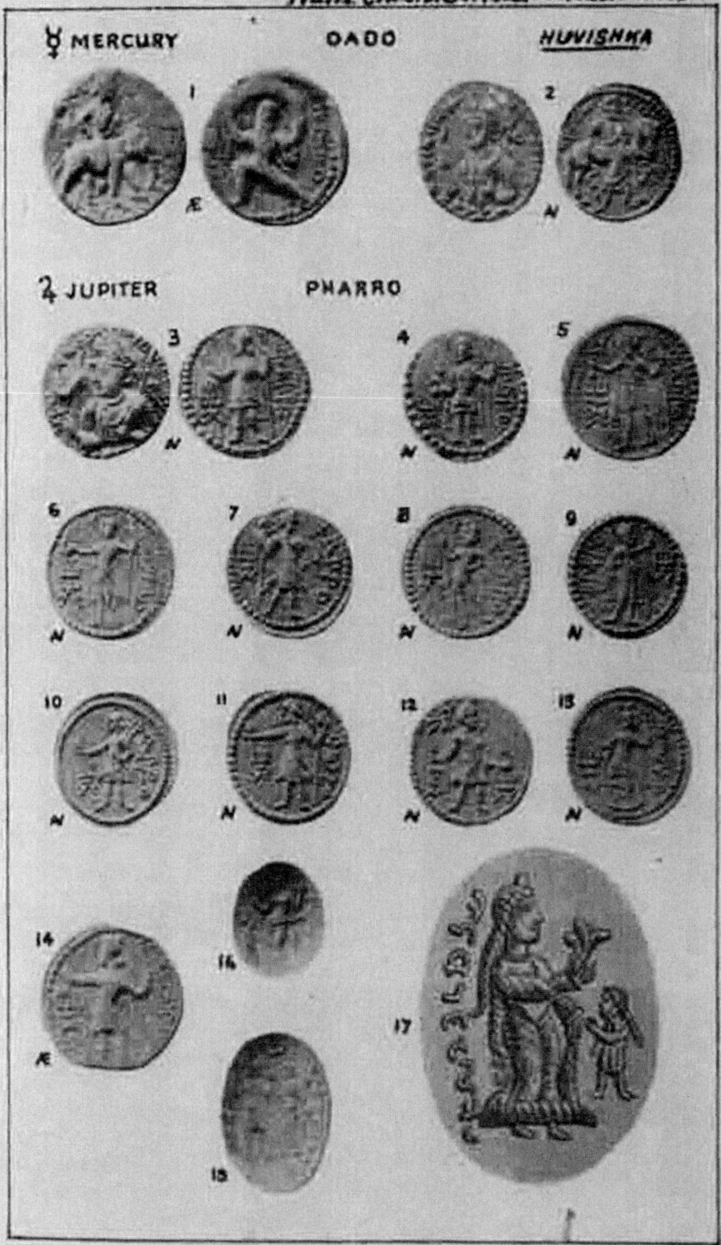

INDO-SCYTHIANS. KUSHANS. PLATE XXI.

Num. Chron. Ser III Vol. XII Pl. XII

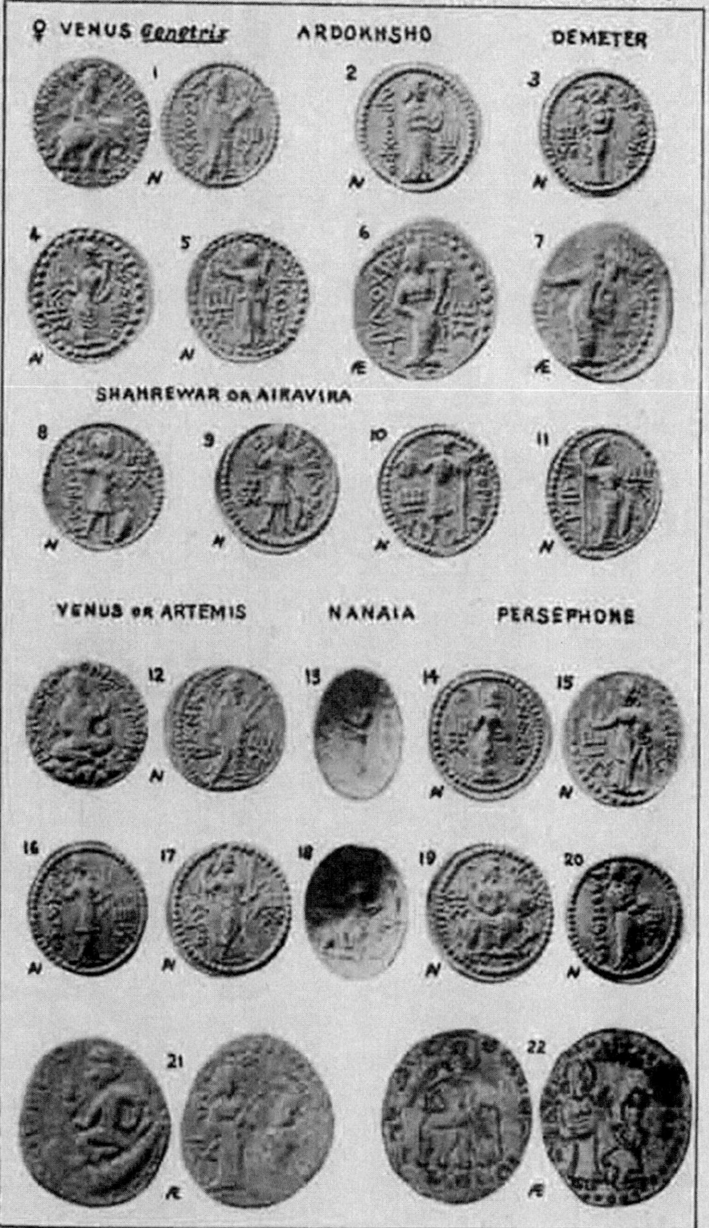

INDO-SCYTHIANS. KUSHANS. PLATE XXII.

Num. Chron. Ser. III. Vol. XII Pl. XIII.

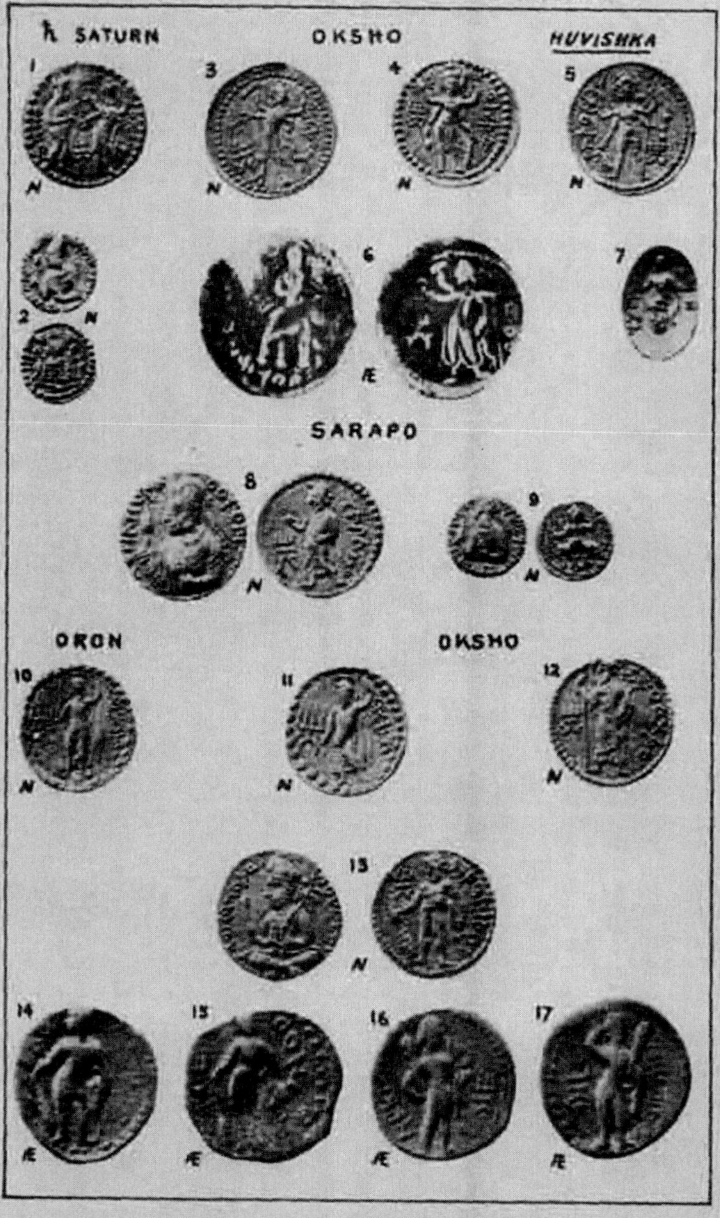

INDO-SCYTHIANS. KUSHANS. PLATE XXIII.

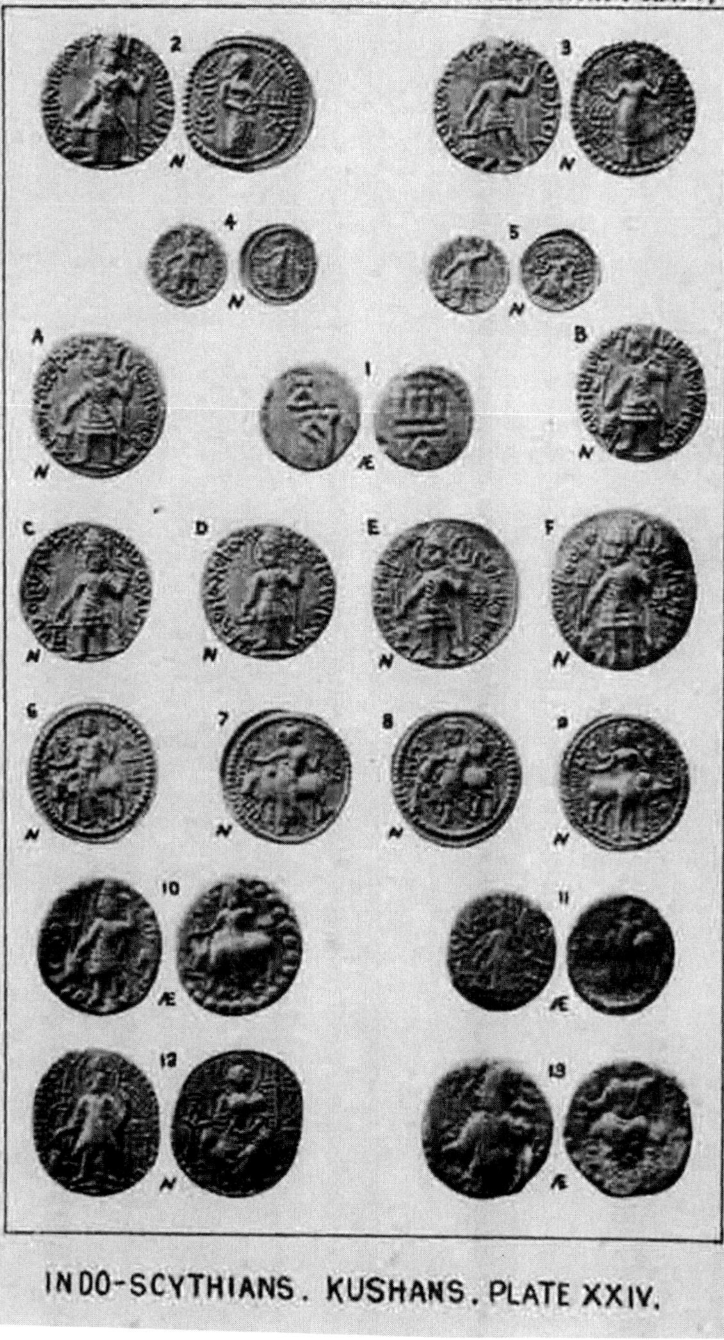

INDO-SCYTHIANS. KUSHANS. PLATE XXIV.